Takeaway English 系列规划教材

Takeaway English 2

（学生用书）

原 著　Peter Loveday
　　　　Melissa Koop
　　　　Sally Trowbridge
　　　　Lisa Varandani
　　　　Edward Scarry
改 编　牛　健　张勇军
　　　　朱佳文　赵港笙
　　　　高　旭

McGraw Hill Education

北京师范大学出版集团
BEIJING NORMAL UNIVERSITY PUBLISHING GROUP
安徽大学出版社

图书在版编目(CIP)数据

Takeaway English.2/(美)洛芙迪(Loveday,P.)等原著;牛健等改编.—合肥:安徽大学出版社,2014.7(2017.1重印)

Takeaway English 系列规划教材.学生用书

ISBN 978-7-5664-0782-5

Ⅰ.① T… Ⅱ.①洛… ②牛… Ⅲ.①英语—教材 Ⅳ.①H31

中国版本图书馆 CIP 数据核字(2014)第 135220 号

Peter Loveday, Melissa Koop, Sally Trowbridge, Lisa Varandani, Edward Scarry

TAKEAWAY ENGLISH STUDENT BK 2 W/CD; TAKEAWAY ENGLISH STUDENT BK 3 W/CD

978-607-15-0588-0; 978-607-15-0591-0

Copyright © 2012 by McGraw-Hill Education.

All Rights reserved. No part of this publication may be reproduced or transmitted in any form or by any means, electronic or mechanical, including without limitation photocopying, recording, taping, or any database, information or retrieval system, without the prior written permission of the publisher.

This authorized English Adaptation is jointly published by McGraw-Hill Education (Asia) and Anhui University Press. This edition is authorized for sale in the People's Republic of China only, excluding Hong Kong, Macao SAR and Taiwan.

Copyright © 2014 by McGraw-Hill Education (Asia), a division of McGraw-Hill Education (Singapore) Pte. Ltd. and Anhui University Press.

版权所有。未经出版人事先书面许可,对本出版物的任何部分不得以任何方式或途径复制或传播,包括但不限于复印、录制、录音,或通过任何数据库、信息或可检索的系统。

本授权英文改编版由麦格劳-希尔(亚洲)教育出版公司和安徽大学出版社有限责任公司合作出版。此版本经授权仅限在中华人民共和国境内(不包括香港特别行政区、澳门特别行政区和台湾)销售。

版权 © 2014 由麦格劳-希尔(亚洲)教育出版公司与安徽大学出版社有限责任公司所有。

本书封面贴有 McGraw-Hill Education 公司防伪标签,无标签者不得销售。

出版发行:	北京师范大学出版集团
	安 徽 大 学 出 版 社
	(安徽省合肥市肥西路 3 号 邮编 230039)
	www.bnupg.com.cn
	www.ahupress.com.cn
印 刷:	合肥远东印务有限责任公司
经 销:	全国新华书店
开 本:	210mm×270mm
印 张:	15
字 数:	285 千字
版 次:	2014 年 7 月第 1 版
印 次:	2017 年 1 月第 2 次印刷
定 价:	37.00 元(含光盘)

ISBN 978-7-5664-0782-5

ISBN 978-7-88105-097-3(光盘)

策划编辑:李 梅 钱来娥 薛淑敏		装帧设计:李 军 金伶智
责任编辑:钱来娥 薛淑敏		美术编辑:李 军
责任校对:程中业		责任印制:赵明炎

版权所有　侵权必究

反盗版、侵权举报电话:0551—65106311

外埠邮购电话:0551—65107716

本书如有印装质量问题,请与印制管理部联系调换。

印制管理部电话:0551—65106311

前　言

"Takeaway English系列规划教材"改编自美国McGraw-Hill Education（麦格劳-希尔教育）2012年出版的TAKEAWAY ENGLISH，是一套在教学理念和教学活动设计方面具有国际领先水平，且又适合我国高职高专院校学生使用的英语教材。本系列教材包括：

Takeaway English 1–3（学生用书 配CD）

Takeaway English 1–3（练习册）

Takeaway English 1–3（教师用书 配DVD）

Takeaway English Online Learning Center（学习网站）

《学生用书》第一、二册由15个单元组成，第三册由10个单元组成，每5个单元后设有一个综合复习单元。每个单元设1个主题，通过12个模块展开：热身（Start）、听力（Listening）、词汇（Vocabulary）、语法（Grammar）、阅读（Reading）、项目（Project）、歌曲/文化（Song/Culture）、语音（Pronunciation）、对话（Conversation）、写作（Writing）、测试（Test）、单元小结（Unit Summary）。

《练习册》是《学生用书》的配套教材，提供了专项补充练习，旨在帮助学生巩固所学知识，强化语言技能训练。

《教师用书》供教师教学使用和参考，内含对《学生用书》中各单元内容的教学指导、教学方法小贴士、对不同水平学生的教学指导、课堂知识拓展、文化知识补充、课文相关背景知识、可能存在的教学问题和可行的解决方案等。

"学习网站"是供学生自主学习的平台，同时也辅助教师课上教学，为教师和学生实施线上、线下相结合的混合式教学模式及翻转课堂教学提供了便利。（注："学习网站"仍以原版教材四册书安排，教师与学生在使用时需与本改编版三册教材对接。）

本系列教材的特色是：

1. 在重视语言知识的基础上，强化语言能力的提高，尤其是口语交流能力。作为口语能力的基础，语音和语调训练在教材中占有一定比例。

2. 选材时尚，体裁广泛，互动活动丰富，富于时代感，话题涵盖日常生活及一般职场，符合高职教学要求。

3. 中文旁注及听、说、读、写策略指导适合学生自学，旨在培养学生的自主学习能力。

4.《学生用书》与《练习册》相互参照，导航明确，方便使用。

5. 线上、线下资源相结合，配套完备，相辅相成，相得益彰。

6. 项目（Project）模块采用项目驱动教学法，引导学生在真实的语境下应用英语，解决实际问题。

7. 歌曲/文化（Song/Culture）模块设计新颖，将语言运用融于歌曲和文化中，既增加了学习趣味性，又帮助学生了解了中西文化异同，提高了跨文化交际意识及能力。

8. 测试（Test）模块独树一帜，在点滴中提高学生的应试能力，增加学生的考试自信心。

9. 单元小结（Unit Summary）模块列出了每单元的单词、短语及表达法，一目了然，方便学生有效学习。

10. 各种附录齐全，能最大程度地满足学生的学习与测试需求。

说明：

1. Takeaway English 1（学生用书），15单元（60学时），达到高等学校英语应用能力考试B级水平；

2. Takeaway English 2（学生用书），15单元（60学时），达到高等学校英语应用能力考试A级水平；

3. Takeaway English 3（学生用书），10单元（40学时），达到大学英语四级水平。

我们希望本系列教材能够助推高职高专英语教学改革，为学生提供优质的教学内容，创设良好的学习平台。由于改编者学识与水平有限，虽经最大努力，教材仍难免有不足之处，敬请使用本系列教材的教师和学生不吝指正。意见和建议请发往邮箱：xsm678@126.com。

编者

2014年5月

CONTENTS

Unit 1	Good luck, bad luck	2
Unit 2	My favorite things	14
Unit 3	Memorable experiences	26
Unit 4	I love chocolate!	38
Unit 5	How can we help?	50
	Review 1	62
Unit 6	World languages	66
Unit 7	Are you fashionable?	78
Unit 8	That's life!	90
Unit 9	Do you know a good story?	102
Unit 10	Home, sweet home	114
	Review 2	126
Unit 11	Doing it for charity	130
Unit 12	How do you stay healthy?	142
Unit 13	Space travel	154
Unit 14	What have you been doing?	166
Unit 15	Great adventures	178
	Review 3	190
	Grammar Takeaway	194
	Irregular Verbs	209
	Key to Phonetic Symbols	210
	Vocabulary	211
	Audioscript	221
	Photo Credits	229
	Audio Track List	230

SCOPE and SEQUENCE

Unit	Start	Listening	Vocabulary	Grammar	Reading
1 Good luck, bad luck *page 2*	Good luck and bad luck customs	A lucky man!	Expressions with *get*	Review: simple past	A lucky thief *Strategy:* Order the sequence of events
2 My favorite things *page 14*	Things people collect	What do you collect?	Vocabulary building	Present perfect	Enthusiastic collectors *Strategy:* Predict
3 Memorable experiences *page 26*	Feelings	A childhood memory	Accidents happen!	Past continuous versus simple past	Experiences to remember *Strategy:* Know your purpose for reading
4 I love chocolate! *page 38*	Made with chocolate	A dessert recipe	Cooking instructions	The passive voice	All about chocolate *Strategy:* Preview the contents
5 How can we help? *page 50*	In need of help	A service trip	Ways to help	Object pronouns	The recycled goats *Strategy:* Know the writer's purpose
Review 1, *page 62*					
6 World languages *page 66*	Understanding languages	Learning languages *Strategy:* Listen for key words	How well do you speak the language?	Simple present and present continuous	The written word *Strategy:* Preview the task
7 Are you fashionable? *page 78*	Formal and casual clothes	What do you wear to work? *Strategy:* Listen for details	Different ages, different clothing	Verb patterns (verb + infinitive or verb-*ing*)	Jeans, jeans, jeans *Strategy:* Read for the main idea
8 That's life! *page 90*	Tell me about your family	How's it going? *Strategy:* Identify relationships	Life events	Present perfect and past perfect	A special family reunion *Strategy:* Identify verb forms to understand sequence
9 Do you know a good story? *page 102*	Classifying animals	An African folktale: *The Eagle and the Tortoise Strategy:* Preview	Giving and responding to information	Simple past and past continuous	A folktale from India *Strategy:* Make a prediction
10 Home, sweet home *page 114*	Apartment for rent	I'm calling about the apartment *Strategy:* Listen for specific information	What's in the living room?	*Should* for advice and the imperative for instructions	Feng Shui *Strategy:* Identify cause and effect
Review 2, *page 126*					
11 Doing it for charity *page 130*	Charity events	A walk for charity *Strategy:* Identify sequence	What do you do and where do you go to stay in shape?	Future forms: *will, be going to,* simple present	A blog about a charity event *Strategy:* Understand the writer's purpose
12 How do you stay healthy? *page 142*	The human body	Let's exercise! *Strategy:* Understand instructions	Where does it hurt?	Modal verb review	A health advice column *Strategy:* Scan for specific information
13 Space travel *page 154*	Fly me to the Moon	A vacation on the Moon *Strategy:* Understand hesitations	Build your vocabulary!	*Would* for hypothetical situations	What about the Moon? *Strategy:* Skim for the main idea
14 What have you been doing? *page 166*	The average American	How long does it take? *Strategy:* Take notes	Time flies!	Present perfect continuous	Have you been waiting long? *Strategy:* Ask and answer questions
15 Great adventures *page 178*	Famous expeditions	Expedition to Lhasa *Strategy:* Focus on what you understand	Equipment for a camping trip	Passive voice	Adventures in Africa *Strategy:* Predict
Review 3, *page 190*					
Grammar Takeaway, *page 194*					

SCOPE and SEQUENCE

Song / Culture	Pronunciation	Conversation	Writing	Test
Culture: Lotteries around the world	*Did* + subject	Responding to good news and bad news *Strategy:* Show surprise	Writing a story about luck *Strategy:* Use time expressions	Understanding sequence
Song: Do you have a heart?	Sentence stress in the present perfect	Talking about things you like *Strategy:* Emphasize your ideas	Writing a descriptive essay *Strategy:* Use the five senses	Text completion questions
Culture: Stories and culture	Vowel sounds /aʊ/ *how*, /əʊ/ *no*, and /ɔː/ *for*	Reacting to a story *Strategy:* Use body language	Writing a story about a memorable experience *Strategy:* Identify the key events and details	Listen for and recognize tone
Song: I drink coffee, I drink tea	Word stress in three-syllable words	Making, accepting, and declining offers *Strategy:* Make your response polite	Writing an encyclopedia entry *Strategy:* Make an outline	Identify pros and cons
Culture: Charitable organizations around the world	Vowel sounds /ʌ/ *up*, /ʊ/ *put*, and /ɪ/ *busy*	Making requests and giving excuses *Strategy:* Use formal vs. informal language	Writing a plan to help others *Strategy:* Use a flowchart	Identify support for an opinion
Song: My one true love	Syllable stress	Asking for clarification *Strategy:* Ask the person to repeat	Writing an ad for a language course *Strategy:* Use advertising techniques	Understand tone and language
Culture: Wedding clothing traditions	Reduction of *to*	Shopping for clothes *Strategy:* Confirm information	Writing an email about clothes *Strategy:* Know your audience	Understand cause and effect
Song: My crazy family	The sounds /ɪ/ *live* and /aɪ/ *life*	Saying goodbye and making plans *Strategy:* Agree strongly	Writing a letter about recent events *Strategy:* Organize your writing by topic sentences	Look for the correct form and part of speech of a word
Culture: Folktales about the Moon	Pronunciation of *-ed* verb endings	Asking for more information about a story *Strategy:* Express surprise	Writing a folktale *Strategy:* Make your writing interesting	Short answer questions
Song: Close the door	Vowel sounds /ʊ/ *wood*, /uː/ *you*, and /ɔː/ *for*	Responding to suggestions *Strategy:* Be polite when responding	Writing an advice letter *Strategy:* Write an effective response	Listening comprehension questions
Culture: Charities around the world	Pronouncing contractions	Showing support and offering help *Strategy:* Use contractions	Writing a blog to promote a charity event *Strategy:* Make a plan	Choose the correct verb tense or form
Song: What can this be?	Sentence stress	Seeing the doctor *Strategy:* Get all the information	Writing an article giving advice *Strategy:* Use graphic organizers	Compare and contrast
Culture: Space food	Contracted *would*	Checking into a hotel *Strategy:* Check understanding	Writing an email to request hotel information *Strategy:* Write a professional email	Vocabulary questions: Select meaning by word
Song: Passing the time	Understanding numbers and times	Apologizing and accepting an apology *Strategy:* Admit responsibility	Writing a survey report *Strategy:* Organize parts of a report	Use context clues to answer questions
Culture: Excursions and transportation around the world	The sound /ɜː/	Shopping for camping equipment *Strategy:* Give feedback	Writing a blog about a trip *Strategy:* Use the active vs. passive voice in writing	Vocabulary questions: Select word by meaning

Takeaway English 系列规划教材

"Takeaway English系列规划教材"改编自美国McGraw-Hill Education(麦格劳-希尔教育)2012年出版的TAKEAWAY ENGLISH,是一套在教学理念和教学活动设计方面具有国际领先水平,且又适合我国高职高专院校学生使用的英语教材。本系列教材包括:

  Takeaway English 1-3(学生用书 配CD)
  Takeaway English 1-3(练习册)
  Takeaway English 1-3(教师用书 配DVD)
  Takeaway English Online Learning Center(学习网站)

1 Good luck, bad luck

In this unit you...
- talk about good luck and bad luck
- use expressions with *get*
- respond to good news and bad news

Grammar
- review: simple past

START

Good luck and bad luck customs

1. Do you believe in good and bad luck? Name one time when you had good luck. Name one time when you had bad luck.

2. Match the sentences about good luck and bad luck to the pictures. Then listen and check.

four-leaf clover
四叶草; 幸运草

1. __G__ A four-leaf clover brings good luck.
2. _____ Some people believe that if you break a mirror, you get seven years of bad luck.
3. _____ In some countries, a horseshoe means good luck.
4. _____ Some people think it's bad luck to walk under a ladder.
5. _____ In some countries, Friday the 13th is an unlucky day.
6. _____ Some people believe that it's bad luck when a black cat walks in front of you.
7. _____ Some people cross their fingers for good luck.
8. _____ You are lucky if you see a shooting star.

shooting star
流星

Talk about it!

3. Work with a partner. Make a list of good luck and bad luck customs or symbols in your culture. Talk about which ones you believe in.

4. Report to the class about the good and bad luck customs. As a class, decide on the most interesting custom for good luck and bad luck.

culture matters

In different cultures, people have different ideas about luck. For example, in some cultures people say that the number 13 means bad luck, and that Friday the 13th is an unlucky day. But in other countries, people say that Tuesday the 13th is unlucky.

请注意不同文化对"运气"的不同理解

Unit 1

LISTENING

A lucky man!

1 Before listening You will hear an interview with Bill Morgan. Look at the pictures of Bill's life. What do you think happened to him? Talk about your predictions with a partner.

HELP listening

Listen for sequence of events
When you listen, pay attention to the sequence (the order) of events. This will help you understand the story.

请注意事件发生的顺序

happen to sb.
某人发生……

2 Listening Listen to the interview. Number the events from 1 to 8.

____ Bill won a car.
____ Bill got his job back.
____ Bill won $100,000.
  1   Bill had a heart attack.
____ Bill got engaged.
____ Bill bought another ticket.
____ Bill was in a coma.
____ Bill bought a lottery ticket.

heart attack
心脏病; 心脏病发作
get engaged
订婚

in a coma
陷于昏迷状态
lottery ticket
彩票; 奖券

3 After listening Read the sentences. Circle *True* or *False*.

1. Bill is a taxi driver.	True	(False)
2. Bill was in a coma for seven days.	True	False
3. Bill's doctors thought he was going to die.	True	False
4. Bill didn't need a new car.	True	False
5. The reporters bought Bill's second ticket.	True	False
6. The reporters didn't believe that he had a winning ticket.	True	False
7. Bill started to cry because he was unhappy.	True	False

have a winning ticket
中奖

Talk about it!

4 Work with a partner. Talk about these questions.

1. In your opinion, what was the luckiest thing that happened to Bill?
2. In your opinion, what was the most unlucky thing that happened to Bill?
3. Talk about a time when your luck went from bad to good, or your luck went from good to bad.

WORKBOOK PAGE 1

Unit 1

VOCABULARY

Expressions with *get*

have... in common
在……有共同之处

1. Check the things that are true about you. Then tell a partner. What word do these expressions all have in common?

☐ get 50 text messages a day ☐ get angry easily
☐ get new clothes every week ☐ get good grades

in bold
黑体; 粗体

2. Read Bill's story. Match the expressions with *get* in bold with the definitions. Then listen and check.
01_03

Two years ago Bill **got a job** as an engineer. That's when he met Lucy. Then he **got sick**. He went to the hospital, and he **got worse**. He nearly died. Then, suddenly, he **got better**. When he came out of the hospital, he **got** a lottery ticket. It had the winning number. He **got rich**. Then Bill and Lucy decided to **get engaged**. Next year they are going to **get married**.

1. <u>got better</u> = started to feel well again
2. _____ = make a plan to get married
3. _____ = became rich
4. _____ = found / obtained work
5. _____ = bought
6. _____ = started to feel sicker
7. _____ = started to feel sick
8. _____ = become husband and wife

3. Write the expressions from exercises 1 and 2 in the correct columns. Then compare with a partner. Add two more expressions with *get* to each column.

become	obtain / receive / buy
get angry	

ENGLISH *express*

Get has different meanings in different expressions.

I **get** angry. (*become*)
I **got** 10 emails. (*receive / obtain*)
I **got** a lottery ticket. (*buy*)

请注意 get 在不同短语中的不同含义

Talk about it!

4. Work with a partner. Ask and answer the questions.

1. Where did you get the clothes you're wearing?
2. What did you get for your last birthday?
3. When was the last time you got sick?
4. Do people in your country get engaged before they get married?
5. How old are most people when they get married?
6. Do you think the economic situation in your country is getting better or getting worse?

Unit 1

GRAMMAR

Review: simple past

ALSO GO TO
Grammar Takeaway
PAGE 194

1 Read the sentences. The past verb forms are underlined. Write them in the correct column of the chart in the base form and the simple past.

1. I just <u>wanted</u> to get back to work. Fortunately, I <u>got</u> my old job back.
2. I <u>had</u> a heart attack. I <u>was</u> in a coma for several days.
3. I suddenly <u>woke up</u> 12 days later. I <u>felt</u> great.
4. I <u>decided</u> to ask my girlfriend to marry me… and she <u>said</u> yes!
5. I <u>bought</u> a lottery ticket. I <u>shouted</u>, "I won $100,000!"

regular		irregular	
base → past		base → past	
want	wanted	get	got

base form
原形

	regular verbs	irregular verbs
affirmative	I wanted my old job back.	I got my old job back.
negative	He didn't want his old job back.	He didn't get his old job back.
yes / no questions and answers	Did you want your old job back? Yes, I did. / No, I didn't.	Did you get your old job back? Yes, I did. / No, I didn't.
information questions	Why did you want your old job back?	When did you get back to work?

2 Complete the conversation with the simple past of the verbs in parentheses. Then listen and check.
01_04

Ann: What (1) _did you do_ (do / you) last weekend?

Bob: On Saturday, I (2) _____ (sleep) late, and then I (3) _____ (clean) my room. In the afternoon, I (4) _____ (go) to the beach.

Ann: You did? Who (5) _____ (go / you) to the beach with?

Bob: Well, I (6) _____ (go) with Jessica, but we (7) _____ (see) lots of other people from school there.

Ann: Really? Who (8) _____ (see / you)? (9) _____ (be) Tom and Billy there?

Bob: Tom (10) _____ (be / not) there, but Billy (11) _____ (be). He (12) _____ (say) that Tom (13) _____ (be) sick.

Ann: Oh, no! I (14) _____ (call) him yesterday, but he (15) _____ (answer / not). I (16) _____ (know / not) he (17) _____ (be) sick! Poor Tom!

Talk about it!

3 Work with a partner. Talk about what you did last weekend.

A: What did you do last weekend?

B: I went shopping on Saturday morning and then I studied in the afternoon.

A: Did you get anything good?

B: Yes! I got a great sweater and some jeans.

WORKBOOK
PAGE 3-4

Unit 1

READING

A lucky thief

1 Before reading Look at the words in the box. They are all from the news article you are going to read. Look up any new words in a dictionary. What do you think the article is about?

DOCTOR THIEF EMPTY SPARE TIRE FLAT TIRE TRUNK SUITCASE

look up
查找

HELP reading
Order the sequence of events
When you read, write small numbers in the story next to each main event to show the sequence. This will help you understand the story.

请注意按事件发生的先后顺序排序

2 Reading Read the article and check your guesses to exercise 1.

THIEF LEAVES WINNING LOTTERY TICKET BEHIND

Trevino, Italy – Last week, local doctor Giovanni Ricci was surprised to find that a thief had robbed him. Even more surprising, however, was the winning lottery ticket that the thief left behind.

Dr. Giovanni Ricci was going to visit a friend on New Year's Eve when he got a flat tire. Another driver stopped to help Dr. Ricci. The man took off the old tire, put the spare tire on, and then drove off. Dr. Ricci looked in his trunk and realized that the man was a thief. Everything from his car trunk—a suitcase, some tools, and a large box of chocolates—was missing. In fact, the trunk was empty! Then the doctor noticed a lottery ticket on the road next to the car. The ticket obviously belonged to the thief, and fell out of his pocket while he was helping Dr. Ricci.

Dr. Ricci kept the lottery ticket. A week later, he discovered that it was the winning ticket! But Dr. Ricci did not keep the ticket. He put an ad in the newspaper, asking the thief to come and get the ticket. The thief answered the ad, apologized to the doctor for robbing him, and took the ticket. When asked why he didn't keep the money, Dr. Ricci told reporters that the ticket wasn't his. "He may be a thief, but I'm not."

fall out of
从……掉出来

leave behind
留下；遗落

get a flat tire
轮胎没气

take off
卸下；拿掉

spare tire
备胎

apologize to sb. for sth.
为某事向某人道歉

car trunk
后备箱

3 Reading Read the news article again. Number the pictures from 1 to 5.

A

B 1

C

D

E

Unit 1

4 After reading Circle the correct words to complete the sentences.

1. The man stopped to help the doctor buy / change a tire.
2. The doctor knew / didn't know the man.
3. The man took the doctor's old tire / suitcase.
4. The man lost / gave the doctor his lottery ticket.
5. The doctor kept / didn't keep the money.
6. The man was / wasn't sorry that he robbed the doctor.

Talk about it!

5 Work with a partner. Talk about the questions.

1. Do you think the doctor did the right thing when he gave the money to the thief? Would you do the same thing? Why or why not?

    A: What do you think? Did the doctor do the right thing?
    B: Yes, I think he did. It's true. The doctor isn't a thief.
    A: Would you do the same thing?
    B: Yes, I would. What would you do?
    A: I think I would keep the money because I found the ticket.

2. What would you do in these situations?
    1. You find a purse in a restaurant.
    2. You find a lot of money on the street.
    3. You see someone drop a lottery ticket on the street.
    4. You buy something in a store and the salesperson gives you too much change.
    5. You see a thief trying to steal a tourist's purse.

> **ENGLISH express**
>
> Use would + verb to talk about situations that aren't real.
>
> What would you do if this happened to you?
>
> I would (not) give the money to the thief.

请注意 would + verb 的含义及用法

##

Work in pairs or small groups. Do research to find out about good luck and bad luck symbols and customs from around the world. Choose one good luck symbol / custom and one bad luck symbol / custom. Prepare and present a short skit for each symbol / custom. The skit should show a person with the symbol / custom and having good or bad luck.

Unit 1

CULTURE

Lotteries around the world

1 Before reading What do you know about lotteries? Read the sentences and circle your guesses.

1. The first lottery was held in the United States / China / Italy.
2. Most early lotteries were operated by businesspeople / governments / schools.
3. The country with the most lotteries is Japan / the United States / Italy.

2 Reading Read the article to check your guesses to exercise 1.

Lotteries more than fun and games

Lotteries may seem like nothing more than a fun game or an easy way to get rich quickly. However, they have a long history and connection with government and social projects. One famous example of this was in China between 205 and 187 B.C. During this time, the Han Dynasty used <u>ancient</u> Keno slips to collect money to make the Great Wall of China. Another example is from the ancient Romans. During this time, it was common to give party guests a prize based on a lottery system. Everyone received a ticket, and after a drawing, people would get prizes.

The first modern European lottery to <u>award</u> money was held in Florence, Italy, in 1530. Just like the earlier Roman-style lottery, all ticket <u>holders</u> received a small prize. The <u>Dutch</u> also gave money as prizes in lotteries. In these lotteries, people had a <u>1 in 4</u> chance of winning a prize. In fact, the English word lottery comes from the Dutch word *loterij*, which comes from the Dutch noun *lot* meaning *fate*, or something that happens because it was supposed to. The Dutch government-owned *staatsloterij* is still the oldest existing lottery.

The first legal lottery in America was held in 1964 in New Hampshire. <u>Proceeds</u> went to support education. In the last 20 or 30 years, instant ticket lotteries have also become popular. These tickets allow players to <u>scratch off</u> a protective coating from a ticket to discover instantly if they have won a prize. The popularity of lotteries is growing all over the world. The United States is <u>currently</u> the country with the most lotteries.

nothing more than
仅仅；只不过

after a drawing
开奖后

1 in 4 chance
1/4的机会

be supposed to
应该；被期望

staatsloterij
国家彩票

New Hampshire
新罕布什尔
(美国州名)

scratch off
擦去；刮掉

3 After reading Match the phrases to complete the information from the article.

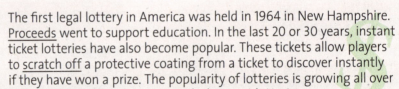

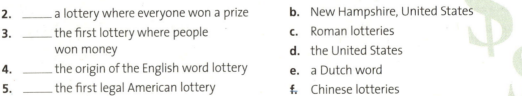

1. __f__ the first lotteries
2. _____ a lottery where everyone won a prize
3. _____ the first lottery where people won money
4. _____ the origin of the English word lottery
5. _____ the first legal American lottery
6. _____ the country with the most lotteries

a. Florence, Italy
b. New Hampshire, United States
c. Roman lotteries
d. the United States
e. a Dutch word
f. Chinese lotteries

4 After reading Circle the correct definitions for the underlined words and phrases in the article.

1. ancient: very new / (very old)
2. award: give / take
3. holders: people who sold tickets / people with tickets
4. Dutch: from Germany / from the Netherlands
5. 1 in 4:   4% / 25%
6. proceeds: money earned / money lost
7. scratch off: write / remove, take off
8. currently: at the moment / possibly

Talk about it!

5 Work with a partner. Talk about the questions.

1. What are the different lotteries in your country?
2. Who organizes them?
3. What is the money used for?
4. Which ones have the biggest prizes?
5. How old do you have to be to participate?
6. Do you know anyone who buys lottery tickets?

PRONUNCIATION

Did + subject

1 (01_07) In past tense questions, we pronounce *Did you* like *Diju*, and *Did he* like *Diddy*.

In writing		In speaking
Did you buy a ticket?	→	Diju buy a ticket?
Did he buy a ticket?	→	Diddy buy a ticket?

2 (01_08) Listen to the questions. Write the missing words.

1. ___Did he___ win that car?
2. _____ have a lottery in ancient times?
3. _____ have a winning ticket?
4. _____ get married?
5. _____ get rich?
6. _____ get sick last night?

Unit 1

CONVERSATION

Responding to good news and bad news

1. How do you respond to good and bad news in your language?

2. Listen to a conversation between two friends. Who do you think has the best news?

3. Complete the conversation with expressions from the box. Then listen again to check your answers.

| That's really a shame | That's amazing | That's great news |
| I'm sorry to hear that | ~~Congratulations~~ | That's too bad |

in a long time 长时间
What's new? 有什么好事？

Maya: Hey, Kate! I haven't seen you in a long time. How are you?
Kate: Hi, Maya! Oh, things aren't too bad.
Maya: What's new?
Kate: Well, I'm getting married next month.
Maya: You are? (1) _Congratulations_ ! Who's the lucky guy?
Kate: His name is Nick. His grandfather's a millionaire.
Maya: (2) _____ !
Kate: Yes, but unfortunately he died last week.
Maya: Wow. (3) _____ .
Kate: Yes, it is. He lived a long life, but we're still very sad. So, what's new with you?

get the promotion 提拔；升职

Maya: Not much. I just found out that I didn't get the promotion I wanted at work.
Kate: Oh… (4) _____ .
Maya: Thank you. And I've been sick all week.
Kate: Really? (5) _____ . I hope you get well soon.
Maya: Thanks. But the good news is that I just bought a lottery ticket and I won $500!
Kate: Really? (6) _____ !
Maya: Thanks! Now I'm going to get a new TV with the money!

CONVERSATION STRATEGY

Show surprise
We usually stress the words in a sentence that show we are surprised or sorry. When we are surprised, we also use a higher pitch (intonation). When we are sorry, we use a lower pitch.

请注意表达"惊讶"的不同方式

Talk about it!

4. Work with a partner. Take turns telling each other good news and bad news. Respond to the news with the words and phrases from exercise 3. Be careful to use the correct intonation.

Tell me more!

Visit the Takeaway English Online Learning Center at http://olcs.mcgraw-hill-education.com/takeaway/

 Check out the *Takeaway TV* video.

 Improve your English with the online activities.

Unit 1

WRITING

Writing a story about luck

HELP writing

Use time expressions
When you write an article, use time expressions—when, while, on, at, before, after, then, that... this... the next...—to help the reader understand the order of events.

请注意使用时间顺序词

1 Before writing Talk about a time you or a friend had good luck or bad luck.

2 Writing model Read the luck story. Is it about good luck or bad luck? Circle the time expressions. Then write the details from the story into the timeline.

left work at 6 p.m.

FRIDAY   SATURDAY   SUNDAY

found a cat

My friend Alina had really good luck last weekend! On Friday night, she left work at 6 o'clock. When she got home, she found an old cat sitting in front of her door. The cat was hungry, so she fed it. She put out a bowl of food and some water. The cat ate the food very quickly, and then continued to sit there. After that, she decided to brush its hair. The cat meowed happily while she brushed it. The next morning, the cat was still sitting in front of her door! So she fed it again, and it meowed happily again. That night, it was raining, so she let the cat sleep in her kitchen. On Sunday, Alina went to the supermarket. She saw a sign with a picture of the cat on it. The sign said, "Missing cat: Please call 555-7810." When she got home, she called the number. The owner of the cat was very happy! Thirty minutes later, he came to her house to get it. When he got there, he gave Alina $50 to say thank you. After he left, she went to the mall and spent the money on a new pair of shoes.

put out
把……放好备用
brush one's hair
梳头发

3 Planning your writing Now plan the details of your own luck story with a timeline.

4 Writing Write your luck story. Use the information in exercises 2 and 3 to help you.

Unit 1

TEST

Test-taking strategy

Understanding sequence   Understanding the sequence, or order of events, can help you better understand the story you are reading or listening to.

Use these steps to help you understand sequence.

1. Pay attention to sequence words like *first, second, then, before, after that, next,* and *finally.*
2. Use any pictures to help you understand the sequence of events.
3. Ask yourself; *What needed to happen before something else could happen?*
4. Number important events to put them in order.
5. If you are listening, take notes.

Example
You read this story.
I usually have very good luck, but not this week. Monday morning I turned on my computer and it crashed. I finished an important paper for school on Saturday, but now it was lost. I couldn't print it. Then I lost my phone. I got it back eventually, but I didn't have it for two days. Finally, I did poorly on a test on Friday. Next week has to be better!

You see this test question.

1. Which event happened first?
   - ~~A.~~ I couldn't print it.   This happened after the computer crashed.
   - **B.** I finished my paper.   This is the correct answer.
   - ~~C.~~ My computer crashed.   This happened after the paper was finished.
   - ~~D.~~ My paper was lost.   This happened when the computer crashed.

PRACTICE

Order the events of the story correctly using the numbers 1 - 8.

_____ I didn't have my phone for two days.
__1__ I finished an important paper.
_____ I couldn't print the paper.
_____ My computer crashed.
_____ I turned on my computer.
_____ I lost my phone.
_____ I did poorly on a test.
_____ I got my phone back.

Unit 1

UNIT SUMMARY

Nouns
cat
clover
horseshoe
ladder
lottery
mirror
money

Expressions with *Get*
get a job
get better
get engaged
get married
get rich
get sick
get worse

Time expressions
After
At
Before
On
That
Then
The next
This
When
While

Expressions—responding to good news
Congratulations!
That's amazing!
That's great news!

Expressions—responding to bad news
I'm sorry to hear that.
That's really a shame.
That's too bad.

2 ▸ My favorite things

In this unit you...
- identify things that people collect
- talk about collections and hobbies
- talk about things you like

Grammar
- present perfect

START

Things people collect

1. What do you see in this picture? Why do you think the owner has so many of these things?

2. Write the names of the things people collect as a hobby under the pictures. Then listen and check.

sports memorabilia	stamps
art	electronics equipment
watches	model airplanes
~~coins~~	stuffed animals

sports memorabilia
体育纪念品
electronics equipment
电子设备
stuffed animal
填充动物玩具

3. Work with a partner. Make a list of five other things that some people collect. Then make a class list. Who collects each thing? Write the names next to the things.

Talk about it!

4. Work with a partner. Ask and answer the questions.

   1. Who do you know that collects something? What do they collect? How many things do they have in their collection?
   2. Do you think collecting is a good hobby? Why or why not?
   3. In your opinion, what is the difference between having a lot of something and collecting something?

1. _coins_   2. _____

3. _____   4. _____

5. _____   6. _____

7. _____   8. _____

Unit 2

LISTENING

HELP listening

Listen for reactions
When you listen to a conversation, pay attention to people's reactions. This will help you understand what they are talking about.

positive reactions	negative reactions
That's awesome!	That's too bad!
That's so cool!	Oh, no!
No way!	What a bummer!

请注意交谈时对方的反应

What do you collect?

1 Before listening   You will hear a conversation between Nancy and Greg. Look at the pictures. What do you think they are talking about?

2 Listening   Listen and check your guesses for exercise 1.

3 Listening   Listen again. Match the sentences and the reactions.

1. __b__ I think I have about 215.
2. _____ I lost some when I was on vacation.
3. _____ I wear a different one every day.
4. _____ I think I have about 80 pairs.
5. _____ I wore my favorite pair to school one day, and they got scratched.

a. Wow! That's awesome!
b. That's so cool!
c. No way!
d. Oh! That's too bad!
e. Oh, no! What a bummer!

on vacation
度假

What a bummer!
真糟糕！真扫兴！
get scratched
有刮痕

4 After listening   Answer the questions.

1. What does Greg collect?
2. How many does he have?
3. When did he start collecting them?
4. How often does he wear them?
5. What does Nancy collect?
6. How many does she have?
7. When did she start collecting them?
8. How often does she wear them?

Talk about it!

5 Work with a partner. Talk about a collection that you have. If you don't have one, talk about a collection that a friend / family member has.

1. What do you collect?
2. How many do you have?
3. When did you start collecting them?
4. Why do you collect this item?
5. Where do you get items for your collection?
6. Do you ever use / wear them?

WORKBOOK PAGE 8

15

Unit 2

VOCABULARY

Vocabulary building

1 Look at the sentences and the underlined words. Write *thing*, *verb*, or *person*. What ending was added to the verb for a person? What ending was added for a thing?

1. Jim <u>collects</u> soccer balls. _____verb_____
2. Jim is a <u>collector</u>. _____
3. He has 35 in his <u>collection</u>. _____

 2 Build your vocabulary by completing the chart. Then listen and check.

verb	person	thing / action
collect	collector	collection
direct	(1) **director**	direction
(2)	actor	action
educate	educator	(3)
illustrate	(4)	illustration
decorate	(5)	(6)
(7)	(8)	instruction

3 Complete the sentences with words from exercise 2. Be sure to use the correct forms.

1. Barbara is an _____ . She draws pictures for books.
2. Every parent wants their children to have a good _____ .
3. My swimming _____ is teaching me how to do the backstroke.
4. We moved into a new apartment, but we still need to _____ it. We want to put art on the walls.
5. Brad Pitt is my favorite _____ . He's been in many movies.
6. Steven Spielberg is a famous _____ . He _____ the Indiana Jones movies.

do the backstroke
仰泳

put art on the walls
在墙上来点艺术

Talk about it!

4 Work with a partner. Ask and answer the questions.

1. Who's your favorite actor? Why?
2. Who's your favorite movie director? Why?
3. Do you think education only happens at school or do people learn outside of school also? Explain your answer.
4. What's your English instructor's name?
5. Do you like to read books with illustrations in them? Why or why not?

GRAMMAR

Present perfect

ALSO GO TO
Grammar Takeaway
PAGE 195

1 Read the sentences. Underline the verbs in the present perfect. Notice when we use this tense. Check (✔) when each thing happened. Then complete the rule.

	started at a non-specific time in the past	started in the past and still happening now
1. I've collected baseball hats since I was in high school.		✔
2. He's been an actor for 10 years.		
3. I've seen a lot of rock bands.		
4. We haven't gone skiing for a month.		
5. She has collected dolls for years.		
6. Have you done the illustrations yet?		

ENGLISH express

We use *for* and *since* with the present perfect to say when something started.
Use *for* before periods of time. *He has collected hats for 12 years.*
Use *since* before a specific time in the past. *I've lived here since 2005.*

请注意 for 和 since 在现在完成时中的不同用法

rock band
摇滚乐团

do the illustrations
插图

We form the present perfect with the present tense of the verb _____ plus a past participle.

Past participles

be – been   go – gone
do – done   see – seen

 Complete the conversation with the present perfect of the verb in parentheses. Then listen and check.

Pam: Hey, Zoe! How do you like my watch from Paris?
Zoe: (1) _Have you been_ (you / be) to Paris?
Pam: No, I (2) _____ (be). My dad went there last year. He brought it back for my watch collection.
Zoe: Really? That's great! How long (3) _____ (you / collect) watches?
Pam: Let's see… I (4) _____ (collect) them since I was 12 years old.
Zoe: That's great! Hey! (5) _____ (you / be) to the antique jewelry store on Elm Street? Sally (6) _____ (got) some cool watches there!
Pam: Yes, I (7) _____ (be) there. I (8) _____ (got) three watches from there. But my favorite place is the flea market on Main Street.
Zoe: Really? I (9) _____ (go / not) to that flea market. How long (10) _____ (it / be) there?
Pam: Oh, it (11) _____ (be) there for years. It's really great!

antique jewelry
古董珠宝

flea market
跳蚤市场
Main Street
大街

 Talk about it!

3 Work with a partner. Ask and answer questions about your hobbies.

A: What's your hobby, Hannah?
B: I make necklaces.
A: Really? How long have you made necklaces?
B: I've made them since I was 13 years old.
A: Have you sold any of your necklaces?
B: No. I usually just make them for my friends.

Unit 2

READING

Enthusiastic collectors

1 Before reading Match the words to the pictures. What do you think the reading will be about?

Fred Flintstone
弗雷德·弗林斯特
Dalmatian
达尔马提亚狗

1   2   3   4

a. teaspoon
b. Fred Flintstone
c. Dalmatian
d. frog

2 Reading Now read the news article to check your guess for exercise 1.
02_05

HELP reading

Predict
Before you read a news article, read the title and subtitle to predict what it will be about.
请注意通过标题预测文章大意

COLLECTING . . . *A family affair*

101 Dalmatians
《101只斑点狗》
(电影名)

collecting fever
收集热潮

a huge collection of
大量的收藏

souvenir teaspoon
纪念品茶匙

If you're looking for a Dalmatian or a Fred Flintstone, a frog, or a teaspoon, you're sure to find it at the home of the Bradleys. The family, from Chicago, are all enthusiastic collectors, from dad right down to little Rebecca.

Five-year-old Rebecca fell in love with Dalmatians after seeing the film *101 Dalmatians*. She now has 284 Dalmatian items in her collection. Her mom Wendy said, "Everything has Dalmatians on it: her schoolbooks, her clothes—even her toothbrush! She has toy Dalmatians of all sizes, and she spends all her money on them."

But she's not the only collector in the Bradley family. Older sister Louise has collected souvenir teaspoons since she was eight. She has now collected 196. "Whenever anyone goes anywhere, they bring her one back," says Mrs. Bradley. She too is an enthusiastic collector. "I'm a Flintstones fan. I have 206 items in my collection. My favorite is my talking Fred doll—he's awesome!"

And that's not all. Ten-year-old son Richard has a collection of 158 frog items. He has been interested in frogs since he saw some in his grandfather's garden a few years ago. Like his sister's Dalmatians, he has frogs on his clothes, his school bag, and his bedroom wall.

Perhaps the collecting fever started with Mr. Bradley. He owns a model shop, and he has a huge collection of model planes. Mrs. Bradley said, "I went into the room to count them, but I gave up because there are so many of them!"

18

3 Reading Read the news article again. Answer the questions.

1. Who collects toy dogs?
2. What does Wendy collect?
3. How long has Louise collected teaspoons?
4. Who collects frog items?
5. What does Mr. Bradley collect?

4 After reading Read the sentences. Circle *True* or *False*.

1. Rebecca's friend had a Dalmatian so she started collecting them.
   True (False)
2. Wendy has Dalmatians on her schoolbooks, her clothes, and her toothbrush.
   True False
3. People bring teaspoons for Louise when they travel.
   True False
4. Mrs. Bradley has 296 Flintstones items.
   True False
5. Richard collects real frogs.
   True False
6. He started collecting frogs after he saw frogs in his grandfather's garden.
   True False
7. Mr. Bradley works in a shop where you can buy model planes, ships, etc.
   True False
8. Mrs. Bradley doesn't know how to count.
   True False

Talk about it!

5 Work with a partner. Talk about these questions.

1. Why do you think the Bradleys collect things?
2. Do you think collecting is a waste of money? Why or why not?
3. Do you think that children should have to use their own money to buy toys? Why or why not?

Work in a group. Do research on the Internet to find out about world records for collections. Make a list of the five most interesting collections. Report back to the class. Have a class vote to decide on the craziest collection in the world.

Unit 2

SONG

Do you have a heart?

1 Before listening What are some famous brands you know? Write two or three brands for each category. Then say what country they come from.

cars	clothes	watches	electronics	sunglasses	shoes
Nissan (Japan)					

2 Before listening Compare your lists with a partner. Do you have any of the things on the list? Do you want any of the things on the list? Which ones?

3 Listening Listen to the song. Write the missing words in the lyrics.
02_06

bored fan friends heart Milan small trees ~~watch~~

Do you have a heart?

Chorus

You have a Rolex (1) __watch__,
Suits by Hugo Boss.
Yes, you like to dress real smart.
You have famous (2) _____,
A Mercedes Benz,
But do you have a (3) _____?

When I talk about my favorite things,
You sit there looking (4) _____.
So I ask you what you'd like to do,
And my question gets ignored.

I know you love those Bonsai (5) _____,
So I bought one from the mall.
But when I brought it home to you,
You said it was too (6) _____.

Chorus

You've been the favorite child since you were small,
And your mom's your biggest (7) _____.
You've lived a life of shopping trips
To New York and (8) _____.

You've always been on the winning team,
With your good looks and pride.
But when you've had enough of them
You cast your friends aside.

Chorus

---

dress smart
着装体面

Mercedes Benz
梅赛德斯·奔驰

get ignored
被忽视

cast...aside
把……丢在一边

4 After listening   Write the underlined expressions in the song next to their meanings.

1. elegantly, with style _____ smart _____
2. is not answered _____
3. abandon your friends _____
4. confidence and positive attitude _____
5. appearance _____
6. put on and wear _____

Talk about it!

5 Work with a partner. Ask and answer these questions.

1. In your opinion, are expensive brands better than cheaper brands? Why or why not?
2. Do you think you should spend your money on expensive brands for some things, but not others? Which ones? Why?
3. What is your opinion about copies of famous brands? Have you ever bought one? Why or why not?
4. Do you think it's more important to have expensive things or to have good friends?

PRONUNCIATION

Sentence stress in the present perfect

1 In present perfect sentences, we stress the words that give the meaning. Listen and repeat.
02_07

> We've <u>lived</u> here for <u>three years</u>.
> She <u>hasn't visited</u> us.
> How <u>long</u> have you <u>lived</u> in <u>Chicago</u>?
>
> <u>Have</u> you <u>been</u> to the <u>market</u>?
> <u>Yes</u>, I <u>have</u>. / <u>No</u>, I <u>haven't</u>.

2 Listen to the sentences. Underline the stressed words.
02_08

1. **A:** <u>Have</u> you <u>eaten</u> <u>breakfast</u>?
   B: No, I haven't.
2. Michael has been to Australia.
3. How long have you worked at the café?
4. They haven't looked online yet.
5. **A:** Has he graduated from college?
   B: Yes, he has.

Unit 2

CONVERSATION

CONVERSATION STRATEGY

Emphasize your ideas
To emphasize your ideas, use words like really, very, and so with adjectives and adverbs.

请注意如何强调自己的观点

Talking about things you like

1 Listen to a conversation between two friends. What things do they like?

Pete: _____   Tara: _____

2 Complete the conversation with the expressions from the box. Then listen again to check your answers.

| interested in | avid | fell in love with | big fan |
| have been hooked | ~~into~~ | my favorite | |

big fan
铁粉

Elvis
埃尔维斯
(猫王，美国著名摇滚明星)

Tara: Hey, Pete. What kinds of things are you interested in?
Pete: Well, I'm really (1) __into__ music.
Tara: What kind of music do you like?
Pete: Well, (2) _____ singer is Elvis. In fact, I'm an (3) _____ collector of Elvis memorabilia.
Tara: Really? What kinds of things?
Pete: Oh, you know, T-shirts, clocks, pens, mirrors... you name it!
Tara: Wow! That's so cool!
Pete: What about you? What kinds of things do you like?
Tara: I'm a really (4) _____ of music too.
Pete: Really? What kind of music?
Tara: Actually, I like all kinds of music. I'm very (5) _____ musical instruments, especially guitars. In fact, I collect guitars as a hobby.
Pete: That's awesome! How did you get interested in guitars?
Tara: Let's see... I (6) _____ guitars after seeing my first rock concert. And I (7) _____ ever since!

Talk about it!

3 Work with a partner. Talk about things you like. Use the words and phrases from exercise 2. Emphasize your ideas when possible.

Tell me more!

Visit the Takeaway English Online Learning Center at 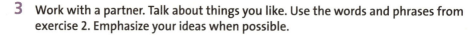 http://olcs.mcgraw-hill-education.com/takeaway/

 Check out the *Takeaway TV* video.

 Improve your English with the online activities.

Unit 2

WRITING

Writing a descriptive essay

1 Before writing Work with a partner. Talk about your favorite possession. It should be an actual *thing* that you can touch with your hand.

> **HELP writing**
> **Use the five senses**
> When you write a descriptive essay, focus on the senses. Describe what you can see, smell, hear, taste, or touch. This will help your reader visualize what you are writing about.
>
> 请注意五种感官的描写

2 Writing model Read the descriptive essay. Which senses does it focus on? Write the details from the description in the chart.

focus on
集中(注意力、精力等)

sight	small,
sound	
smell	
taste	
touch	

My favorite possession is my toy giraffe. I've had it for 15 years. I got it when I went to the zoo when I was five years old, so it's really special.

My toy giraffe is small and colorful. It's about three inches tall, and it fits in the palm of my hand. It has a beige body with brown spots on it. It has horns on the top of its head and two big ears. It has four pointy legs and a long tail that hangs down in the back. It's so cute.

My toy giraffe is very light when you pick it up. It feels soft and smooth when you touch it. You can feel small bumps where the brown spots are. When you push the bottom of the green stand, the giraffe's legs bend and it sounds like it's breaking. But when you stop pushing the bottom, it goes back together.

toy giraffe
长颈鹿玩具

beige body
浅褐色身体

hang down
垂下

3 Planning your writing Now plan the details of your descriptive essay in the chart. Use at least three senses.

sight	
sound	
smell	
taste	
touch	

4 Writing Write about your favorite possession. Use the information in exercises 2 and 3 to help you.

WORKBOOK PAGE 12-13

23

Unit 2

TEST

Test-taking strategy

Text completion questions   Many tests ask you to fill in the blanks in a sentence or paragraph with the correct words or phrases.

Use these steps to help you answer text completion questions.

1. Look at the words before and after each blank space.
2. Make sure it is the correct part of speech (noun, verb, adjective, etc.).
3. Does the word or phrase make sense in the sentence or paragraph?
4. Make sure you answer all the questions. You may understand better than you think.

> *Example*
> You see this test question.
>
> 1. John is a coin _____. He has money from all over the world.
>
>   ~~A.~~ collecting   This verb form does not work here.
>
>   ~~B.~~ collection   This noun does not work in the blank.
>
>   C. collector   This is the correct answer. A noun works here.

PRACTICE

Fill in the blanks with the words to complete the paragraph.

| acting | collector | dance | actor | dancing |

Julia is a coin (1) __**collector**__. She has money from all over the world. Her brother, John, wants to be an (2) _____. He thinks (3) _____ is the best job in the world. John and Julia's parents like to (4) _____. They go (5) _____ every Saturday night.

UNIT SUMMARY

Nouns
art
coin
electronics equipment
model airplane
sports memorabilia
stamps
stuffed animal
watch

Advebs
really
so
very

Expressions—talking about things you like
I am a big fan…
I am interested in…
I fell in love with…
I have been hooked…
My favorite…

3 ▶ Memorable experiences

In this unit you...
- talk about your feelings
- talk about childhood memories
- describe accidents
- react to a story

Grammar
- past continuous versus simple past

START

Feelings

1 How do you feel right now? How did you feel yesterday?

2 03_01 Write the adjectives for feelings under the pictures. Then listen and check.

| angry | exhausted | scared | ~~thrilled~~ | embarrassed | nervous | surprised | worried |

1. thrilled
2. _____
3. _____
4. _____
5. _____
6. _____
7. _____
8. _____

3 Choose the best adjective from exercise 2 to describe how you feel in each situation.

fall down
跌倒

1. I fell down in front of my class. **embarrassed**
2. My sister broke my cell phone.
3. I heard a strange noise outside my window last night.
4. I won the lottery.
5. It's very late. My parents haven't come home yet.
6. I saw an old friend at the mall.
7. I have a very important test tomorrow.
8. It's 2 a.m. I want to go to bed.

Talk about it!

4 Work with a partner. Describe a time you had one of the feelings from exercise 2. Your partner guesses the feeling. Take turns.

jump out of
跳出
feel scared
感到害怕

A: Last year, I was in my bed and I saw a big spider on my pillow. I jumped out of bed and yelled for my dad to help me.
B: Did you feel scared?
A: Yes!

Unit 3

LISTENING

A childhood memory

1 Before listening Do you have many memories from your childhood? What is one thing or event that you remember?

2 Before listening Look at the pictures of Tim's childhood memory. What do you think happened? Number the pictures in order.

A B C D E F

3 Listening Listen and check your guesses to exercise 2.
03_02

4 Listening Listen again. Circle *True* or *False*.
03_02

1. Tim was about four years old.	True	False
2. The bridge was new.	True	False
3. Tim was wearing red sandals.	True	False
4. His sister didn't see him fall.	True	False
5. His sister rescued him from the river.	True	False
6. Tim wasn't scared.	True	False

rescue from
抢救；营救

5 After listening Work with a partner. Retell Tim's story in your own words. Take turns telling the different parts of the story. Use the pictures in exercise 2 to help you.

A: One summer, when Tim was a little boy, he was walking on an old bridge with his sister.

B: The bridge was very old...

Talk about it!

6 Work with a partner. Talk about a childhood memory you have. Answer the questions.

1. When did it happen?
2. Where were you?
3. Who were you with?
4. What happened?
5. How did you feel?

HELP listening

Summarize

After you listen, summarize the story in your own words. Include the main idea and important details. This helps you understand and remember what you listened to.

请注意用自己的语言总结听到的内容

Unit 3

VOCABULARY

Accidents happen!

1 Have you ever had an accident? What happened? How did you feel?

2 Complete the descriptions of accidents with the words from the box. Then listen and check.
03_03

| burned | cut | fell down | ~~slipped on~~ | crashed into | dropped | fell off | trip on |

1. He _slipped on_ the wet floor.
2. We _____ a tree.
3. He _____ the stairs.
4. She _____ her bike.
5. She _____ her notebooks.
6. I _____ my finger.
7. Don't _____ the curb.
8. She _____ the cake.

3 Complete the chart with more examples of accidents. Use the verbs in exercise 2 and the words in the box. Some words can go with more than one verb.

burn	my hand,
crash into	
cut	
drop	
fall down	
fall off	
slip on	
trip over	

a banana peel	a skateboard
a box	my backpack
a bridge	my hand
a chair	my plate
a hole	the cookies
a ladder	the dog
a motorcycle	the ice
a sign	a wall

crash into
撞到……上; 闯入

fall off
跌落

slip on
滑倒

trip over
被……绊倒

Talk about it!

4 Work with a partner. Ask and answer the questions.

1. What are accidents that happen when riding a bike, a skateboard, a motorcycle, etc.?
2. What are accidents that happen in different rooms in the house? (bedroom, bathroom, garage, etc.)

ride a skateboard
滑滑板

Unit 3

GRAMMAR

Past continuous versus simple past

ALSO GO TO
Grammar Takeaway
PAGE 196

1 Look at the examples of the past continuous. Then complete the rule.

affirmative	I was walking with my sister. We were walking on an old bridge.
negative	I wasn't watching where I was going. They weren't watching the movie.
yes / no questions and answers	Were you watching? Yes, I was. / No, I wasn't.

To form the past continuous, we use the past tense of _____ with the main verb + _____ .

2 Read Tim's story. Underline the verbs in the past continuous. Circle the verbs in the simple past. Then circle the correct answers to complete the rule.

My sister and I were walking over an old bridge near our house. I wasn't watching where I was going. I fell off the bridge into the river. I remember I was wearing red plastic sandals. I remember that I saw those red plastic sandals and the blue sky as I was falling. My sister didn't see me fall! She continued walking over the bridge and talking to me! Luckily, there were some people who were swimming in the river. They saw me fall in and rescued me.

- We use past continuous / simple past to describe completed actions in the past. These things happened one time and then finished.
- We use past continuous / simple past to describe actions in progress in the past, or to give a description of the situation or scene.

plastic sandals
塑料凉鞋

fall in
跌入;投进

3 Complete each sentence with the past continuous or simple past form of the verb in parentheses.

1. I __was working__ (work) late and the lights __went out__ (go out).
2. She _____ (run) for the bus, and she _____ (fall down).
3. A: _____ on Friday when the new boss came in? (work / you)
   B: Yes, I _____ .
4. He _____ (sleep) when the storm _____ (start).
5. A: What _____ yesterday? (do / she)
   B: She _____ (shop).

go out
熄灭

Talk about it!

4 Work with a partner. Talk about your first-time experiences. What do you remember? Who were you with? What were you doing? What happened?

The first time I...
- met my best friend
- drove a car
- took a photo

A: I remember the first time I took a photo.
B: Oh, really? When was that?

take a photo
拍照

Unit 3

READING

Experiences to remember

1 Before reading Look at the pictures of the emergency providers. Match the names with the pictures. What emergencies can they help you with?

emergency provider 急救人员

1. ___ ambulance
2. ___ fire department
3. ___ police

fire department 消防队

> **HELP reading**
>
> Know your purpose for reading
> When you read, have a clear purpose, or reason, for reading the text. Think about what you want to find out before you read.

请注意明确阅读目的

2 Before reading Read the key words from each story. What do you think the stories are about? Talk about it with a partner. Then read the stories to check your predictions.

1. friend
   candle
   grass
   fire

2. *wife*
   baby
   car
   ambulance

large pumpkin 大南瓜

3. new job
   elevator
   night
   police

fall over 倒下; 跌倒

3 Reading Read the stories to check your predictions in exercise 2.
03_04

Lucy: I remember when I first met you, Andy.

Andy: Really? When was that?

Lucy: When I was a child.

Andy: What were we doing?

Lucy: We were in a field near my house. It was in the fall, and the grass was very dry. We were trying to cook a large pumpkin with a candle.

Andy: I don't remember that. What happened?

Lucy: Well, unfortunately, the candle fell over and the grass started to burn. The fire department came. I remember we felt very embarrassed.

2

... and here is this week's EXCITING MOMENTS

letter from Costa Rica.

My son Harry was born two weeks early. Jean, my wife, suddenly had labor pains. We got in the car and started to drive to the hospital. We were driving through the center of town and Jean called out, "The baby is coming!" I stopped the car and helped my wife. I was very nervous and worried. I was holding the baby when the ambulance arrived. Fortunately, the baby and my wife were fine. We are thrilled with our new son!

3

Dear Ian,

Nice to hear from you. My new job is going well. I like it a lot. But last week, the craziest thing happened! I was working at night in my office on the tenth floor, and suddenly the lights went out. The elevator wasn't working. I went to the emergency exit, but it was locked. I went to the window. I wrote, "Help! I can't get out! Call the police!" on some pieces of paper. Then I threw the pieces of paper out of the window to people on the street. Finally, someone read one and called the police. I was very tired and angry by then. The next day, the people at work told me never to work at night. They said they think the building has a ghost in it! I don't really think there's a ghost, but I don't plan to stay late anymore!

Hope all is well with you!

Talk to you soon!

Angie

4 Reading Read the stories again. Answer the questions.
03_04

1. Which story is about work?
2. Which story happened when the writer was a child?
3. Which story is about a baby?
4. Which person was alone when this story happened?

5 After reading Work with a partner. Talk about the emotions the people in the stories felt. Who was angry, thrilled, exhausted, nervous, scared, surprised, or worried?

Talk about it!

6 Work with a partner. Talk about an unusual emergency that you or a friend / family member has had. What happened? How did you / he / she feel?

A: Have I ever told you about when there was a huge snake in my mom's yard?
B: No! What happened?
A: Well, my mom was walking outside, when she saw it on the front steps. It was lying in the sun, and it wasn't moving.
B: Wow! How scary! What did she do?
A: Well, she called the police.

PROJECT

Work in a small group. Choose one of the three stories on pages 30-31. Prepare a dramatic presentation of the story to present to the class. The class votes on the best presentation.

labor pain
分娩时的阵痛

drive through
开车穿过

be thrilled with
非常兴奋；极为激动

on the tenth floor
在10楼
some pieces of paper
几张纸
call the police
打电话报警

Unit 3

Unit 3

CULTURE

Stories and culture

1 Before reading What is the name of a famous story you know from your culture or country? What is it about?

2 Before reading Match the story types to their definitions.

1. _d_ an anecdote
2. ___ a fable
3. ___ a fairy tale
4. ___ an urban legend

a. These are stories told to entertain children. They are usually about princesses, monsters, and faraway kingdoms. These stories are often made into movies.

b. This is a short story about animals, plants, or objects that have human qualities. These stories always end with a moral or lesson.

c. This is a modern story of things that people think are true but, in fact, are exaggerated or made sensational. These stories are often circulated by email.

d. This is a true story about real life. It is often about a funny or surprising situation.

faraway kingdoms 遥远的王国
make into movies 拍成电影
fairy tale 童话；神话故事
urban legend 都市传奇
sensational 耸人听闻的

3 Reading Read about some urban legends.

Urban Legends

Everybody has heard that in northern continents, like Asia, water turns in one direction when it goes down the drain, but turns in the opposite direction in southern continents, like Australia. This, in fact, is not true. This urban legend has appeared on a number of TV programs, in episodes of *The Simpsons*, *X-files*, and even in a school textbook! Another popular urban legend is that there are alligators living under the streets of New York City, or that someone once put a wet cat in a microwave oven to dry it. You may also have heard that it is possible to see the Great Wall of China from the moon. None of these urban legends is true, although these stories are often accepted as facts.

microwave oven 微波炉

The Simpsons 《辛普森一家》（美国动画片）
X-files 《X档案》(美剧)

4 After reading Check (✓) the three pictures that illustrate the urban legends.

A ☐ B ☐ C ☐ D ☐

Unit 3

5 Reading 　Now read an anecdote about the American actor Cary Grant.

Cary Grant
加里·格兰特
(美国演员)

TELEGRAM CABLE COMPANY
TELEGRAM

Cary Grant was a popular Hollywood actor. He was in a lot of movies, often with actresses who were much younger than he was. His age was always kept secret. One day, when he was in his agent's office, a telegram arrived from a journalist who wanted to know how old Cary Grant was. The telegram said:

HOW OLD CARY GRANT?

Cary Grant read the telegram and immediately sent a reply:

OLD CARY GRANT FINE. HOW YOU?

6 After reading 　Explain why the anecdote about Cary Grant is funny.

Talk about it!

7 Work with a partner. Do you know any urban legends? Tell your partner about an urban legend you've heard. If you don't know any, look some up on the Internet.

PRONUNCIATION

Vowel sounds /aʊ/ how, /əʊ/ no, and /ɔː/ for

Three common vowel sounds in English are /aʊ/ as in *how*, /əʊ/ as in *no*, and /ɔː/ as in *for*. Listen and put the words into three groups according to their vowel sounds.

| ~~course~~ | down | four | hold | now | or |
| close | found | go | more | phone | house |

/aʊ/ how	/əʊ/ no	/ɔː/ for
		course

33

Unit 3

CONVERSATION

Reacting to a story

1 How do people react to stories in your culture? What words, sounds, and body language do they use to show they are listening?

2 Listen to a conversation between Ron and Jen. Who is Jen?
03_08
  a. Tim's mother   b. Tim's friend   c. Tim's sister

3 Complete the conversation with expressions from the box. Then listen again to check
03_08 your answers.

| He really got lucky | Is he OK | Poor Tim |
| Really | That's terrible | ~~What happened~~ |

Ron: Hey, Jen. What did you do last weekend?
Jen: Well, most of the weekend was boring, but there was a terrible accident on Sunday!
Ron: Really? (**1**) _What happened_ ?
Jen: Well, Tim and I were walking over the old bridge, and he fell off it!
Ron: Really? (**2**) _____ ! How did it happen?
Jen: Well, he wasn't paying attention. He was leaning on a rail, and it broke!
Ron: Oh, no! (**3**) _____ ?
Jen: Yes, he's fine. There were some people swimming in the river and they helped him.
Ron: Wow! (**4**) _____ !
Jen: Yes, he did! But he wasn't so lucky when we got home.
Ron: (**5**) _____ ? What happened?
Jen: Well, my mom wasn't very happy when she found out why he was wet. So he got in trouble. He's not allowed to watch TV for a week!
Ron: Oh, no! (**6**) _____ !

lean on
倚;靠

get in trouble
遇到麻烦

CONVERSATION STRATEGY

Use body language
When we listen to a story, we use body language, such as eye contact, leaning forward, and nodding our heads. This shows the speaker that we are listening.

请注意使用肢体语言给对方回应

Talk about it!

4 Work with a partner. Talk about an accident or memorable event you were part of. Use the words and phrases from exercise 3 to react to your partner's story. Also use body language to show you're listening.

Tell me more!

Visit the Takeaway English Online Learning Center at http://olcs.mcgraw-hill-education.com/takeaway/

 Check out the *Takeaway TV* video.   Improve your English with the online activities.

Unit 3

WRITING

Writing a story about a memorable experience

HELP writing

Identify the key events and details
Before you write a story, use a graphic organizer to list the key events. After you have the key events, fill in the details. Try to balance the number of details for each key event.

请注意列出要点事件

1 Before writing Work with a partner. Talk about a memorable experience from your past. It can be a good or bad experience.

2 Writing model Read the story. Match three details to each key event.

Key events

1. coming home / storm
   _c_ ____ ____
2. the last bridge
   ____ ____ ____
3. the next day
   ____ ____ ____

Details

a. getting late / one more bridge
b. we could cross the bridge
c. crossed a lot of bridges / rivers getting higher
d. exhausted when we got home
e. driving home from vacation one summer
f. father drove car to top of hill / slept in car
g. terrible storm / rain very heavy
h. very happy and cheered
i. water covering bridge

One summer we were driving home from our vacation, and there was a terrible storm. We crossed a lot of bridges. The rain was really heavy. We saw that the rivers were getting higher and higher. It was getting dark, and we had one more bridge to cross. Unfortunately, the water was covering this bridge. My father drove the car up the hill and we slept in the car all night. Luckily, in the morning we could cross the bridge. We were thrilled and all cheered! When we finally arrived home, we were exhausted. That was the thing I remember most about that vacation—driving home.

get dark
变黑

3 Planning your writing Now plan the key events and details of your story. On a piece of paper, make a graphic organizer like the one shown here. Put the key events in the boxes on the left and the details in the boxes on the right.

4 Writing Write a story about your memorable event. Add illustrations. Then present your story to the class.

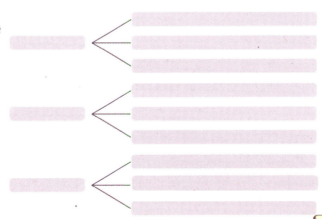

Unit 3

TEST

Test-taking strategy

Listen for and recognize tone Tone is the way in which something is said. Tone is very important because it can determine the meaning of what is said.

Use these steps to understand tone.

1. Listen for the tone of the speaker. Is it angry, happy, sarcastic, sweet, excited, afraid, friendly, funny, or sad?
2. What volume is the speaker using? Is it loud, natural, or quiet?
3. If you can see the speaker, what does his or her body language or facial expression tell you?
4. The exact same words can have completely different meanings depending on the tone.
5. The exact same question can have completely different meanings depending on the tone.
6. Different languages and cultures can have different tones. It is important to understand these differences to communicate clearly.

facial expression
面部表情

Example
You hear this speaker.

The hotel we stayed in was just great. The people in the next room were partying all night long and I didn't sleep. In the morning I was exhausted and then there was no hot water in the shower. I really think you should stay there on your next vacation. It's the best!

You see this test question.

1. Listen. What is the tone of the speaker?
    - ~~A.~~ happy   The speaker is not happy.
    - ~~B.~~ afraid   This speaker is not afraid.
    - C. sarcastic   This is the correct answer. The speaker hated the hotel.
    - ~~D.~~ funny   The speaker is not being funny. .

PRACTICE

Choose the correct answer. Mark the letter on the Answer Sheet.

1. Listen. In what sentence are the speaker's words true?
    - A The hotel we stayed in was just great.
    - B In the morning there was no hot water in the shower.
    - C I really think you should stay there on your next vacation.
    - D It's the best!

03_09

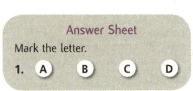

Answer Sheet
Mark the letter.
1.   A   B   C   D

WORKBOOK PAGE 21

UNIT SUMMARY

Nouns
anecdote
fable
fairy tale
urban legend

**Verbs—
accidents**
burn
crash into
cut
drop
fall down
fall off
slip on
trip over

**Expressions—
React to a story**
He / She really got lucky!
Is he / she OK?
Poor (name of the person)!
Really?
What happened?

4 ▶ I love chocolate!

> **In this unit you...**
> - talk about food made with chocolate
> - discuss recipes
> - give quantities
> - make, accept, and decline offers
>
> **Grammar**
> - passive voice

START

Made with chocolate

1 How often do you eat chocolate or something made with chocolate?

2 Write the names of some foods made with chocolate under the pictures. Then listen and check.
04_01

a box of chocolates	a chocolate cake	a cup of hot chocolate
a chocolate bar	chocolate chip cookies	a glass of chocolate milk
~~chocolate sauce~~	a chocolate-covered ice cream bar	

chocolate chip cookies
碎粒巧克力饼干
sauce
汁/酱

1. chocolate sauce   2. _____   3. _____   4. _____

5. _____   6. _____   7. _____   8. _____

3 Which three foods in exercise 2 are your favorites? Number them from 1 (your most favorite) to 3. Compare lists with a partner.

ENGLISH express

There are different types of chocolate. Three of the most common types are milk chocolate, dark chocolate, and white chocolate.

请注意巧克力的不同种类

Talk about it!

4 Work with a partner. Ask and answer the questions.
1. Which type of chocolate do you like best? Milk, dark, or white? Why?
2. What's your favorite chocolate dessert?

Unit 4

LISTENING

HELP listening

Spell words

As you are listening, take notes. Some words in English are not spelled as you expect. If you hear a word that you don't know how to spell, make a guess. Then look up the spelling in a dictionary later. Knowing how to spell a word helps you remember its meaning.

请注意听时记笔记并学会拼写单词

dessert recipe
甜点食谱

A dessert recipe

1 **Before listening** Who do you know that's a great cook? What recipes does he / she make?

2 **Before listening** Brandon gives Monica a recipe for chocolate sauce. Look at the list of ingredients (the things used to make a food product). Circle the ingredients that you think are in the recipe.

| chocolate | eggs | lemon juice | sugar |
| cream | honey | milk | water |

3 **Listening** Listen and check your guesses to exercise 2.
04_02

4 **Listening** Listen again. Check (✓) the correct quantity of each ingredient.
04_02

1.	baker's chocolate:	1 ounce	3 ounces	✓ 4 ounces
2.	cream:	1/2 cup	a cup	3 cups
3.	milk:	1/4 cup	1/2 cup	a cup
4.	honey:	1 teaspoon	1 tablespoon	3 teaspoons

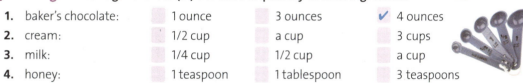

5 **After listening** Circle *True* or *False*.

1.	Monica is planning a dinner party.	**True**	False
2.	Monica knows what she's making for an appetizer.	True	False
3.	The chocolate sauce is difficult to make.	True	False
4.	The chocolate sauce is made with water.	True	False
5.	Monica decides not to make chocolate sauce.	True	False
6.	Brandon is probably a good cook.	True	False

Talk about it!

6 Work with a partner. Describe a dessert. Use a dictionary for ingredients you don't know. Your partner guesses what the dessert is.

A: You make this dessert with flour, eggs, oil, and chocolate. You cook it in the oven. People serve it for birthdays.

B: Is it chocolate cake?

A: Yes!

WORKBOOK PAGE 22

39

Unit 4

VOCABULARY

Cooking instructions

1 Do you like to cook? Why or why not? What's your favorite thing to cook or eat?

2 Match the cooking instructions to the pictures. Then listen and check.
04_03

| 1. ~~bake~~ | 2. boil | 3. cut | 4. fry | 5. mix | 6. pour | 7. serve | 8. stir |

A  B  C

D

E  F  G  H

3 Complete the sentences with the cooking verbs from exercise 2.

1. ___Fry___ the vegetables in a pan with oil.
2. _____ the chicken with rice and vegetables.
3. _____ the sauce while you're cooking it.
4. _____ the chocolate into small pieces.
5. _____ the hot milk over the chocolate pieces.
6. _____ the water before you pour it over the tea bag.
7. _____ the cake in the oven for 35 minutes.
8. _____ all of the ingredients together in a bowl.

> **ENGLISH express**
>
> We often use prepositions—
> in, into, for, to, over—with
> cooking verbs.
>
> Cut the meat into small pieces.
> Pour the sauce over the fruit.
>
> 请注意与烹饪动词搭配使用的介词

Talk about it!

4 Think of a food that you know how to prepare. Choose an appetizer, a main course, or a dessert. Make a list of the ingredients. Then make notes on how you make it. Use the verbs from exercise 2.

main course
主菜

5 Work with a partner. Use your notes from exercise 4 to explain your recipe.

This is a recipe for …
First…

GRAMMAR

The passive voice

ALSO GO TO
Grammar Takeaway
PAGE 197

1 Read these sentences. Then use the passive voice. Circle the *be* verb forms. Underline the past participle forms.

1. Baker's chocolate is made with less sugar than regular chocolate.
2. It's often used in cooking.
3. Chocolate sauce isn't made with water!
4. It's served on ice cream or fruit—or both.

ENGLISH express

To form passives, we use the verb *be* plus the past participle of the main verb.

请注意被动语态的形式

2 Look at the chart. What is the subject of each sentence? How are the active and passive sentences different?

	active voice	passive voice
affirmative	People make chocolate from cacao beans.	Chocolate is made from cacao beans.
negative	Rita doesn't make chocolate sauce with water.	Chocolate sauce isn't made with water.
yes / no questions and answers	Do you make chocolate sauce with cream? Yes, I do. / No, I don't.	Is chocolate sauce made with cream? Yes, it is. / No, it isn't.

cacao bean
可可豆

3 Read the sentences. Check (✔) A (active) or P (passive).

		A	P
1.	Monica plans the meal in advance.	✔	
2.	Chocolate is used in many different foods.		
3.	Fruit is often put on the plate for decoration.		
4.	Brandon helps Monica in the kitchen.		
5.	People sometimes eat cookies for dessert.		
6.	Honey is used in Brandon's recipe.		
7.	Candy makers make chocolate into many shapes.		

in advance
率先; 预先

4 On a piece of paper, rewrite the active sentences in exercise 3 in the passive.

1. The meal is planned in advance by Monica.

Talk about it!

5 Work with a partner. Describe an object for your partner. Use passive sentences. Your partner guesses what the object is.

A: I'm thinking of an object. It's sold at a jewelry store. It's made of gold or silver. It's worn on the wrist. It's usually worn by women.

B: Is it a bracelet?

A: Yes!

Unit 4

READING

HELP reading

Preview the contents
When you read an online encyclopedia entry, read the *Contents* list to find the sections that you are looking for. You can click on the section title names in the contents list to get to each section quickly.

请注意查找目录

All about chocolate

1 Before reading What do you know about chocolate? Circle your answers.

Portuguese explorers
葡萄牙探险家
neither...nor...
既不……也不

1. The Aztecs ate / **drank** chocolate at first.
2. Chocolate was brought to Europe by Spanish / English / Portuguese explorers in 1500.
3. Chocolate was first manufactured in the United States in 1665 / 1765 / 1865.
4. Chocolate is good / bad / neither bad nor good for your teeth.
5. Chocolate is possibly / isn't addictive.
6. People eat the most chocolate in Portugal / Spain / Switzerland.

2 Reading Read the online encyclopedia entry about chocolate.
04_04 Write the section titles in the entry.

http://www.encyclodopedia-chocolate.com

encyclopedia

Contents
▶ Facts or urban legends?   ▶ ~~What is it?~~
▶ Chocolate today   ▶ History

_____ **What is it?**

be native to
原产于;源于……的
hot climates
热带

Chocolate is made from the bean of the cacao tree. These trees are native to tropical South America. Cacao grows today in hot climates all over the world. Cacao beans are found in the fruit of the cacao trees. Cacao has been cultivated for thousands of years in Central America and Mexico.

_____

Aztec
阿兹特克人
(墨西哥印第安人)

The Mayans and Aztecs first used chocolate as a drink. Chocolate was first brought to Europe and then Asia by Spanish colonizers in 1500. It was first manufactured in the United States in 1765.

_____

scientific basis
科学基础
acne
痤疮; 粉刺
antioxidant
抗氧化剂

There are many popular beliefs about chocolate, but most of these don't have a scientific basis. For example, it is believed that eating chocolate can cause acne and other skin problems. In fact, pure chocolate contains antioxidants, and these are good for your skin. Many people also believe that chocolate is addictive, and that it is bad for your teeth. However, scientists believe that neither of these beliefs is true; it is not addictive, and it is the added sugar in chocolate products that is bad for your teeth, not the chocolate.

_____

Most of the chocolate that is consumed today is made into bars, using cacao, fats, and sugar. It is one of the most popular foods in the modern world, with Switzerland being the country where the most chocolate is eaten.

3 Reading Read the entry again. Check your answers to exercises 1 and 2.
04_04

Unit 4

4 After reading Match the underlined words from the text to the definitions.

1. _f_ native
2. ___ cultivated
3. ___ colonizers
4. ___ manufactured
5. ___ beliefs
6. ___ basis
7. ___ addictive
8. ___ consumed

a. causes a habit, your body needs it
b. eaten or drunk
c. factual support
d. grown, produced
e. ideas, opinions
f. originally from
g. made
h. people who try to make other countries part of their country

culture matters

In many English-speaking countries, chocolates are given as a gift on special days, like Valentine's Day (February 14). On other special days, such as Easter Sunday, chocolate eggs, rabbits, and other figures are given to children.

请注意西方节日时常送的礼物

Valentine's Day
情人节
(圣瓦伦丁节)

Talk about it!

5 Work with a partner. Talk about the questions.

1. When do people in your country give each other chocolate as a gift? Are there special shapes for the chocolate?

   A: I buy chocolate for my girlfriend on Valentine's Day.
   B: Really? What do you buy?
   A: Well, I buy different things, such as a box of chocolates or a chocolate heart.

2. What are the most popular ways to eat or drink chocolate in your country?

3. Are there any special days or times when people eat or drink chocolate in your country? When?

4. Are there any typical dishes in your country that contain chocolate? What are they?

CONVERSATION STRATEGY

Give examples
Use phrases like such as, for example, and like to give examples.

typical dishes
特别的菜肴

请注意"举例"的不同表达方式

PROJECT

Work in a small group. Find a recipe for a dish that has chocolate in it. Look in cookbooks or on cooking websites on the Internet. Write up the recipe to share with the class. Put all the recipes together to make a class cookbook. If possible, make one recipe at home. Bring in the dish for everyone in the class to try. Explain the recipe to the class as they try your dish.

Unit 4

SONG

I drink coffee, I drink tea

1 Before listening Match the drinks to the descriptions.

1. __c__ black coffee
2. _____ cappuccino
3. _____ espresso
4. _____ mocha latte
5. _____ Earl Grey

a. a drink made with espresso, chocolate, and a lot of hot milk
b. a small cup of very strong coffee
c. a cup of coffee with no sugar, milk, or cream in it
d. a type of tea
e. a drink made with espresso and a little bit of steamed milk

black coffee 不加奶的咖啡; 清咖啡
cappuccino 卡布奇诺
espresso 意大利式黑咖啡 (用蒸汽加压煮出的)
strong coffee 浓咖啡
mocha latte 摩卡拿铁
Earl Grey 伯爵茶

2 Listening Listen to the song. Put the verses in order. Number them from 1–5.
04_05

I drink coffee, I drink tea

CHORUS
My friends tell me
Give it up now
I'm not ready
One more cup now

☐ Mocha latte
Chocolate shake
I love to sit
In a street café

☐ I should try
Ice-cold lemonade
But without my caffeine
I get the shakes

[1] I drink coffee
I drink tea
I drink hot chocolate
More fool me

☐ Double espresso
To take away
With milk or cream
It makes my day

☐ Cappuccino
Strong Earl Grey
Sit inside
Or take away

ice-cold 冰冷的

the shakes 混合饮料

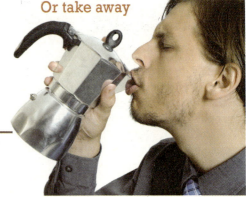

Unit 4

3 After listening Write the underlined expressions in the song next to their meanings.
1. it's a good idea to try ___I should try___
2. stop having it _____
3. when your hands move and are not steady, like when you're nervous _____
4. very cold _____
5. the thing in coffee that wakes you up _____
6. a type of drink made from ice cream and milk _____

Talk about it!

4 In your opinion, what are the best drinks to have in the morning? Number these drinks from 1 (best) to 8 (worst).

___ chocolate shake   ___ tea
___ orange juice   ___ cappuccino
___ coffee with cream ___ espresso
___ hot chocolate   ___ black coffee

5 Work in a small group. Compare your lists. Talk about which drinks you think are the best and why. As a group, decide on the best drink.

chocolate shake
巧克力奶昔

PRONUNCIATION

Word stress in three-syllable words

1 There are different word stress patterns in three-syllable words. Listen and repeat.
04_06

| cho<u>c</u>olate (●••)   Ko<u>re</u>an (•●•)   under<u>stand</u> (••●) |

2 Put the words into three groups according to their word stress pattern.
04_07 Then listen and check.

| ~~accident~~ | ambulance | decorate | Italian | Mexican | remember |
| addictive | anything | espresso | Japanese | recipe | seventeen |

1st syllable ●••	2nd syllable •●•	3rd syllable ••●
accident		

45

Unit 4

CONVERSATION

Making, accepting, and declining offers

1 How do people make polite offers in your language? How do they accept or decline the offers?

2 Listen to three conversations. Was the offer in each conversation accepted or declined? Check (✔) the correct box.

1. ☐ accepted ☐ declined
2. ☐ accepted ☐ declined
3. ☐ accepted ☐ declined

CONVERSATION STRATEGY

Make your response polite

When you decline an offer, give extra information. This makes the response more polite.
A: Would you like an apple?
B: No, thank you. I already had one.

请注意如何礼貌地拒绝他人

3 Complete the conversations with expressions from the box. Then listen again to check your answers.

| Are you sure | Do you want... | Here, have... | No, thanks |
| Thanks, anyway | Thanks very much | ~~Would you like...~~ | Yes, please |

1. **Rob:** It's my birthday. _Would you like_ a chocolate?
   Sara: _____. I'll have that one—the square one.
   Rob: But that's my favorite!

2. **Don:** Oh...I don't have any water.
   Tim: _____ some of mine.
   Don: _____.

3. **Josh:** I'm going to the store. _____ anything?
   Liza: _____. I have everything I need.
   Josh: _____?
   Liza: Yes. _____.

Talk about it!

4 Work with a partner. Role play a conversation between two people. One is making an offer, and the other is accepting or declining the offer.

make an offer
提出要求
accept/decline the offer
接受/拒绝请求

Tell me more!

Visit the Takeaway English Online Learning Center at http://olcs.mcgraw-hill-education.com/takeaway/

 Check out the *Takeaway TV* video.

 Improve your English with the online activities.

Unit 4

WRITING

Writing an encyclopedia entry

1 Before writing Make a list of ten common foods that would appear in an encyclopedia.

2 Writing model Read the encyclopedia entry about coffee. Write the missing details into the outline.

HELP writing

Make an outline
Before you write an article, make an outline. An outline is a system of short phrases that help you organize your paper. You use Roman numerals, letters, and numbers in an outline.

请注意写作时如何列出大纲

ENGLISH express

Roman numerals are a number system.
Roman numerals 1-10:
I, II, III, IV, V, VI, VII, VIII, IX, X

请注意罗马数字1-10的书写方式

---

http://www.encyclodopedia-coffee.com

encyclopedia

Coffee

What is it?
Coffee is a popular drink all over the world. It is prepared from the beans of the coffee plant. The coffee plant is native to Ethiopia and Yemen. It needs a temperate climate to grow.

The history
Coffee was first discovered in the mountains of Ethiopia, where it was first consumed in the 9th century. The coffee was taken to Yemen and then Europe to be sold. It quickly became popular. Aside from being a popular drink, it was also used in religious ceremonies in Africa and Yemen.

Myths or facts?
The health effects of coffee are not clear. Coffee is a good source of caffeine, which is a common stimulant. People like coffee because it wakes them up in the morning. Some studies have shown that caffeine can cause health issues such as heart disease and stomach problems. People say that children should not drink coffee because it will stop their growth.

Coffee today
Coffee is one of the most popular hot drinks today. It is drunk all over the world. There are many different ways to drink coffee—black, with cream and sugar, or as an espresso drink such as a cappuccino or a latte.

Outline
Coffee
I. What is it?
  A. popular drink
    1. all over world
  B. How prepared
    1. beans of _coffee plant_
    2. plant is native to _____, _____
      a. temperate climate
II. History
  A. _____ in Ethiopia
    1. first consumed in ___ century
  B. Taken to other countries
    1. Yemen and Europe
      a. popular _____
      b. used in _____
III. Myths or facts?
  A. Health effects not clear
    1. stimulant
      a. wakes people up
    2. health issues
      a. _____ disease
      b. stomach problems
      c. bad for _____
      d. stops growth
IV. Coffee _____
  A. very popular
    1. all over world
  B. many ways to drink coffee
    1. black
    2. _____ and sugar
    3. espresso drink
      a. _____
      b. latte

aside from
除……以外
religious ceremonies
宗教仪式
common stimulant
常见刺激物
health issues
健康问题

3 Planning your writing Choose one of the common foods to write an encyclopedia entry about. On a piece of paper, make an outline to plan the details of your entry. Be sure to use Roman numerals, letters, and numbers in your outline.

4 Writing Write your encyclopedia entry. Use the information in exercises 2 and 3 to help you.

Unit 4

TEST

Test-taking strategy

pros and cons
利与弊; 支持与反对

Identifying pros and cons   *Pros* are good things and *cons* are bad things. Many readings or listenings on tests will give both pros and cons on a certain topic or issue. Pros and cons can also be called advantages and disadvantages.

Use these steps to identify pros and cons.

in favor of
赞同; 支持

1. Pros are arguments in favor of, or supporting, a particular issue. Look for words like *advantage, positive, better, best, wonderful, fantastic,* etc.
2. Cons are arguments against a particular issue. Look for words like *disadvantage, negative, bad, worse, terrible, horrible,* etc.
3. Words and phrases like *but, though, although, however,* and *on the other hand* often introduce the opposite opinion of what was just said.
4. Writers or speakers will often give both pros and cons. Which argument do they make stronger?

> *Example*
> You see this test question
> 1. In the following sentence, what is the pro and what is the con?
>   *Putting cream in your coffee is delicious, but it does have a lot of fat.*
>   Pro = <u>coffee with cream is delicious</u>
>   Con = <u>cream has a lot of fat</u>

PRACTICE

Read the following paragraph. Write all the pros in one column and all the cons in the other column.

Everybody loves chocolate, right? It is so sweet and tasty. However, it does have a lot of sugar and fat. Some doctors say that dark chocolate is good for your heart. This is not true of milk and white chocolate. People have strong opinions about which chocolate is best. Some people say dark chocolate has the strongest flavor, but others say it is too strong and not sweet enough. Many people love the color and flavor of white chocolate, though others say it is too sweet. Milk chocolate is the most popular. It is creamy and medium sweet.

medium sweet
中等甜度

| Milk chocolate, dark chocolate, and white chocolate. ||
Pros	Cons
chocolate is sweet and tasty	

Unit 4

UNIT SUMMARY

Nouns
chocolate
cream
egg
honey
lemon juice
milk
sugar
water

Nouns—units of measure
cup
ounce
tablespoon

Nouns—Beverages
black coffee
cappuccino
chocolate shake
coffee
Earl Grey
espresso
hot chocolate
mocha latte
orange juice
tea

Verbs—cooking instructions
bake
boil
cut
fry
mix
pour
serve
stir

Prepositions
in
into
for
to
over

Expressions—making, accepting, and declining offers.
Do you want…
No, thanks.
Thanks, anyway.
Thanks very much.
Would you like…
Yes, please.

5 ▸ How can we help?

In this unit you...
- talk about people in need of help
- identify natural disasters
- discuss ways to help people
- make requests and give excuses

Grammar
- object pronouns

START

In need of help

1 Who in your community, your country, or the world needs help? Why do they need help?

2 Write the words about people who need help in the sentences. Then listen and check.
05_01

| disabled | elderly | homeless | orphaned | earthquake | flood | hungry | ~~poor~~ |

1. They have no money. They're __poor__.
2. He's very old. He's _____.
3. He needs food. He's _____.
4. He cannot walk. He's _____.

5. There was an _____.
6. He lives on the street. He's _____.
7. There was a _____.
8. They have no parents. They were _____.

natural disasters
自然灾害

3 Which of the words in exercise 2 are adjectives that describe people? Which are natural disasters? Write the words in two lists. Then add more words to each list.

adjectives that describe people	natural disasters
poor,	

ENGLISH express

A natural disaster is an emergency that is caused by a problem in nature, such as a hurricane, a flood, or an earthquake.

请注意了解自然灾害

Talk about it!

4 Work with a partner. Answer these questions for each picture in exercise 2.
1. What do you see in the picture?
2. What kind of help do the people need?

Unit 5

LISTENING

A service trip

1 Before listening What do you usually do when you have a vacation?

2 Before listening Look at Sara's spring break photos. Where do you think she was? What do you think she did? Who was she with?

> **culture matters**
>
> In the United States, most universities give students a week of vacation during the spring. This is called *spring break*. Many students go to the beaches in Florida and Mexico.
>
> 请注意了解美国的"春假"

spring break
春假

3 Listening Listen to Sara's conversation with Brad. Check your predictions from exercise 2.
05_02

4 Listening Listen again. Check (✔) who said each statement or question.
05_02

	Brad	Sara
1. We spent lots of time on the beach and we went to lots of great parties.	✔	
2. I did have a great time, but I didn't go to any parties.		
3. A service trip? What's that?		
4. We built a house for a family that lost their house in last year's hurricane.		
5. Dr. Collins in the French department is organizing the next one to Haiti.		
6. I'd like to go on a service trip for my next vacation.		

service trip
服务旅行

5 After listening Answer the questions. Compare your answers with a partner.

1. What did Brad do for his spring break?
2. What is a *service trip*?
3. What does Brad think about Sara's spring break?
4. Will Sara go on the service trip to Haiti? Why or why not?

> **HELP listening**
>
> **Make inferences**
> After you listen, make inferences—guesses based on what you heard and what you know—about people's actions and reactions. This will increase your comprehension of what you heard.
>
> 请注意听力练习中学会推理

Talk about it!

6 Work with a partner. Talk about the questions.

1. What did you do for your last vacation from school or work?
2. What do you think about going on a *service trip*?
3. If you went on a service trip, who would you want to help?

Unit 5

VOCABULARY

Ways to help

1 What are some ways that you can help people in need?

in the brochure
小册子里的

2 Write the words for helping people in the brochure. Then listen and check.

| aid | ~~charity~~ | donate | lend | raise | sponsor | visit | volunteer |

Eight Ways to help

1. Get a job working for a ___charity___ or other organization that helps people.
2. _____ by working for no pay at an organization that helps people in need.
3. _____ money by selling things, such as cookies. Then give all of the money to an organization that helps people.
4. _____ ! Give money or things you don't use anymore to a local organization.
5. _____ someone that is participating in a walk, run, or other event to raise money for a good cause. Then you give all of the money to the organization that supports the cause.
6. Travel to an area where there are problems. Offer them _____ , or help.
7. _____ money to those who need it. Make an agreement that they will give it back to you later.
8. _____ the sick, elderly, or lonely. Spend time with them so that they don't feel alone.

make an agreement
达成协议; 达成共识

feel alone
感到孤独

Talk about it!

3 Work with a partner. Describe a situation where people were in need of help and what other people did to help them.

A: After the earthquake in Haiti, there were many people without houses, food, or water. Many people traveled there from other countries to give aid. They brought food, fixed houses, and helped people that were hurt.

B: That's true. And other people helped without going there. They raised money by having concerts where people paid for tickets. Then they gave all of the money to charities that helped the Haitians.

give aid
提供帮助

Unit 5

GRAMMAR

Object pronouns

ALSO GO TO
Grammar Takeaway
PAGE 198

1 Pronouns take the place of nouns. Circle the pronouns in these sentences. Then complete the chart.

take the place of
代替; 取代

1. (She) brought (you) this t-shirt.
2. Habitat for Humanity helped them.
3. I'll give him your name.
4. Can you tell me what a *service trip* is?
5. You can give help to the people who need it.

subject pronouns	I	you	she	he	it	we	they
object pronouns	me		her			us	

subject pronouns
人称代词主格
object pronouns
人称代词宾格

2 Read the sentences in the chart. Where does the object pronoun go?

verb + noun / pronoun + noun	verb + noun + to + noun / pronoun
Give the homeless people the clothes. Give them the clothes. The organization lent my friend money. The organization lent her money.	Give the clothes to the homeless people. Give the clothes to them. We donated money to the organization. We donated money to it.

3 Complete the sentences. Write object pronouns for the nouns in parentheses.

1. The teacher told ___them___ a story. (**the children**)
2. I gave _____ my coat. (**the homeless man**)
3. I want to show _____ the new brochure. (**my female boss**)
4. Can you give _____ a ride? (**me and my friend**)
5. She sent _____ money. (**the poor people**)
6. I like to throw _____ the ball. (**the dog**)
7. The government lent _____ some money. (**the businessman**)

ENGLISH express

Most verbs follow the pattern:
verb + noun + to + noun / pronoun.
Some verbs like *give*, *lend*, and *tell* can also follow the pattern:
verb + noun / pronoun + noun.

请注意动词的搭配形式

Talk about it!

4 Work in a small group. Take turns telling other students about a person who needs help. The group gives suggestions of how to help that person.

A: A man doesn't have a job or money. He wants to work, but he doesn't know how to get a job. How can we help him?

B: Well, we could give him clothes to wear to an interview.

C: Or we could send him to an organization that helps people find jobs.

D: We could also help him write a good résumé...

Unit 5

READING

The recycled goats

1 Before reading Label the picture with words from the box.

| goat | milk | manure | crops |

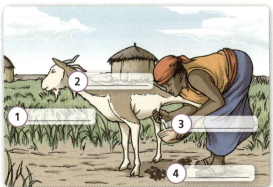

Burundi 布隆迪(非洲国家)
civil war 内战

constant fear 持续的恐惧

aid organization 援助机构

2 Before reading Look at the words in the box below. They are all from the news article. Look up any new words in a dictionary. What do you think the article is about?

widow, fear, Burundi, aid organization, poor, recycle, money, gift, education, clothes, sell, goat, milk, manure, crops

3 Reading Read the article and check your guess in exercise 2.
05_04

> **HELP reading**
>
> **Know the writer's purpose**
> When you read, consider who wrote the article and his or her purpose in writing it. Knowing the writer's purpose can help you understand what you are reading.
>
> 请注意阅读时考虑作者的写作意图

One goat — one small gift of $4 a month

That's all it takes for people like Gerthrude Bukuru to survive.

Gerthrude Bukuru lives in Burundi, a country <u>ruined</u> by years of civil war. During the war some of her <u>neighbors</u> were killed. Gerthrude has lived in constant fear. She is a poor woman in a poor country. But she is not going to <u>give up</u>. She and some other women from her village asked for help. That help came in a surprising way.

An aid organization gave the women ten goats. And by "<u>recycling</u>" these

54

goats, the women's lives have been changed forever.

The goats produced milk, and this meant that Gerthrude's children had good milk to drink.

The goats also produced manure. The women used the manure to fertilize their small plots of land. This improved the quality and quantity of their crops. There was even enough food to sell. This meant that the women had more money to pay for necessities like clothes, medicine, and education for their children.

In time, the goats produced their own goats. The first ten baby goats were given back to the aid organization. The women were able to keep their original ten goats. Most importantly, they didn't need help any more.

A small gift—one goat costs $4 a month— is all it takes to make a big difference.

4 Reading Read the article again. Answer the questions.
05_04

1. What's the widow's name?
2. Who helped her?
3. How many goats did they give the women?
4. What did they do with the manure?
5. Why did they give back the baby goats?
6. What was the writer's purpose?

5 After reading Write the underlined words in the text next to the definitions.

1. destroyed or broken _____ruined_____
2. give nutrients (food) to plants _____
3. made it possible for _____
4. made better _____
5. people living near _____
6. pieces, areas _____
7. stop, stop having hope, surrender _____
8. using something again and again _____

Talk about it!

6 Work with a partner. Discuss other aid projects that help people to help themselves.

A: Let's see. There is an organization for homeless people. They make their own newspapers and sell them on the street.

B: Right. This means that these people are working and making a little money.

A: Yes, and they are also telling other people about the lives of homeless people.

B: What else?

PROJECT

Work in a small group. Think of a situation in which people give help in some way. Write a script for a scene about the situation, including dialogue that explains the situation, what help is needed, what people do, and how people feel. Present your scene to the class. The class votes on the best scene.

manure
肥料; 粪肥

plots of land
地块

make a big difference
有很大影响;
意义重大

Unit 5

55

Unit 5

CULTURE

Charitable organizations around the world

charitable organization
慈善组织

1 Before reading   What are the names of some charitable organizations in your community and country? What do they do?

2 Reading   Read about the charities. Who do they help?
05_05

3 After reading   Read the sentences. Circle *True* or *False*.

Big Brothers and Big Sisters
兄姐会
Oxfam (Oxford Committee for Famine Relief)
牛津饥荒救济委员会
CARE (Cooperative for American Relief to Everywhere)
美国援外合作署
suffer from
忍受; 遭受
Meals on Wheels
上门送餐服务
match up with
和……相配
role model
榜样
be dedicated to
致力于

1. Big Brothers and Big Sisters helps teenagers learn to babysit their brothers and sisters.	True	**False** (circled)
2. Oxfam works to fight hunger.	True	False
3. CARE only helps people in the United States.	True	False
4. Doctors Without Borders helps people and areas that are suffering from disease.	True	False
5. The people that work at Meals on Wheels are all young.	True	False

Great Charitable Organizations

Big Brothers and Big Sisters of America is an organization whose goal is to help low-income children achieve success in life. They do this through mentoring, or matching up children with adults that act as friends and role models to them.

Oxfam is an international organization that is dedicated to fighting hunger around the world. They focus on helping people learn to help themselves. They also send help after natural disasters or war.

natural resources
自然资源

CARE is a worldwide charitable organization. They work to improve education, health, and the environment, and to protect natural resources around the world. They do most of their work with women because they believe that women have the power to help whole families. They also help people rebuild after war and natural disasters.

Doctors Without Borders
无国界医生组织
war-torn areas
遭受战争破坏的地区
medical professionals
医学专家
medical care
医疗护理
housebound
不能离家外出的

Doctors Without Borders is an organization that is working to fight the spread of disease in developing and war-torn areas around the world. They do this by sending doctors, nurses, and other medical professionals to provide medical care to people who are suffering from disease and other health issues.

The **Meals on Wheels** program works to bring food to low-income people who aren't able to leave their house. The most common population they serve is the elderly, but they also help disabled and other low-income people who are housebound. Most of the volunteers for the Meals on Wheels program are also elderly, but they are still able to get around, drive, etc. The program is found in a variety of English-speaking countries worldwide, including Canada, Australia, the United Kingdom, and the United States.

4 After reading Match the people's problems to the charities that help them.

1. _____Oxfam_____ : Asari is from a small village in Indonesia. His family lost everything in a recent earthquake. They have no home, no clean water, and very little food.
2. _____ : Ibibo lives in a small village in Nigeria. Many people in the village are dying because there is an epidemic of smallpox.
3. _____ : Bill is 92 years old and lives alone in a small apartment. He cannot walk or see well. He doesn't have any family and has very little money.
4. _____ : Luz is from a very poor community in Ecuador, where they have little money and resources. Everyone in the community has a low education level. Luz wants to help her family and community.
5. _____ : Janiya is 9 years old. She lives in a poor neighborhood in New York City. She lives with her mother and two younger brothers. Her mother works all day at a fast food restaurant, but they still have very little money.

epidemic of smallpox
天花的流行

low education level
文化程度低

Talk about it!

5 Work with a partner. Talk about the questions.

1. Do you think charitable organizations can make a difference in people's lives? Why or why not?
2. Do you think charitable organizations can help make the world a better place? Why or why not?
3. Who do you think should be required to give money to charitable organizations? Explain your answer.

PRONUNCIATION

Vowel sounds /ʌ/ up, /ʊ/ put, and /ɪ/ busy

1 Three common vowel sounds for the letter *u* are /ʌ/ as in *up*, /ʊ/ as in *put*, and /ɪ/ as in *busy*.
05_06

2 Put the words into three groups according to their vowel sounds. Then listen and check.
05_07

| ~~brush~~ | business | cup | hurry | number | rush |
| bus | butcher | hungry | minute | push | sugar |

/ʊ/ up	/ʌ/ put	/ɪ/ busy
brush		

Unit 5

CONVERSATION

Making requests and giving excuses

1. When do you make formal and informal requests? How are formal and informal requests different in your language?

CONVERSATION STRATEGY

Use formal vs. informal language
We use different words for formal and informal requests. In general, the more formal the request, the more words we use.

Can you open the window, please? (informal)
Excuse me. Would you mind opening the window, please? (formal)

请注意正式和非正式请求的不同表达方式

2. Listen to three conversations. Is the request in each conversation formal or informal?

3. Complete the conversations with expressions from the box. Then listen again to check your answers.

give sb. a hand
给予某人帮助

Can you give me a hand	I don't know how…
I'm really busy	~~Would you mind…~~
I'm doing my homework	I'm in a hurry
I was wondering if I could…	

1. **Eve:** Excuse me. __Would you mind__ helping me, please? How does this thing work?
   Ned: I'm sorry, I can't help you. _____ it works.
   Eve: Oh, well. Thank you anyway.

2. **Dad:** Hey, Tina. _____ ?
   I'm cleaning up.
   Tina: Sorry. _____ .
   Dad: Come on! It won't take long.
   Tina: _____ . I'll help later.

clean up
清理; 大捞一笔

3. **Jodie:** Excuse me. _____ ask you a few questions.
   Marc: I'm sorry, _____ .
   Jodie: OK. Thank you anyway.

Talk about it!

4. Work with a partner. Practice making requests and giving excuses. Then perform your requests and excuses for the class. The class says if the requests are formal or informal.

Tell me more!

Visit the Takeaway English Online Learning Center at http://olcs.mcgraw-hill-education.com/takeaway/

 Check out the *Takeaway TV* video.

 Improve your English with the online activities.

Unit 5

WRITING

Writing a plan to help others

1 Before writing Make a list of ways that you could help others in need.

HELP writing
Use a flowchart
To prepare a plan, use a *flowchart*. A flowchart is a graphic organizer that shows a chain of events, or the cause and effect of different actions.
请注意写作时使用流程图

in need
在困难时;
在灾难中

2 Writing model Read Marla's essay about her plan to help others. Write the missing details in the flowchart.

- collect _____old_____ bicycles from friends and family
- give the bicycles to _____
- the people use the bicycles to get to _____
- the people make _____ at their jobs
- the people use their money to _____
- they give the original biycles to _____
- the people can achieve success and become _____

achieve success
取得成功;获得成功

A plan to help others

I start by collecting old bicycles from my friends and family. I then work with the school to find people that are unemployed, but would like to work and don't have transportation. We give the bicycles to the unemployed people. They use the bicycles to get to job interviews. After they get jobs, they use the bicycles to get to work. The people make money at their jobs and learn skills. They save enough money to buy their own bicycles. They then give the original bicycles to other unemployed people. These people use the bicycles for the same process. With this plan, the people are able to achieve success. They become better citizens, and this make the world a better place.

3 Planning your writing On a piece of paper, make a flowchart to write the details of your plan. Use one of the ideas below or your own idea.

- Give a smart child a dictionary.
- Give a poor family a garden.
- Give a disabled person a laptop.
- Give a homeless person $100.

4 Writing Write your essay about your plan to help others. Use the information in exercises 2 and 3 to help you.

Unit 5

TEST

Test-taking strategy

Identifying support for an opinion Writers or speakers use facts or statements to support their opinions. It is important to be able to identify this support.
Use these steps to identify support for an opinion.

back up
支持; 援助

1. First identify the opinion.
2. Next identify any statements or facts that support or back up that opinion. Does the writer or speaker also give support for the facts?
3. Recognize the difference between an opinion and a fact.
4. Writers or speakers will often give both sides of an argument before giving their opinion. Is the support for their opinion strong and convincing?

> *Example*
> You read these two opinions.
>
> (**1**) I don't think we should help homeless people. Most homeless people use drugs and alcohol. Many homeless are criminals. If you give money to the homeless they will buy more drugs and alcohol. They don't want to change.
>
> (**2**) I think it's very important to help the homeless. Everybody needs a warm, clean place to sleep. Nobody can have a good life without a home. I think a lot of homeless people use drugs and alcohol and commit crimes because they are so sad.
>
> **You see this test question.**
>
> 1. What do both writers agree on?
>   - ~~A.~~ Homeless people are criminals. — Only the first writer says this.
>   - B. Homeless people use drugs and alcohol. — This is the correct answer.
>   - ~~C.~~ Homeless people are not happy and need help. — Only the second writer says this.
>   - ~~D.~~ Homeless people choose to be homeless. — Only the first writer says this.

commit crimes
犯罪; 做坏事

PRACTICE

Choose the correct answer. Mark the letter on the Answer Sheet.

1. Why does the second writer say that the homeless commit crimes?
   - A Because they don't want to change.
   - B Because they use drugs and alcohol.
   - C Because they are sad.
   - D Because they need money for drugs and alcohol.

2. What is the opinion of the first writer?
   - A Homeless people want to change.
   - B Homeless people commit crimes to get drugs.
   - C The homeless are sad and no good.
   - D Don't help the homeless.

3. What two things do both writers agree on?
   - A Homeless people use drugs and commit crimes.
   - B Homeless people use alcohol and want to change.
   - C Homeless people are sad and want to change.
   - D Homeless people are criminals and don't want to change.

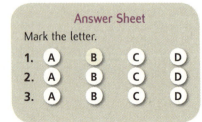

Answer Sheet
Mark the letter.
1. A B C D
2. A B C D
3. A B C D

WORKBOOK
PAGE 35

Unit 5

UNIT SUMMARY

Nouns
charity
disease
earthquake
flood
homeless
hunger
orphan
volunteer

Verbs
aid
donate
lend
raise
recycling
sponsor
visit

Adjectives
broken
disabled
elderly
hungry
orphaned
poor

Expressions—making requests and giving excuses
Can you give me a hand?
I don't know how to…
I'm in a hurry.
I'm really busy.
I was wondering if you could…
Would you mind…

Review 1

VOCABULARY

1 Complete the crossword.

Across
1. this is what people in the movies do
4. child whose parents die has been _____
6. start to feel well again after being sick (two words)
8. an organization that helps people in need
10. a hot drink made of milk and chocolate (two words)
11. very old
12. a teacher
14. decide to get married (two words)

Down
2. small pieces of metal money
3. when you touch something very hot and get hurt
5. a big storm in the ocean
7. to cook something in the oven
9. a small clock that you wear on your wrist
11. feeling very tired
13. to put food on a plate and give it to someone to eat

Review 1

GRAMMAR

1 Write the verbs in the simple past, past continuous, or present perfect.

1. She _____ (**eat**) a hamburger for dinner last night.
2. David _____ (**never / eat**) meat. He's a vegetarian.
3. How long _____ (**you / live**) in Seoul?
4. _____ (**you / ever / fly**) in an airplane?
5. While I _____ (**drive**) to work, I _____ (**crash**) into another car.
6. We _____ (**go**) to the movies last night.
7. Christina _____ (**be**) to that restaurant. She _____ (**go**) there last week.
8. I remember the first time I _____ (**meet**) you. We _____ (**walk**) to school.

2 **Error correction** If the sentence is wrong, rewrite the sentence correctly. If it is correct, write **C** next to the sentence.

1. I have shopped last week.
2. Have you ever eaten a whole pizza?
3. Paper is make from trees.
4. Mona is lived in London for two months.
5. That glass was falling down last night and it was breaking.
6. I made dinner because my mother was sick.
7. We asked for a dictionary and the teacher gave one to we.
8. The lightbulb was invented by Thomas Edison.
9. The old man was walking down the street and he has fallen.

Review 1

LISTENING

A special gift

1 Before listening What's the best gift you've ever gotten? Why was it special? Who gave it to you? Do you still have it?

2 Listening Listen to someone describing an object that is special for him. Which object is it? Check the box.
05_R1_01

 A
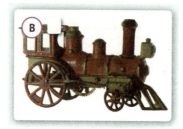 B
 C

3 Listening Listen again. Complete the notes.
05_R1_01

Once, someone gave me a (1) _____. It was made in
(2) _____. My (3) _____ bought it when she
was (4) _____. It was a souvenir from a museum.
It's a (5) _____ with a sail. I have it (6) _____,
(7) _____. I (8) _____
a lot. I (9) _____ Spain, but I would
(10) _____ one day.

Talk about it!

4 Work with a partner. Talk about an unusual or interesting gift you've received. Use the phrases to help you.

Once, someone gave me a...	I love / don't like / hate it.
It was the best / strangest / worst present.	I keep it in / under / on...
It is (not) very...	I use / wear / put it...

5 Tell the class about your partner's gift. As a class, decide on who had the most unusual or interesting gift.

Review 1

CONVERSATION

1 Look at the picture. Where are the people? What are they talking about?

2 Listen to a conversation between two friends.
1. What's Tina doing next week?
2. What's she doing over the summer?

3 Complete the conversation with the words in the box. Then listen to check your answers.

| a big fan of | Congratulations | Thanks very much | That's terrible |
| an avid | Poor | That's amazing | Would you like... |

Nora: Hey, Tina! What are you doing this summer?

Tina: Well, you know I'm graduating next week, right?

Nora: You are? **(1)** _____ !

Tina: Thanks! I'm really excited because after graduation I'm going on a hiking trip in Costa Rica this summer to celebrate.

Nora: Wow! **(2)** _____ !

Tina: Yeah—I'm looking forward to it. I'm **(3)** _____ hiker, and I'm also **(4)** _____ unusual animals, so I think it will be the perfect trip for me.

Nora: It sounds like it! Who are you going with?

Tina: Well, Janet was planning to go with me, but she just broke her leg.

Nora: Really? **(5)** _____ ! **(6)** _____ Janet!

Tina: I know.... So I'm looking for someone to go with me. Hey, **(7)** _____ to go?

Nora: Wow! **(8)** _____ ! That would be great!

Talk about it!

4 Work with a partner. Talk about your upcoming plans.

6 ▸ World languages

In this unit you...
- talk about different languages
- discuss learning languages
- say how you do things
- ask for clarification

Grammar
- simple present and present continuous

START

Understanding languages

1 Do you recognize these words? What do you think they mean? What languages are they?

1. Hello
2. Marhaba
3. Guten Tag
4. Ola
5. Ni Hao
6. Privet
7. Hola
8. Konnichiwa

2 Match each language to the country where
06_01 it is spoken. Then listen and check.

a. __2__ German   e. _____ Spanish
b. _____ Arabic   f. _____ Japanese
c. _____ Portuguese   g. _____ Chinese
d. _____ English   h. _____ Russian

3 Listen to eight people talking. Do you
06_02 recognize each language? Write the correct
language from the list in exercise 2.

speaker 1 __English__   speaker 3 _____   speaker 5 _____   speaker 7 _____
speaker 2 _____   speaker 4 _____   speaker 6 _____   speaker 8 _____

Talk about it!

4 With a partner, ask and answer these questions.

1. How many languages do you speak? Which languages are they?
2. What languages can you say "hello" in? Or count to 10 in? Demonstrate for your partner.
3. Are there words in your language that come from other languages? Make a list together.
4. When do you listen, speak, read, or write in another language? At home? At school? When traveling?

Unit 6

LISTENING

Learning languages

1 Before listening Which sentences have similar meanings?

1. _e_ My native language is Korean.
2. ____ I speak fluent Korean.
3. ____ I speak broken Korean.
4. ____ I picked up some Korean on vacation.
5. ____ I know some Korean slang.
6. ____ I can get by in Korean.

a. I have basic Korean.
b. My Korean is not grammatically correct.
c. I speak Korean easily and naturally.
d. I know some informal Korean words.
e. The first language I learned is Korean.
f. I learned some Korean words without studying.

pick up
不费力地学会

get by
过得去

2 Before listening Work with a partner. Use these words from exercise 1 to talk about your language skills.

| native language | fluent | broken | pick up | slang | get by in |

native language
方言

A: I can get by in French. How about you?

3 Listening (06_03) Listen to Amal and Nancy talk about languages. Circle the languages that each person speaks.

| Amal | French | Chinese | English | (Arabic) | Italian | Japanese |
| Nancy | French | Chinese | English | Arabic | Italian | Japanese |

HELP listening

Listen for key words
Listen for key words and expressions related to a certain topic. This can improve your overall understanding. In this conversation, listen for the language expressions you have learned and practiced.

请注意听时抓住核心词与关键句

4 Listening (06_03) Listen again. Circle True or False for each sentence.

1. Amal speaks four languages. **(True)** False
2. Amal's native language is French. True False
3. Nancy studied French in Paris. True False
4. Nancy picked up slang in French. True False
5. Nancy is fluent in Chinese. True False

5 Listening (06_04) Listen to the rest of the conversation. Check (✔) what Nancy and Amal do to help them learn Chinese and Italian.

Do they...	Amal	Nancy
1. do grammar exercises?	✔	
2. speak with friends in person?		
3. surf the Internet for websites and blogs?		
4. listen to music / watch movies?		
5. write email and chat with an e-pal?		
6. read books / magazines / news articles?		

chat with an e-pal
和网友聊天

Talk about it!

6 Look at exercise 5. Do you do any of these things? Tell your partner what you do.

Unit 6

VOCABULARY

How well do you speak the language?

1 How well do you speak your native language? How well do you speak English? How well do you speak another language?

2 Listen to the sentences. Look at each underlined word. Can you guess the word's meaning from the way it is used? Discuss with a partner.
06_05

1. Kumi learns new English expressions easily. She remembers everything she studies.
2. Carl's mother is Colombian and his father is American. He speaks both Spanish and English fluently.
3. Sometimes my Spanish teacher speaks too quickly. I wish she would speak more slowly.
4. Tina is Mexican, but she speaks English so naturally I thought it was her native language.
5. Kim normally speaks English, but when he visits his grandparents he speaks Korean.
6. The teacher speaks very clearly. I understand almost everything he says.

3 Complete the sentences with the words from the box. Check your answers with a partner.

| clearly | loudly | naturally | quickly | normally | fluently | easily | ~~slowly~~ |

1. Sometimes the teacher speaks very ___slowly___ so the students can understand.
2. I can't hear you. Please speak _____ .
3. Native speakers are difficult to understand because they often speak very _____ .
4. I speak English _____ with my teacher, but it's more difficult with native speakers.
5. Nick doesn't speak _____ . Do you understand what he says?
6. One day, after many years of study, I hope to speak English _____ .
7. I _____ study English every day, but I didn't today.
8. He doesn't speak English _____ . He still has a strong accent.

strong accent
很重的口音

4 *Fluently* is only used to describe the way a language is spoken. The other words in exercise 3 can be used to describe other activities. Use the words to make sentences about other things you do.

At a soccer match, sometimes I yell very loudly.

Talk about it!

5 With a partner, compare your lists. Ask more questions.

A: What are some other things that you do easily?
B: Well, I fall asleep easily, but I don't wake up easily.
A: Me too!

fall asleep
入睡; 睡着

Unit 6

GRAMMAR

Simple present and present continuous

ALSO GO TO
Grammar Takeaway
PAGE 199

1 With a partner, look at these pairs of sentences. Discuss how the meaning of the two sentences is different.

> I speak English. / I am speaking English now.
> He writes letters to all his friends. / He can't come with us, because he's writing a letter.
> She studies English every day. / She's studying English to get a better job.

2 Look at the chart. When do you use the simple present? When do you use the present continuous?

simple present	present continuous
She likes learning languages.	I'm learning Chinese for work.
How often do you write to your Chinese e-pal?	Why is she studying Japanese?

3 Read the conversation. Circle the correct form of the verb. Then listen and check.
06_06

Amal: How often (**1**) do you write / are you writing to your Chinese e-pal?

Nancy: Oh, about twice a week. I (**2**) tell / am telling her about my friends, my family, and my hobbies.

Amal: And (**3**) do you usually practice / are you usually practicing speaking too, or just writing?

Nancy: Just writing for now, but we (**4**) think / are thinking of having an online chat in the future.

Amal: That's cool. So why (**5**) do you study / are you studying Chinese? (**6**) Do you have / Are you having friends in China?

Nancy: No, not yet! I've never been to China. But I'd really like to visit. And I (**7**) think / am thinking Chinese is going to be a really important language in the future for work.

> **ENGLISH to go**
>
> **Say** and **tell**
> She says (that) learning Japanese is a hobby.
>   say + (that) + something
> I tell her things about my friends and hobbies.
>   tell + someone + something

请注意 say 和 tell 的不同用法

have an online chat
在线聊天

Talk about it!

4 With a partner, ask and answer these questions.

1. Why are you studying English?
2. What are some of the different ways that you study?
3. What do you think are the best ways to study English? Explain.

WORKBOOK
PAGE 43-44

Unit 6

READING

The written word

1 Before reading Do all languages use the same alphabet? Write the correct language beside each writing sample.

> English   Greek   ~~Russian~~   Korean   Arabic   Chinese

1. Привет _Russian_
2. 喂 _____
3. السلام _____
4. Γειά _____
5. 안녕하세요 _____
6. Hello _____

2 Reading Read the magazine article about writing systems. Then choose and fill in the correct title for each paragraph.
06_07

> How writing developed   Modern changes
> ~~The origins of writing~~   The organization of letters and symbols

HELP reading

Preview the task
Read the true / false statements in exercise 3 first. This will help you focus on the important information in the reading.

请注意阅读前读题

1. **The origins of writing**

the distant past 远古
historical events 历史事件
cultural traditions 文化传统
Mesopotamia 美索不达米亚
Mesoamerica 中美洲
adapt to 使……适合
text messaging 手机短信发送

In the distant past, people told stories and sang songs to remember important historical events and cultural traditions. When people started to trade, writing was developed to record information in a more permanent way. Writing first appeared in four different places: Mesopotamia (modern day Iraq, Iran, and Syria), Egypt, China, and Mesoamerica (modern day Southern Mexico and much of Central America).

2. _____

Around the world, writing systems developed in different and complex ways. Some writing systems used symbols to represent ideas. For example, in Chinese, the symbol 龟 means *tortoise*. Other languages used symbols to represent syllables or combinations of sounds. In Japanese, the symbols ホテル represent the three syllables in the Japanese word for *hotel*: ho-te-ru. Other writing systems developed letters to represent sounds. In the English word *cat*, each letter represents a sound: /kæt/.

3. _____

Writing systems also differed in the way they were organized for people to read. For example, Greek (and later Latin and all European languages) was written horizontally from left to right, but Arabic was written horizontally from right to left. Traditionally, Chinese, Japanese, and Korean were written vertically from right to left. Nowadays, these languages can also be written horizontally from left to right. This is partially because of the influence of English and the use of computers.

4. _____

Writing systems change over time to adapt to the needs of the people who use them. Recently, Internet chatting and text messaging with cell phones are changing the way people use words. People write abbreviations like "ttyl" for "Talk to you later" or use numbers to represent words. In Chinese, the numbers 520 sound like the words for "I love you" and in English the numbers 2 and 4 replace the words *to* and *for*.

70

Unit 6

3 **After reading** Check (✔) T (true) or F (false) for each statement. Also <u>underline</u> the information in the reading that corresponds to the statement.

		T	F
1.	The Egyptians invented writing.		✔
2.	Humans developed writing to help them remember important information.		
3.	Writing systems around the world are very similar.		
4.	Chinese uses letters to represent sounds.		
5.	Changes in technology influence writing systems.		

Talk about it!

4 What things do you write? Check (✔) the boxes. Then compare your list with a partner.

- ☐ shopping lists
- ☐ meeting notes
- ☐ class notes
- ☐ email to friends
- ☐ notes in my diary
- ☐ notes for myself
- ☐ text messages on my cell phone
- ☐ instant messages on my computer
- ☐ letters
- ☐ reports for work
- ☐ essays for college
- ☐ other: _____

instant message
即时信息

5 Read the descriptions below. Find one classmate who does each thing. Ask why and take notes.

Find someone who . . .   Name   Notes

1. sends letters by mail (not using the computer)
2. likes writing by hand
3. writes stories, poetry, or songs
4. has a blog
5. sends more than 20 text messages every day
6. has nice handwriting

by hand
用手

6 Share your answers from exercise 5 with the class.

Peter has a blog because he has strong opinions and likes to write.

PROJECT

Work in a group to research one of the languages listed on page 66. Find out where the language is spoken, how many people speak it, its origin, and any other interesting information about the language. Also research and learn ten expressions in the language (such as: *What's your name? My name is... I speak English.*). Present your information to the class and teach the class the expressions.

Unit 6

SONG

My one true love

1 Before listening Do you know someone (a friend or a famous person) who fell in love with someone from another country? Describe their story.

2 Before listening Songs often use words that rhyme at the ends of the lines. Say each pair of words from the song aloud. Do the words rhyme? Check (✓) *yes* or *no*.

1. head / said ✓ yes ☐ no
2. girl / world ☐ yes ☐ no
3. there / care ☐ yes ☐ no
4. stars / ours ☐ yes ☐ no
5. good / school ☐ yes ☐ no

3 Listening 06_08 Listen to the song. Use the words from exercise 2 to complete it. Then listen again and check your answers.

4 Listening 06_08 Listen to the song again. Then correct the sentences below so that they are true.

1. The singer's girlfriend lives in the same city.
2. The singer is good at learning languages.
3. The singer and his girlfriend have long conversations.
4. The singer's girlfriend gets angry when she doesn't understand.

5 After listening Match these definitions to the underlined words in the song.

1. real ___true___
2. might or possibly _____
3. a feeling of surprise or admiration _____
4. with hands together _____
5. move your head to agree _____
6. everybody including me _____

a feeling of admiration
崇拜感

CHORUS

Because my one <u>true</u> love
Is the love of a girl
From the other side of the (1) _____.
My one true love
Is the love of a (2) _____
From the other side of the world.

I was never any (3) _____
At learning languages at (4) _____.
But there are things that <u>even</u> I
  can understand.
Like the beauty and the meaning and
  the <u>wonder</u> in her eyes
When she looks at me and touches
  my hand.

CHORUS

If I tell her how I'm feeling
I know she'll <u>nod</u> her (5) _____.
My words <u>may</u> have no meaning
But she'll smile at what I've (6) _____.
We'll sit there <u>holding hands</u>
And looking at the (7) _____.
We speak in fluent silence
That describes this love of (8) _____.

CHORUS

We communicate in kisses
A few words here and (9) _____.
Some we understand
The rest we just don't (10) _____.

CHORUS

If I tell her how I'm feeling
I know she'll nod her head.
My words may have no meaning
But she'll smile at what I've said.

CHORUS

Unit 6

Talk about it!

6 Think of a time when you had to talk with someone who spoke a language you didn't understand. How did you communicate? Discuss with a partner.

A: I remember one day when someone stopped me in the street and . . .

Communicate effectively
Successfully communicating information doesn't always require fluency in a language. Using a word or phrase, drawing a picture, or even using your body to point or act something out can sometimes be effective.

请注意有效交流信息的方式

PRONUNCIATION

Syllable stress

06_09

In English, syllable stress does not always follow predictable patterns. Therefore, when you learn a new word, also pay attention to the stress.

Listen to the countries and nationalities.

Then listen again and underline the stressed syllables.

Countries	Nationalities
1. Mexico	Mexican
2. Vietnam	Vietnamese
3. Sweden	Swedish
4. China	Chinese
5. Japan	Japanese
6. Brazil	Brazilian
7. Norway	Norwegian
8. Canada	Canadian
9. Korea	Korean
10. Peru	Peruvian

Unit 6

CONVERSATION

Asking for clarification

1 The students in the following conversations are asking the teacher to clarify something. Complete the conversations with expressions from the box. Then listen and check. (Note: More than one answer is possible.)

> Can you give me an example?
> Can you say that again, please?
> Would you mind repeating that?
> Excuse me. I didn't catch that.
> ~~I don't understand what "..." means.~~
> What are we supposed to do?

CONVERSATION STRATEGY

Ask the person to repeat
If you don't understand what someone says, it's best to ask the person to repeat it. Otherwise, you can become more and more confused.

请注意交谈中适时让对方重复说过的话

be supposed to do
应该做……

slang words
俚语

refer to
指的是

1
- Student: Excuse me. **(1)** _I don't understand what "slang" means_.
- Teacher: Slang words are informal words.
- Student: I still don't understand. **(2)** _____?
- Teacher: Sure. Let's see . . . In the U.S. you can say "bucks" or "greenbacks" when you are referring to dollars.
- Student: OK. I get it. Thanks.

2
- Student: Excuse me. **(3)** _____?
- Teacher: Read the text on page 17 and answer the questions with a partner.
- Student: I'm sorry. **(4)** _____?
- Teacher: Sure. First open your book to page 17. Then answer the questions with a partner.

2 Practice the conversations with a partner.

Talk about it!

3 With a partner, create and practice your own conversations using at least three of the expressions.

Tell me more!

Visit the Takeaway English Online Learning Center at http://olcs.mcgraw-hill-education.com/takeaway/

 Check out the *Takeaway TV* video.

 Improve your English with the online activities.

WRITING

Writing an ad for a language course

1 Before writing
Work with a partner. Talk about five things a language course should have or do.

2 Writing model
Read the ad for a language course.
   a. Identify the titles and main points.
   b. Are they complete sentences?

3 Planning your writing
Choose a language to write an ad for. Answer the five "Ws" about your language course: *Who, What, Where, When,* and *Why.* Write the information in a chart.

HELP writing
Use advertising techniques
In some ads, clarity and briefness are important. Long, complete sentences might bore the reader. In the ad below, do the titles (in **bold**) and main points (marked by a bullet "■") give the information in a clear and brief way?

请注意广告用语的特点

Come and study Maori at the Abel Tasman University!

TĒNĀ RA KOUTOU KATOA

GREETINGS TO YOU ALL!

Why study Maori?
- To learn about New Zealand's culture
- To find new job opportunities

Who should take this course?
- People who speak no Maori— Start at beginner level!
- People who speak a few words of Maori or broken Maori— Start at elementary level, or do a special intensive course!

What kind of Maori do you learn?
- At lower levels you learn "standard Maori"
- At advanced levels you also learn about some Maori dialects

What do you learn about the language?
- Pronunciation / Grammar / Vocabulary
- And most importantly, how to use these to speak to people in Maori

And finally . . .
- Stay with a New Zealand family and speak Maori to them!
- Travel around New Zealand and speak Maori to the local people!

Abel Tasman University
亚伯塔斯曼大学

broken Maori
蹩脚的毛利语
elementary level
初级阶段
intensive course
精读课程

4 Writing Now create your ad. Remember to use bullet points. Also add pictures.

5 After writing Hang your ad on the wall and compare it to your classmates' ads. Say which ad you like best and why.

bullet points
要点

Unit 6

75

Unit 6

TEST

Test-taking strategy

Understand tone and language A writer's tone tells you how the writer thinks and feels about a subject. The language is the exact words and punctuation that the writer uses to express his / her thoughts and feelings.

Look at the example below. Use these steps to help you understand the writer's tone and answer questions.

1. What words does the writer use to let us know how he / she feels?
2. Pay attention to punctuation like question marks (?), exclamation points (!), or capital letters (ABC).
3. Read between the lines. What is the writer trying to say without saying it?
4. Try to understand the writer's tone before looking at the answer options.

exclamation points
感叹号

> **Example**
> **What are the writer's feelings in this sentence? Choose the correct answer.**
>
> 1. I can't believe that she speaks five languages fluently!
>   A. The writer doesn't believe her.   The expression *doesn't believe* shows surprise here.
>   B. The writer is very angry.   Nothing indicates that the writer is angry.
>   C. The writer is excited.   The information is more surprising than exciting.
>   D. The writer is very surprised.   This is the correct answer. Speaking five languages fluently is unusual, and the writer is very surprised. Note the use of the exclamation point.

PRACTICE

Read the paragraph below. Answer the questions. Mark the letter on the Answer Sheet.

> I don't understand my teacher. All of the students tell him what we want to discuss, but he doesn't hear us. Our words have no meaning!

1. What does "he doesn't hear us" mean?
   A. The teacher can't hear the students.
   B. The teacher doesn't listen to the students.
   C. The teacher doesn't believe the students.
   D. The teacher doesn't speak to the students.

2. How do you think the writer feels?
   A. happy
   B. excited
   C. unhappy
   D. sick

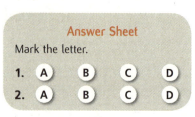

Answer Sheet
Mark the letter.
1. A B C D
2. A B C D

WORKBOOK PAGE 47

Unit 6

UNIT SUMMARY

Nouns
native language
slang
wonder

Nouns—Languages
Arabic
Chinese
English
German
Japanese
Portuguese
Russian
Spanish

Nouns—Countries
Brazil
China
Egypt
Germany
Japan
Mexico
New Zealand
Russia

Adjectives
basic
broken
fluent
informal
true

Verbs and verb phrases
get by in
hold hands
may
nod
pick up

Adverbs
clearly
easily
even
fluently
loudly
naturally
normally
quickly
slowly

Ask for clarification
Can you give me an example?
Can you say that again, please?
Excuse me. I didn't catch that.
I don't understand what "…" means.
What are we supposed to do?
Would you mind repeating that?

7 ▶ Are you fashionable?

In this unit you...
- talk about clothes
- discuss clothing worn by different age groups
- shop for clothes

Grammar
- verb patterns

START

ENGLISH express
Another way to say *casual* is *informal*.
请注意 casual 的另一种表达方式

Formal and casual clothes

casual clothes 休闲装

1 Match the clothing words to the pictures. Then listen and check your answers.
07_01

A jeans
B shirt
C tie
D T-shirt
E sneakers
F sweatshirt
G dress
H shorts
I suit
J shoes

2 Look at the pictures. Circle the correct word to complete sentences 1 and 2.

Jake is wearing **formal** clothes.

Sue is wearing **casual** clothes.

1. People usually wear casual / formal clothes at home or on vacation.
2. People usually wear casual / formal clothes to work or to a wedding.

3 Work with a partner. Say which clothes from exercise 2 are casual, formal, or both.

A: A dress is both casual and formal.

casual	formal	casual or formal
sneakers		

Talk about it!

4 What are some places or events where people wear formal clothes? What about casual clothes? What kinds of clothing? Discuss with a partner. Make a list.

Formal clothes
interview: suit, dress

Casual clothes
school: jeans, T-shirt

Unit 7

LISTENING

What do you wear to work?

1 Before listening Work with a partner. Complete the descriptions of the people with the words in the box.

checkered	faded	baggy	plain	bright
~~leather~~	shiny	striped	tight	

1. The man is wearing black pants, a black ___leather___ belt, a _____ blue shirt, a _____ tie, and _____ black shoes.
2. The boy is wearing _____ jeans, a red T-shirt—the color is very _____ —and white sneakers. His jeans are old and _____ .
3. The woman is wearing a _____ jacket, _____ jeans, and black boots.

2 Listening Listen to three women—Pat, Kim, and Sam—talk about the clothes they wear for work. Write each woman's name under her picture.
07_02

A B C

_____ _____ _____

HELP listening

Listen for details
Sometimes it's important to listen for details. Know what details you are listening for before you start.

请注意听细节内容

3 After listening Which people in exercises 1 and 2 are wearing formal clothes? Which people are wearing casual clothes?

Talk about it!

4 Work in a group. Take turns describing what people in class are wearing. The other students in the group guess who it is.

A: This person is wearing tight blue pants, a striped sweatshirt, and casual shoes.
B: Is it Lily?
A: Yes, that's right! Now it's your turn to describe someone.

striped sweatshirt
条纹运动衫

Unit 7

VOCABULARY

Different ages, different clothing

1 How old are you? What clothes do people at your age usually wear?

2 These words describe people of different ages. Match the words with each age group. Then listen and check.

| a person in his / her twenties | a teenager | an adult | an elderly person |
| a middle-aged person | a toddler | a baby | a kid / a child |

0–1 __a baby__ 1–12 _____ over 18 _____ 40–65 _____
1–3 _____ 12–18 _____ 21–29 _____ 65+ _____

3 Complete each sentence with the correct word(s).

| teenager | elderly people | middle-aged people | adults | babies |

1. Many __adults__ go to business and social events and have to wear formal clothes.
2. When I was a _____, I wore what all the other kids were wearing.
3. _____ never have to think about what they're going to wear!
4. Some _____ dress too young for their age. I think they want to be teenagers again.
5. _____ often dress for comfort and warmth, especially if they have physical problems.

4 Match the pictures to the descriptions.

A  B  C  D

1. _____ I like to wear earrings.
2. _____ I put on my make-up every morning.
3. _____ My toddler can get dressed by himself now.
4. _____ I carry an umbrella when the weather is bad.

put on one's
make-up
上妆

Talk about it!

5 Work with a partner. Find photos of people in this book. Describe their age and what they are wearing and carrying.

A: The woman on page 80 is an adult. She's in her twenties. She's wearing a plain white shirt. She's carrying a lipstick.

GRAMMAR

Verb patterns

ALSO GO TO
Grammar Takeaway
PAGE 200

ENGLISH express

A *trend* is what is popular now. If something is *trendy*, it is the latest fashion.

请注意 trend 的含义

1 Read the paragraph. Pay attention to the underlined words.

Teenagers <u>want to look</u> good, but they don't always have a lot of money to spend. They <u>like wearing</u> the same clothes as their friends. They <u>hate to feel</u> different or uncool. They don't <u>like to wear</u> the same styles as their parents! They usually <u>prefer wearing</u> casual clothes like jeans and T-shirts. They <u>want to wear</u> trendy clothes.

trendy clothes
流行服饰

> The verbs *like*, *love*, *prefer*, and *hate* follow the pattern:
>
> verb + verb-*ing* + adjective / noun   OR   verb + infinitive + adjective / noun
> I like wearing bright t-shirts.   I like to wear bright t-shirts.
>
> The verb *want* can only follow the pattern:
>
> verb + infinitive + adjective / noun
> I want to put on a warm sweatshirt. I'm cold.

2 Use these words and the patterns you have learned to make sentences. Give two answers when possible.

1. carry / in a backpack / my books / I / prefer
   I prefer to carry my books in a backpack. / I prefer carrying my books in a backpack.

in a backpack
背包里面

2. put on / a suit / My father / every day / hates
   _____

3. We / eat breakfast / get dressed / prefer / we / before
   _____

4. clothes / trendy / wear / loves / Max
   _____

5. wedding / a new dress / She / wear / wants / to her sister's
   _____

6. wear / jeans / Some people / like / tight
   _____

7. wants / Rita / her interview / put on / earrings / for
   _____

Talk about it!

3 With a partner, talk about what you like and don't like to wear at different times.

A: On the weekend, I like wearing casual clothes during the day. But I love to wear more formal clothes at night when I go out. During the week, I don't like…

on the weekend
周末

Unit 7

READING

HELP reading
Read for the main idea
The first time you read an article, just read for the main idea. This will help you decide a title for the reading.
请注意首次阅读时抓住文章大意

Jeans, jeans, jeans

1 Before reading How many pairs of jeans do you own? Are they all alike? If not, how are they different?

2 Reading Read the magazine article about jeans and circle the best title.

A. The shrinking world of jeans   B. The changing color of jeans   C. The changing world of jeans

Levi Strauss
李维斯·史特劳斯
(Levi's的创始人)
sweatpants
(美)宽松长运动裤
gold diggers
淘金者
horseback riding
骑马

ban from
禁止
house insulation
房屋隔热
go out of style
过时

Jeans are one of fashion's longest survivors. People started wearing jeans over a hundred years ago, when Levi Strauss introduced
5 jeans as tough clothes for gold diggers in San Francisco. The dark blue color of denim was very practical, since it was difficult to wash clothes frequently. Jeans were also a favorite with cowboys. The tough denim
10 material was perfect for horseback riding and working outside. Actors like James Dean made jeans popular among young people in the 1950s. But not everyone liked
15 jeans at this time. Some schools in the U.S. banned students from wearing denim to school in the 50s. Later, in the 1960s, hippies drew pictures and embroidered flowers on
20 their jeans.

In the 1990s, jeans became popular with different age groups. Some teenagers didn't think that jeans were trendy anymore when they saw their parents wearing them. They
25 turned to other clothing uch as sweatpants and sweatshirts, preferably with the logo of a fashionable brand name.

Nowadays, jeans are more popular than ever. Everyone seems to wear them, from teenagers
30 to politicians. You can even spend hundreds of dollars on designer jeans. According to one website, the average North American has seven pairs of jeans! They come in an endless number of styles
35 and colors. What happens to all the old pairs of jeans? Some "green" companies recycle old denim and use it as house insulation. It seems that jeans will never go out
40 of style! Are you wearing jeans today?

Are you wearing jeans today?

3 Reading Read the article again. Then answer the following questions.

1. When did people start wearing jeans?
2. When did actors start making jeans popular?
3. Who didn't like jeans in the 1950s?
4. When did people start putting pictures on their jeans?
5. What kind of clothes did some young people prefer in the 1990s?
6. What kind of people wear jeans these days?

Unit 7

4 After reading Write the underlined words in the article next to the definitions below. Then work with a partner. Make your own sentences using each underlined word.

1. sewed as a design onto clothes _____embroidered_____
2. strong _____
3. the symbol, design, or way of writing a name on a product _____
4. didn't permit, prohibited _____
5. a type of cloth used to make clothes, especially jeans _____

5 After reading Answer the questionnaire. Circle the letter for each answer.

Are you a fashionista*?

1. The oldest item in your wardrobe is…
   a. less than 1 month old.
   b. about 1 year old.
   c. from the 1990s.
2. Do you ever wear second-hand clothes?
   a. No way.   b. Sometimes.   c. Yes.
3. You are invited to a party tonight. Do you…
   a. wash your favorite jeans?
   b. buy new clothes?
   c. wear the clothes you put on this morning?
4. A friend starts to wear the same clothes as you. What's your reaction?
   a. You're happy.
   b. You think your friend is a little strange.
   c. You don't notice.
5. Brand-name clothes are…
   a. cool.
   b. too expensive.
   c. boring.

*fashionista= an informal word to describe a person who is very enthusiastic about fashion

fashionista
赶时髦的人

second-hand clothes
二手衣服
brand-name clothes
品牌服装

Talk about it!

6 Work with a partner. Ask and answer questions about the questionnaire.

A: What's the oldest item in your wardrobe?
B: That's tough to say. Maybe my sneakers.

A: Are they more than one year old?
B: Totally! Much older.

7 Based on your partner's answers, describe him / her for the class. For example:

- He's / She's a fashionista! It's all about the clothes.
- He's / She's stylish. He / She likes fashion and tries to look good.
- Designer clothes just aren't very important to him / her.

ENGLISH express

You can say Totally! in an informal situation to show that you agree strongly with a statement.

请注意 totally 的用法

PROJECT

Work in a group. Prepare and present a fashion show for the class. Use real clothing or pictures of clothing. Give complete descriptions of all clothing items.

83

Unit 7

CULTURE

Wedding clothing traditions

1 Before reading What are the bride and groom in this picture wearing? Are they wearing formal or casual clothes? How is this wedding similar to or different from a typical wedding in your country?

be similar to
类似的; 相同的

2 Reading Where do you think the man in the picture below is from? Who is he? What is he wearing? Read the text to find out.
07_05

Is that a skirt?

Abby and José decided to follow tradition on their wedding day. "My husband and I got married in Glasgow, my hometown in Scotland," says Abby. "I wore a white wedding dress and José wore a kilt. He's from Spain and he was a little worried that some of his friends would laugh at a groom in a 'skirt'. Actually he looked really cool—all the guys wear
5 kilts at a Scottish wedding." They exchanged rings in Abby's local <u>church</u>. Abby threw her flowers to the guests after the <u>ceremony</u> and her younger sister caught them. Will she be the next to get married?

wear a kilt
穿苏格兰裙

The <u>reception</u> was in a hotel. There was a luxurious four-course lunch with a wedding cake, followed by live music and dancing. There were about 200 guests; lots of them
10 were from Spain. Abby noticed a difference between the Spanish and Scottish guests.

live music and dancing
现场歌舞表演

"The Spanish guests wore much more elegant clothes than our Scottish family and friends. The women wore amazing dresses and some of them were in black—a color that most Scots don't wear at weddings." Another difference was that the Scottish guests bought the <u>newlyweds</u> gifts. The Spanish gave them envelopes full of money. Abby didn't
15 change her name. "In Britain, a wife often takes her husband's last name, but this doesn't happen in Spain," she explained. The day after the wedding Abby and José left for a two-week <u>honeymoon</u> in Mexico.

newlyweds
新婚夫妇

3 Reading Read the text again. Write who...
07_05
1. wore a white dress _the bride_
2. wore a kilt _____
3. wore black dresses _____
4. threw some flowers _____
5. had lunch in a hotel _____
6. bought gifts for the newlyweds _____
7. gave money to the newlyweds _____
8. went to Mexico _____

4 After reading   Match the underlined words in the text with the definitions.
1. a religious building ___church___
2. the formal actions at an important event _____
3. the meal and party after a wedding _____
4. a vacation after a wedding _____
5. a couple who got married very recently _____

Talk about it!

5 Work with a partner. Read the information about wedding traditions in different countries. Add a tradition for your country.

http://www.worldwideweddingtraditions.com/countries

Worldwide Wedding Traditions

#	Country	Tradition
1	EGYPT	To announce that the wedding is going to begin, there is a musical procession with men carrying swords.
2	U.S.	It is unlucky for the groom to see the bride's wedding dress before the wedding ceremony.
3	JAPAN	The bride changes her clothes several times during the wedding day.
4	U.K.	The bride wears something old, something new, something borrowed, and something blue at the wedding.
5	POLAND	The guests traditionally pay to dance with the bride at the reception. The money is used for the honeymoon.
6	ITALY	The groom's tie is cut into pieces and sold to the wedding guests.
7		_____

musical procession
音乐队伍

at the reception
在接待处

Discuss which traditions are the same and which are different in your country.

PRONUNCIATION

Reduction of *to*

1 The word *to* is often reduced. Listen to the short pronunciation /tə/ in these sentences.
07_06

> Teenagers hate to feel different or uncool.   They like to wear the latest styles.
> They prefer to wear casual clothes to school.

2 Work with a partner. Practice pronouncing the reduced *to*.
1. What do you like to wear to work?
2. I prefer to carry my books in a backpack.
3. Where do you like to shop?
4. Wanida loves to wear earrings.
5. Joe hates to wear formal clothes.

Unit 7

CONVERSATION

Shopping for clothes

1 What size is each sweater? Then listen and check.

A   B   C   D   E

The red sweater is an extra small.

ENGLISH express

Sizes

XS S M L XL

XS = extra small
S = small
M = medium
L = large
XL = extra large

请注意尺寸大小的英文表达方式

2 Complete the conversation in a store with the expressions. Then listen and check.
07_07

Salesperson	Customer	
~~Can I help you?~~	I'm just looking.	I'd like to see…
What size…?	Do you have it / them in a (medium)?	I'll take it.
Here you are.	Can I try it / them on?	

Salesperson: (1) _Can I help you_ ?
Customer: No, thanks. (2) _____ . Actually…
 (3) _____ one of these sweaters.
Salesperson: Sure. (4) _____ are you?
Customer: A medium.
Salesperson: A medium. (5) _____ . But I think it's a little big.
Customer: It's fine. I like to wear baggy sweaters.
Salesperson: Yes. Baggy is fashionable these days.
Customer: I like it! (6) _____ . Umm… I'd like to buy some jeans too.
Salesperson: Great. How about these?
Customer: Those look nice. (7) _____ medium?
Salesperson: Yes, we do. Here you are.
Customer: OK. (8) _____ ?
Salesperson: Sure. The dressing room is over here.

baggy sweaters
宽松的毛衣

dressing room
更衣室; 化妆室

Talk about it!

3 Work with a group. Each of you wants to buy two different items. Role-play a shopping scene. Present your scene to the class.

CONVERSATION STRATEGY

Confirm information
One way of confirming information in a conversation is to repeat what the other person said.
A: I'd like an extra large.
B: Extra large. OK. Here you are.

请注意对话中如何确认信息

Tell me more!

Visit the Takeaway English Online Learning Center at http://olcs.mcgraw-hill-education.com/takeaway/

 Check out the *Takeaway TV* video.

Login   Improve your English with the online activities.

Unit 7

WRITING

Writing an email about clothes

1 **Before writing** How do you usually communicate with friends and family who live in other places? How often do you send emails? What do you usually write about?

HELP writing

Know your audience
Be sure that your writing style matches your audience. If your audience is a friend, use a familiar style and informal language.

请注意根据读者确定写作风格

2 **Writing model** You received this email from a friend in the U.S. What does your friend want to do? Does this seem like a good idea to you? Why or why not?

From: pat@mymail.com
Subject: next summer

Hi!

How's it going? Thanks for inviting me to stay with your family next summer. I want to bring some clothes from the U.S. as gifts for you and your family, but I don't know what's trendy in your country. Let me know what kinds of clothes everyone wears, what styles they like, what sizes they wear, and any brand names that are popular.

I want to go shopping when I'm over there. I want to buy gifts to bring back to my family. What are some good things to buy? Let me know.

See you soon,

Pat

3 **Planning your writing** Use the chart to make some notes about yourself and members of your family.

family member	clothes	color, style	size	brand
me	jeans	black, tight	small	Levi's

4 **Writing** Write an email reply to Pat. Use the information in exercises 2 and 3 to help you.

Unit 7

TEST

Test-taking strategy

Understand cause and effect A *cause* makes something happen. An *effect* is what happens. Understanding cause and effect can help you better understand what you are reading or listening to during a test.

Look at the example below. Use these steps to understand cause and effect and choose the correct answer.

1. The cause happens first. The effect happens second.
2. Pay attention to connecting words that link cause and effect. Some examples of connecting words are *because*, *so*, *as a result of*, and *since*.
3. To find a cause, ask questions like *Why did that happen?* or *How did that happen?*
4. To find an effect, ask questions like *What did that do?* or *Then what happened?*

connecting words
连接词

denim jeans
斜纹布料的牛仔裤

Example
Read the sentence. Choose the correct answer.
Levi Strauss's denim jeans were very tough, so they were popular with gold diggers and cowboys.

1. In the sentence, what is the *effect*?
   A. Levi Strauss made jeans. — This is not a cause or an effect.
   B. Jeans were made of denim. — This is a cause, not an effect.
   C. Jeans were tough. — This is a cause, not an effect.
   D. Jeans were popular with cowboys. — This is the correct answer. Cowboys liked jeans because they were tough.

PRACTICE

Read the paragraph. Choose the correct answer. Mark the letter on the Answer Sheet.

wedding cake
结婚蛋糕; 喜饼

Sarah and Michael had a traditional wedding because their parents are old-fashioned. They asked all their guests to wear formal clothing. They had the ceremony in a big church, even though they aren't religious. The reception had music and dancing, and a big wedding cake.

1. Sarah and Michael had the wedding ceremony in a church _____ .
   A. because they are religious
   B. because they are traditional
   C. so their parents would feel comfortable
   D. so there was enough room for all the guests

2. The guests wore formal clothing _____ .
   A. so Sarah and Michael would be surprised
   B. because the bride and groom requested it
   C. since the reception had music and dancing
   D. because the ceremony was in a church

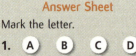
Answer Sheet
Mark the letter.
1.
2. A B C D

UNIT SUMMARY

Nouns
adult
baby
belt
boots
bride
ceremony
child
church
clothes
denim
dress
extra large
extra small
fashionista
groom
guest
honeymoon
jacket
jeans
kid
large
logo
medium
newlywed
pants
reception
shirt
shoes
shorts
size
small
sneakers
suit
sweatshirt
teenager
tie
toddler
trend
T-shirt
wedding

Adjectives
baggy
bright
casual
checkered
faded
fashionable
formal
informal
leather
plain
shiny
striped
tight
tough
trendy

Verbs and verb phrases
ban
carry
embroider
get dressed
put on
wear

Expressions
a middle-aged person
a person in his/her twenties
an elderly person
Totally!

Shop for clothes
Can I help you?
Can I try it/them on?
Do you have it/them in a (medium)?
Here you are.
I'd like to see…
I'll take it.
I'm just looking.
What size…

Unit 7

8 ▶ That's life!

In this unit you...
- talk about families
- tell recent news
- discuss life events
- say goodbye and make plans

Grammar
- present perfect and past perfect

START

Tell me about your family

1. Who are the people in the picture? What do you know about this family?

2. (08_01) Listen to two people talking about the picture. Underline the family words that you hear. Listen again to check your answers.

husband	mother
brother-in-law	grandmother
kids	grandsons
only child	father
grandchildren	children
wife	daughter-in-law

ENGLISH express

The expression ...-in-law means *by marriage*.
Your brother's wife is your sister-in-law.

请注意 -in-law 的含义

3. Organize the words and expressions from exercise 2 into three groups. Add at least two more family words to each group.

male	husband,
female	
male or female	

Talk about it!

4. With a partner, ask and answer questions about your families.

A: Tell me about your family. Do you have a sister?
B: Yes, I do. She's married. My brother-in-law's name is Victor.

Unit 8

LISTENING

How's it going?

1 **Before listening** Look at the photo. Who do you think the people are? What do you think they are talking about?

1. The men are co-workers / old friends / brothers.
2. The men are talking about travel and sports / work and family / pets and movies.

2 **Listening** Now listen to the two men talking. Check your answers to exercise 1.
08_02

3 **Listening** Use the words and phrases in the box to complete the conversation. Listen again to check your answers. Then practice the conversation with a partner.
08_02

what have you   are you still   what about you   how's it going   time flies   have you been

Ken: Dylan!
Dylan: Hi, Ken! Long time no see.
Ken: Yeah, I haven't been here since last summer.
Dylan: So (1) _how's it going_ ? How (2) _____ ?
Ken: Great! We have a new baby son, and we moved last year.
Dylan: Wow! Congratulations.
Ken: Thanks. But (3) _____ ? (4) _____ been up to?
Dylan: Not much, really. We still live in the same place and no kids yet—just a cat. I was in the U.S. for a couple of weeks last month...
Ken: For work?
Dylan: Yes. I had always wanted to go there and then this opportunity came up. And you? (5) _____ working at the bank?
Ken: Yes, I've been there for five years now.
Dylan: Really? (6) _____ , doesn't it?
Ken: Yes, you're right. Anyhow...

HELP listening

Identify relationships
When you listen, don't just listen for *what* people say. Also listen to *how* they say it. This tells you about their relationship. Do the people sound excited? Are the questions personal? Is their language formal or informal?

请注意听说话人的语气和讲话方式

Talk about it!

4 With a partner, role-play a conversation like the one in exercise 3. Ask and answer questions about recent events in your life.

A: Hi. Long time no see. What have you been up to? How's your family?
B: Everybody's great. My mother just got a new dog. What about you?

up to
忙于……
在做……

Unit 8

VOCABULARY

Life events

1 Read these two sentences. Which sentence describes Claudia now (her state)? Which sentence describes an action or event?

Claudia got married.   Claudia is 27 years old.

2 Put the words and phrases into two groups. Then listen and check your answers. Also add your own examples.
08_03

~~be alive~~	be born	be sick	get married	be an adult	be married
~~turn 18~~	get divorced	die	be divorced	be a good driver	get a job
get sick	be pregnant	be dead	get pregnant	get a driver's license	be employed

get/be divorced
离婚
get/be pregnant
怀孕
driver's license
驾照

state	event
be alive	turn 18

ENGLISH express

Except for *be born*, *be* + participle or adjective describes a state.

My sister <u>is</u> employed.

Get + participle or adjective describes an action.

She <u>got</u> divorced last year.

请注意 get 和 be 用法的区别

culture matters

In most English-speaking countries, children usually have just one surname (family name)—the father's.
- Is this the same in your country?

请注意西方人的姓

3 Use the words and phrases from exercise 2 to talk about your own life and family.

I turned 18 last year.
I am not married yet.

Talk about it!

4 Work with a partner. Talk about some important events in your life. How did you feel? How did your life change?

A: I got my driver's license this year.
B: How did it feel?
A: It felt great. I can go everywhere now!

GRAMMAR

Present perfect and past perfect

 ALSO GO TO Grammar Takeaway PAGE 201

1 Think about something in your life that started in the past and is continuing now. For example:

I have been taking karate classes for three years.
(= I started taking karate classes three years ago, and I am taking them now.)
My life: _____

karate
空手道

Now think about two events in your life in the past that have ended. Which one happened first? For example:

I had learned to drive before I bought a car.
My life: _____

2 When do you use the present perfect?

| present perfect | He has worked there since 2009. They have studied English for two years. How long have you been at this school? |

When do you use the past perfect?

| past perfect | She had read the book before she saw the movie. She saw the movie after she had read the book. |

3 Circle the correct word to complete each sentence.
1. I've used this book (for)/ since more than two months.
2. She had bought the dress before / after he invited her to the party.
3. I've known my English teacher for / since January.
4. My parents have been married for / since 20 years.
5. Before I started this English course, I had / have never met any of my classmates.
6. How long has / had the Internet existed?

Talk about it!

4 Work with a partner. Ask and answer questions using the present perfect and past perfect.

A: Did you win your soccer match?
B: Yes, I did.
A: Had you practiced a lot before the match?
B: Yes, I had!
A: Do you have an MP3 player?
B: Yes, I do.
A: How long have you had it?
B: I have had it since I was 15.

Unit 8

READING

A special family reunion

family reunion 家庭团聚

1 Before reading A reunion is when people come together. Does your family have reunions? How often? Who comes?

be apart 分别；离别
Bristol 布里斯托尔

2 Reading 08_04 Read the newspaper article about a special family reunion and complete the sentences about the people.

1. Gloria is Ruth's _____ .
2. Harold is Ruth's _____ .
3. David and Philip are Gloria's _____ .
4. John was Harold's _____ .
5. Ted is Gloria's _____ .

> **HELP reading**
>
> **Identify verb forms to understand sequence**
> When you know the sequence of events, you can understand a story better. Identifying the verb forms used in the story help you put these events in order.
> _____
> Ted found Ruth, whose name had changed from…
> … had changed… = past perfect
> This happened *before* Ted found Ruth.

请注意如何根据动词形式确定事件发生的顺序

3 Reading 08_04 Read the text again and put these events in the order that they occurred from 1 to 8.

- ☐ Gloria moved to Australia.
- ☐ Gloria asked Ted to help her.
- ☐ Ruth and Gloria spoke on the phone.
- **1** Their parents' marriage failed.
- ☐ Gloria was adopted.
- ☐ Gloria's father told her about her family.
- ☐ Gloria started trying to find her family.
- ☐ Ted found Ruth.

break up 结束；破碎

take care of 照顾；抚养
cope with 处理；应付

I've found you at last… together again after 50 years!

Two sisters are going to meet again after being <u>apart</u> for 50 years. Ruth Cable of Bristol, England, said that it will be an emotional reunion with
5 **(1)** <u>her</u> sister Gloria, who now lives in Australia.

Ruth Cable from England

Gloria is flying to the U.K. next month after looking for her family since 1986. Big sister Ruth had also
10 searched for Gloria for more than 30 years. The family reunion will include two <u>surviving</u> brothers, David and Philip, as well.

The sisters were separated after
15 **(2)** <u>their</u> parents' marriage <u>broke up</u>. Ruth's father, Harold, was left to take care of five young children. But **(3)** <u>he</u> couldn't <u>cope with</u> baby Gloria, and he gave **(4)** <u>her</u> up for
20 adoption. Gloria's search began

after (5) she moved to Australia in 1979. She started looking when her adoptive father gave her details about her family. That's when she learned about Ruth and her brothers.

Gloria Young from Australia

But her search nearly ended very quickly. She soon found out that her brother John had died. She was so devastated that she nearly gave up looking. But she returned to Bristol six times over the years, always looking for her family.

Then Gloria asked friend and former police officer Ted Jones to help. Ted found Ruth, whose name had changed from (6) her maiden name of Young.

Gloria called Ruth. "Talking to Ruth and (7) my brothers, it felt like I had known (8) them for years."

Gloria is planning a month-long trip to England to get to know Ruth and her brothers.

"There will be lots of hugs and tears," said Ruth. "Gloria and I have discovered that (9) we have so much in common!"

4 After reading Match the numbered words in the text with the people they refer to.

Ruth: __1 her__ / _____
Gloria: _____ / _____ / _____
Harold: _____
Ruth and Gloria: _____ / _____
Ruth and her brothers: _____

5 After reading Write the underlined words in the article next to the definitions.

1. take care of a difficult situation __cope with__
2. alive; not dead _____
3. not together _____
4. stopped working / functioning correctly _____
5. stopped _____
6. discovered new information _____

Talk about it!

6 With a partner, discuss these questions.

1. Was it a good idea for Ruth to look for her family? Why or why not?
2. Do you know a similar story? Tell the story.
3. Who is more important to you—your family or your friends? Explain your answer with specific examples.

PROJECT

Work with a partner. Create a survey to ask your classmates about their families. For example:

How many people are there in your family?
Does everyone live nearby?
Does anyone live in another country?

Conduct your survey, summarize your results, and report your findings to the class.

Most people in this class come from big families. They are...

maiden name
(女子的)婚前姓

feel like
感觉像是……

a month-long trip
为期一个月的旅行

conduct survey
展开调查

Unit 8

SONG

My crazy family

1 Before listening Match the phrases to the pictures. Which family situation do you live in?

1. _____ a nuclear family
2. _____ a single-parent family
3. _____ an extended family

settle down 定居
nuclear family 小家庭

extended family 大家庭

2 Listening Read the song lyrics and put the verses in order. Then listen and check.
08_05

wait up for (为……而)熬夜等候

3 Listening Listen again. Put the events described in the song in order from 1 to 7.
08_05

☐ He met a girl.
☐ He left home.
1 The singer's sister got married.
☐ He decided to return to his family home.
☐ He called his family.
☐ He started a family.
☐ He went to Boston.

4 After listening Match the underlined words and phrases in the song to the definitions.

well-paid job 高薪工作

1. good, well-paid job _flying high career_
2. often went _____
3. I'm leaving _____
4. married again _____
5. returning _____
6. she's happy again _____
7. no news from home _____
8. made a home and had an organized life _____

discotheque 迪斯科舞厅

My crazy family

A
I moved to Boston
To live with Uncle Bob.
Found myself a girl
And I found myself a job.
I settled down
And had a family of my own.
Five long years
No word from home.
I wondered what was happening
So I picked up the phone.

B
I've had enough.
I'm leaving home.
My bags are packed.
I'm going to hit the road.
I'm out of here.
I'm history.
Won't be home for dinner.
Don't wait up for me.
I'm looking for someone
Who wants to make a family.

C
A new club's opened.
They're going out to dance.
My sister's got divorced.
And she's just come home from France.
My mother has remarried,
The smile's back on her face.
My brother's had a baby
And rejoined the human race.

D
I've heard enough.
I'm going back.
We're on our way.
Our bags are packed.
My wife and kids
Are going to meet my family.
My wife and kids
Are going to meet my crazy family.

1 E
The discotheques have closed
Where we used to go to dance.
My sister's just got married
And she's gone to live in France.
My mother hasn't smiled much
Since my daddy disappeared.
And my brother's just too busy
With his flying high career.

5 **After listening** Circle *True* or *False* for each statement.

1. The singer had a brother-in-law. (True) False
2. He has a stepfather. True False
3. His father doesn't have a daughter. True False
4. He's a father. True False
5. He's not an uncle. True False

Talk about it!

6 With a partner, discuss if the statements are true for your country.

1. People usually leave home when they are eighteen.
   - **A:** Here, people usually leave home when they are…
   - **B:** I don't think so. I think they…
   - **A:** Yes, I agree with you.
2. Most people get married in their twenties.
3. Children, parents, and grandparents don't usually live together.
4. Members of the same family often live in different areas or different countries.
5. Divorce isn't very common.

PRONUNCIATION

The sounds /ɪ/ *live* and /aɪ/ *life*

1 The letters *i* and *y* can have different sounds: /ɪ/ and /aɪ/. Listen to how these words are pronounced.

| lived | goodbye | since | die | sister | child |
| ring | divorced | life | kids | my | wife |

2 Put the words into two groups. Then listen and check your answers.

/ɪ/	/aɪ/
lived	

Unit 8

CONVERSATION

Saying goodbye and making plans

1 Say three things you remember about Ken and Dylan from the Listening on page 91.

2 Listen to the next part of Ken and Dylan's conversation. What do they decide?
   A. They decide on a time to meet next weekend.
   B. They decide to talk on the phone next weekend.

3 Listen again and complete the conversation with the expressions in the box.

> Great to see you...   I need to check...   Take care.   Can I call you...
> get together   I'd better be going. How about... be in touch

be in touch
保持联系

Ken: Yes, you're right. Anyhow, (1) _I'd better be going_.
        Why don't we (2) _____ sometime soon?
Dylan: Absolutely! I'd love to. (3) _____ next week?
Ken: Well, (4) _____ with my wife first.
        (5) _____ on the weekend?
Dylan: Sure. Here's my card. Say hello to your family for me.
Ken: I will. Thanks. Hello from me as well.
Dylan: OK. (6) _____ again, Ken.
Ken: Yeah, you too. (7) _____. I'll (8) _____.

as well
也; 此外

CONVERSATION STRATEGY

Agree strongly
You can say *Absolutely!* in an informal situation to show that you agree strongly with someone.

请注意 absolutely 的用法

4 Practice the conversation with a partner.

Talk about it!

run into
偶遇

5 Work in a group of three. You run into each other in the park. Role-play a conversation about what's going on in your lives, then say goodbye and make plans to get together later. Refer to the conversation above and the one on page 91.

Tell me more!

Visit the Takeaway English Online Learning Center at http://olcs.mcgraw-hill-education.com/takeaway/

 Check out the *Takeaway TV* video.   Improve your English with the online activities.

Unit 8

WRITING

Writing a letter about recent events

1 Before writing Think about recent events in your life. What have you been doing? How have you been? Any problems? Any good news?

2 Writing model Complete the letter with the topic sentences. Be sure the rest of each paragraph supports the topic sentence.

- Over here, things are going fine.
- Have you thought any more about vacation?
- The only problem we've had recently was with my mother.
- ~~I hope all is well with you.~~

> **HELP writing**
>
> **Organize your writing by topic sentences**
>
> Organizing your letter in clear paragraphs makes it easier to read. Each paragraph should have one main idea followed by information that supports it. This main idea is called the topic sentence.
>
> 请注意写好主题句

Dear Lisa,

1 **I hope all is well with you.** I thought it was about time I got in touch. Time flies! How have you been? How are Nick and the kids? Tell me what everyone is doing!

2 _____ As you know, Billy has started college and he loves it. Kate's great too. She's the star player on the school basketball team.

3 _____ She got sick again and had to go to the hospital. They had to do a lot of tests. But she's OK now and staying with us—that way we can keep an eye on her!

4 _____ We booked the beach house I told you about. Of course, we still want you to join us. We have the house from July 21st to the 30th. Let me know what you decide. You could always come for just a few days.

Anyway, that's about all for now. Write back soon.
Lots of love,
Susana

get in touch
取得联系

keep an eye on
照看；留意

3 Planning your writing Choose three or four recent events or pieces of news from your life. For each event write a topic sentence. This will determine the number of paragraphs in your letter. Think of what you want to include in the supporting information.

event / news	topic sentence	supporting info
got a job	I'm happy to report that I finally got a job!	type of work, hours, pay, etc.

4 Writing Write a letter to a friend you haven't seen recently. Tell him or her your recent news. Organize your letter in clear paragraphs. Don't forget to ask how your friend is doing!

Unit 8

TEST

Test-taking strategy

Look for the correct form and part of speech of a word A word can have different forms and can be used as different parts of speech. For example:

live = verb (I live in China.)
alive = adjective (My grandmother is still alive.)
life = noun (My life is very busy.)

Exams include questions and answers with different forms of the same word. Knowing the part of speech of the word you are looking for will help you choose the correct answer.

part of speech 词性

Look at the example below. Use these steps to help you choose the correct word.

1. Read the sentence carefully.
2. Try to identify the part of speech (verb, noun, adjective, etc.) of the missing word.
3. Look at the answer choices. What part of speech is each word?
4. Try each answer in the blank. Which one makes the most sense?

on a date 约会

> **Example**
> **Choose the correct answer.**
> 1. No, you can't ask my sister out on a date. She's _____!
>   A. marriage   A noun with no article does not make sense in the blank.
>   B. marry   This is a verb. A verb in the base form does not follow a form of *be*.
>   C. married   This is the correct answer. This is an adjective. An adjective often follows a form of *be*.

PRACTICE

Choose the correct answer. Mark the letter on the Answer Sheet.

1. I can't believe you had a baby. _____!
   A. Congratulated
   B. Congratulations
   C. Congratulate

2. At what age can you _____ in your country?
   A. drive
   B. driver
   C. driving

3. We have a family _____ every 5 years.
   A. reunite
   B. reunited
   C. reunion

4. It's too late. She already _____ the course.
   A. failed
   B. failure
   C. fail

Answer Sheet
Mark the letter.

1. A B C
2. A B C
3. A B C
4. A B C

UNIT SUMMARY

Nouns
brother-in-law
children
daughter-in-law
event
father
grandchildren
grandmother
grandson
husband
life
mother
reunion
wife

Adjectives
apart
surviving

Verbs and verb phrases
adopt
be a good driver
be alive
be an adult
be born
be dead
be divorced
be employed
be married
be pregnant
be sick
break up
cope with
die
find out
get a driver's license
get a job
get divorced
get married
get pregnant
get sick
give up
go back
hit the road
remarry
settle down
turn 18

Expressions
Absolutely!
an only child
extended family
flying high career
no word from home
nuclear family
single parent family
the smile's back on her face
time flies
used to

Say goodbye and make plans
be in touch
Can I call you…
get together
Great to see you…
How about…
I need to check…
I'd better be going.
Take care.

9 ▸ Do you know a good story?

In this unit you...
- talk about animals
- discuss folktales and the moral of a story
- give and respond to information
- ask for more information about a story

Grammar
- adverbs
- simple past and past continuous

START

Classifying animals

1 Do you have any pets? If so, what kind? If not, what pet would you want?

2 Complete the descriptions of the five types of animals. Then listen and check.

cold/warm-blooded animal
冷/温血动物

mammal
amphibian
reptile
bird
~~fish~~

1. A ___fish___ is a cold-blooded animal that can't live outside of water.
2. A _____ has feathers, a beak, and lays eggs.
3. A _____ is a warm-blooded animal that drinks mother's milk when it's a baby.
4. A _____ is cold-blooded and usually lays eggs.
5. An _____ lives in water like a fish when it's born. When it grows up, it lives on land and in the water.

Talk about it!

3 Work with a partner. Classify the animals into the five groups. Explain your answers. Add more animals to each group.

A rabbit B swan C tuna D snake E tiger G eagle H fox I salmon J frog F tortoise K iguana L monkey

mammal	reptile	bird	amphibian	fish
rabbit				

Unit 9

LISTENING

An African folktale: *The Eagle and the Tortoise*

HELP listening

Preview
Before you listen, preview any pictures, titles, and questions. This information will help you understand the listening better.

请注意听前预览图片、标题、问题等信息

1 Before listening Every culture has folktales— traditional stories with a special message. What is a folktale from your culture?

2 Before listening You are going to listen to an African folktale about an eagle and a tortoise. Circle the adjectives you think will describe the eagle and the tortoise.

| tortoise: | kind | selfish | ungrateful | hospitable | generous |
| eagle: | kind | selfish | ungrateful | hospitable | generous |

3 Listening Listen to the folktale and check your answers to exercise 2.

4 Listening Number the pictures in order from 1 to 7. Then listen again and check.

A   B   C **1** D   E   F   G

5 After listening What do the animals say in the pictures? Write the letter of the picture from exercise 3 next to each sentence. Check your answers with a partner.

1. __C__ "Hello, Eagle. How nice to see you again," the tortoise said.
2. _____ "Ha! Ha! I can visit the tortoise on the ground, but he can never reach my nest on the mountain!" laughed the eagle.
3. _____ "Take me home! You have insulted me and my family's hospitality," the tortoise complained.
4. _____ "Why are you kind to the eagle?" the animals asked. "He is selfish and ungrateful," they explained.
5. _____ "Would you like a basket of food to take home?" asked the tortoise.
6. _____ "Let go! Let go!" the eagle begged. "Only after you take me home!" the tortoise replied.
7. _____ "Why don't you climb into a basket of food? Then you can hear how he insults you," the animals suggested.

on the ground
在地面上

Talk about it!

6 Folktales usually contain a moral, or message, about what is right and wrong. With a partner decide which of these three morals best describes the story, and explain why.

- **A** Don't be too generous. People will take advantage of you.
- **B** Selfish people have no friends.
- **C** For a friendship to work, both people have to contribute.

take advantage of
利用

Unit 9

VOCABULARY

Giving and responding to information

relate to
涉及; 有关

1 There are many verbs in English that relate to giving and responding to information. Two examples are *ask* and *answer*. Think of three other examples.

My friend offered an opinion. I responded to it angrily.

2 Complete the sentences with the simple past verbs. Then listen and check.

| promised | complained | suggested | explained | said | asked | replied | begged |

1. "This is the worst book I have ever read," Eric _____complained_____.
2. "I won't be late to work ever again," Caroline _____.
3. "Why don't we see a movie tonight?" _____ Josh.
4. "I was at the bus stop when I heard the alarm," he _____ to the police.
5. "Hello," she _____. "My name is Nicole. I'm the new French teacher."
6. "Yes, of course," he _____. "I'd love to go out for dinner."
7. "Do you like to read folktales?" _____ Rachel.
8. "Please, please, please don't tell!" she _____.

3 An adverb describes a verb. It tells you *how* something is said or done. Change these adjectives into adverbs.

1. nervous _____nervously_____
2. happy _____
3. angry _____
4. stubborn _____
5. quiet _____
6. proud _____

ENGLISH express

Most adverbs are formed by adding -ly to the corresponding adjective. If the adjective ends in *y*, the *y* changes to *i*.

selfish / selfishly
lucky / luckily

请注意形容词如何转化为副词

4 Complete the sentences with an adverb from exercise 3. Then listen and check.

1. "I hate vegetables. I won't eat them," the boy said _____stubbornly_____.
2. "The baby is sleeping," the man said _____.
3. "My daughter won first prize at the science fair," she said _____.
4. "I won the lottery!" she shouted _____.
5. "I apologize for being late. It won't happen again," he said _____.
6. "You should call if you know you're going to be late!" she said _____.

win first prize
获得一等奖
the science fair
科学博览会

5 Listen to the same sentence said in four different ways. Write the number of the sentence for the correct adverb that describes *how* it is said.

"I'm going on a plane trip tomorrow."   ☐ angrily   ☐ happily   **1** nervously   ☐ quietly

Talk about it!

6 Work with a partner. Take turns giving the information in exercises 2 and 4 in different ways. Talk about *how* your partner says each sentence.

Unit 9

GRAMMAR

Simple past and past continuous

ALSO GO TO Grammar Takeaway PAGE 202

1 Give examples of times when you were doing something and you were interrupted.

I was eating dinner last night when my phone rang.

2 Read the sentences in the chart.

When do you use the simple past?

When do you use the past continuous?

	simple past	past continuous
affirmative	Alan arrived yesterday.	She was watching a movie when Alan arrived.
negative	She didn't arrive yesterday.	She wasn't reading.
question	Did they arrive yesterday?	Was she watching a movie?

3 Match the two sentence parts to complete the story on page 103. Underline the verbs in the simple past. Circle the verbs in the past continuous.

1. Soon all the animals _____
2. The tortoise _____
3. The tortoise was hiding in the basket _____

a. hid in the basket.
b. when he heard the eagle insult him.
c. were talking about the selfish eagle.

4 Read Olivia's story. Write the verbs in parentheses in the simple past or past continuous. Then listen and check.

Olivia: <u>Did</u> I <u>tell</u> (**1.** tell) you my story about the yak?

Charles: No. Tell me what happened.

Olivia: Well, five years ago I _____ (**2.** go) to Nepal on vacation. One day I _____ (**3.** walk) quietly along a path when I _____ (**4.** see) a yak. It _____ (**5.** stand) on the path in front of me.

Nepal
尼泊尔

Charles: Really? What _____ you _____ (**6.** do)?

Olivia: Well, I _____ (**7.** continue) walking towards it. When I _____ (**8.** pass) it, the yak _____ (**9.** try) to attack me with its long horns.

Charles: Wow! Were you scared?

Olivia: Yes, I was! I _____ (**10.** turn) my back, and it _____ (**11.** hit) my backpack once with its horns.

Charles: And then what happened?

Olivia: Well, I _____ (**12.** walk) past it quickly, and I _____ (**13.** no / look) back. A few minutes later, I _____ (**14.** turn) around, and it _____ (**15.** stand) there just like before.

Talk about it!

5 Work with a partner. Take turns telling a story about an animal. It can be a story about something that happened to you or another story that you know.

Unit 9

READING

HELP reading

Make a prediction
Before reading, think about the title, any visuals, and any information you have about the topic. This will help you predict what will happen in the reading.

请注意借助相关信息预测文章大意

A folktale from India

1 Before reading Match the animal descriptions to the pictures.

1. It's a member of the cat family. ___tiger___
2. He is a Hindu of the highest caste (social class) and a wise man. _____
3. It's a domestic animal in India. _____
4. It's a type of wild dog that lives in Africa and Asia. _____

social class 社会地位

2 Reading 09_07 Read the first part of the story. What does the tiger promise the Brahmin?

Brahmin 婆罗门

The Tiger, the Brahmin, and the Jackal *an Indian folktale*

One day a wise Brahmin was walking in the forest when he came across a tiger trapped in a cage.
"Oh, Brahmin," he begged. "Please, free me from this cage."
"No," replied the Brahmin, "If I set you free, you will eat me."
"No, I won't," the tiger promised.
The Brahmin didn't believe the tiger, but he opened the door of the cage.

free from 使摆脱; 免于

3 Reading 09_08 Predict what the tiger did when the Brahmin opened the door of the cage. Then read the next part of the story and find out.

pounce on 猛扑向; 突然袭击

At once the tiger pounced on him. "Fool! People say you are wise, but how could you believe the word of a tiger? Now I'm going to eat you."
"But, that's not fair," said the Brahmin.
"It is fair. I am a tiger and tigers eat people," replied the tiger.
"But you promised," said the Brahmin.
"I promised so you would help me, but I am still going to eat you," said the tiger.
"Wait," replied the Brahmin. "Let me walk through the forest. I will ask the first three things that I meet what they think. If they believe you have been unfair, you let me go. But if they say you have been fair, you can eat me."
"Very well," said the tiger. "I understand the laws of the jungle. Everyone will agree with me."

the laws of the jungle 丛林法则

4 After reading Circle *True* or *False* for each statement.

1. The tiger thought the Brahmin was very wise. True False
2. The tiger kept his promise. True False
3. The Brahmin asked the tiger to let him ask other forest creatures if the tiger was fair. True False
4. The tiger agreed to let the Brahmin talk to other forest creatures. True False

keep one's promise 守信

Unit 9

5 Reading — Now read the rest of the story.

First, the Brahmin explained his problem to a tree. "Fair?" replied the tree. "I offer shade and shelter to everyone, but people cut off my branches to make houses and for their fires. The tiger is right."

Next, the Brahmin explained his problem to a buffalo. "The tiger is right," answered the buffalo. "I give people milk, but when I have no more, they will kill me and eat me. This is the law of the jungle," answered the buffalo.

Finally, the Brahmin saw a jackal and explained his story. "I'm sorry," the jackal said, "but I don't understand."

Again the Brahmin explained, but still the jackal didn't understand. "Come with me," said the Brahmin, "Let's ask the tiger to explain."

So the tiger explained, but once more the jackal shook his head. "Let me see... The Brahmin was in the cage and…" said the jackal.

"No, you fool! I was in the cage," said the tiger angrily.

"Ah, yes, I was in the cage," replied the jackal.

Now the tiger was furious. "Look! *I* was in the cage." And he walked back to the cage and walked inside it for the jackal to see.

"Ah, now I understand," said the jackal smiling. And very quickly he closed the door of the cage. The tiger roared, but it was too late.

"Oh, thank you," said the Brahmin.

"Don't thank me. I just wanted to understand the situation, and now I do. Continue to be wise and good, Brahmin. Goodbye," said the jackal as he walked away.

"I will," said the Brahmin, looking sadly at the tiger. "And if you were wise and good, you wouldn't still be in that cage."

offer shade and shelter 遮阴和庇护
cut off 砍下; 切断

6 After reading — Complete the sentences.

1. The ___tree___ and the _____ agreed with the tiger.
2. The _____ didn't understand the situation.
3. The _____ and the _____ tried to explain the situation to the _____.
4. The _____ walked into the cage to help the _____ understand.
5. The _____ was happy to be free but sad for the _____.

Talk about it!

7 Which of these three morals do you think is best for the story? With a partner, discuss and explain your choice.

A. Never believe what people say. They often don't tell the truth.
B. Never be afraid to say you don't understand.
C. If you trick people and tell lies, it will come to no good.

come to no good 失败; 没有好结果

Work with a group. Find a folktale about an animal from your culture or another culture. Make a cartoon series of pictures to illustrate the story. Write captions under each picture. Be sure to include the moral of the story. Then present and / or act out your story for the class.

Unit 9

CULTURE

Folktales about the Moon

come to one's mind
(突然)想起

1 Before reading What comes to your mind when you think of the Moon? When you look at the Moon, do you see any images on its surface?

bolded words
黑体字

2 Reading 09_10 What do you think the article is about? Look at the title, bolded words, and visuals. Read the text and check your predictions.

The Moon

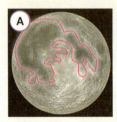

The Moon is the biggest and brightest object in the night sky. When we look at the Moon, we can see the surface is covered with dark spots. For centuries, people around the world have looked up at the Moon's spots and seen different images. To explain these images, they told folktales.

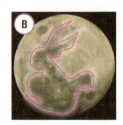

get tired of
厌烦;
对……感到厌倦

A **Hawaiian** tale explains that a woman got tired of working and went to the Moon to rest by walking on a rainbow bridge.

disguise oneself as
把某人伪装成……

In the **Japanese** version of an Indian tale, the god Sakra disguised himself as a beggar and asked a monkey, a fox, and a rabbit for food. The rabbit offered its own body as food and jumped into a fire. Sakra saved the rabbit for its generosity and took him to the Moon, where he works making *mochi* (rice cakes).

A **Native American** story tells how a frog jumped to the Moon to escape a wolf that was madly in love with her.

A **German** story explains that a man who was cutting wood on a Sunday was banished to the Moon for working on a religious day.

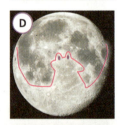

become trapped
被困住

The **Maori** people of **New Zealand** see a woman named Rona, who became trapped on the Moon for cursing it when the Moon went behind a cloud and she tripped in the dark.

the pill of
immortality
长生不老药
float up
飘起来
Angola
安哥拉

The **Chinese** tell different folktales about Chang E who swallowed the pill of immortality and floated up to the Moon. She lives with a rabbit who is constantly working to make more medicine for the gods.

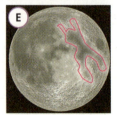

The **Kimbundu** tribe of **Angola** see a frog who acted as a messenger between the king of Earth and the king of the Moon.

One native **Mexican** tale explains how two gods wanted to be the Sun. As only one god could be the Sun, a rabbit was thrown into the face of one of the two Sun gods, making it darker and turning it into the Moon.

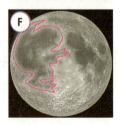

3 **After reading** Match the sentence parts below. Also circle the correct answer for each. Then read each sentence aloud. Is it a good summary of the text?

1. A German man was sent to the Moon __f__
2. A woman went to the Moon on a rainbow bridge _____
3. In the Maori folktale, Rona got angry _____
4. The rabbit in the Chinese folktale _____
5. In one story, a wolf chased a frog _____
6. The Japanese story is about _____
7. The Angolan folktale is about a frog _____
8. In an ancient Mexican tale, a rabbit _____

a. to work / rest in a Hawaiian folktale.
b. was making rice cakes / medicine.
c. that took rice cakes / messages between Earth and the Moon.
d. because it was hungry / was in love with her.
e. was thrown into a sun to turn it into the Moon / a star.
f. for cutting wood / (working on a religious day.)
g. a selfish / generous rabbit.
h. with the Moon for tripping her / for not lighting her way.

Talk about it!

4 With a partner, look at the six pictures (A–F) of the Moon in the article on page 108. Find the man, woman, rabbit, and frog. Do you see any other images?

A: Look. This could be a rabbit's head.
B: OK. I see it. And look here, this looks like the frog.

PRONUNCIATION

Pronunciation of -ed verb endings

09_11

Sometimes the -ed ending on a verb is pronounced as a separate syllable. Sometimes it isn't. Say the words aloud. Put them in two groups. Then listen and check your answers. When is the -ed a separate syllable?

| suggested | ~~replied~~ | repeated | decided | returned |
| insulted | explained | arrived | promised | predicted |

two syllables	three syllables
replied	

Unit 9

CONVERSATION

Asking for more information about a story

1 Listen to Lynn tell Yoon what happened this morning. Circle the correct words in the sentences below.

1. The conversation is taking place at Lynn's house / at work.
2. Lynn is late to work because a bird got into the house / her neighbor needed help.
3. The bird died in the house / left the same way it came in.

2 Complete Lynn and Yoon's conversation with expressions from the box. Then listen again to check your answers.

Lynn: Sorry I'm late, Yoon. A strange thing happened to me this morning.

Yoon: No problem, Lynn. The boss isn't here yet. (1) <u>What happened?</u>

Lynn: Well, I was making breakfast when I heard a crazy sound.

Yoon: A crazy sound? (2) _____

Lynn: Well, it's hard to describe. But it sounded like someone was in my living room breaking things!

Yoon: You're kidding! (3) _____

Lynn: Well, I went into the living room, and there was a bird flying around. It was really confused and scared.

Yoon: No way!

Lynn: Yes! So I ran across the street to my neighbor's house.

Yoon: (4) _____

Lynn: I didn't know what to do! I thought maybe someone could help me.

Yoon: OK. (5) _____ the bird?

Lynn: Well, I went back to my house with my neighbor, but the bird was gone. I guess it flew back out the open window.

> Really? Why did you do that?
> What do you mean?
> But what about…
> ~~What happened?~~
> So what did you do?

CONVERSATION STRATEGY

Express surprise
To respond to information someone gives you, use You're kidding! or No way! to express surprise or disbelief.

请注意如何表达"惊讶"或"怀疑"

run across
跑着穿过

Talk about it!

3 Think of your own unusual or strange story. Share it with a partner. While your partner is telling a story, ask for more information using the expressions from exercise 2.

Tell me more!

Visit the Takeaway English Online Learning Center at http://olcs.mcgraw-hill-education.com/takeaway/

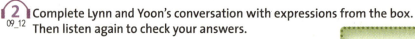

Check out the Takeaway TV video.

 Improve your English with the online activities.

WRITING

Writing a folktale

1 Before writing Review the story of *The Tiger, the Brahmin, and the Jackal* on pages 106-107. Then match the sequence words with the sentence parts to put the story in the correct order.

1. First, __d__
2. Next, ____
3. Then, ____
4. After that, ____
5. Finally, ____

a. they asked the tree if it was fair.
b. the jackal locked the tiger in the cage.
c. they asked the buffalo if it was fair.
d. the Brahmin freed the tiger and it jumped on him.
e. they asked the jackal if it was fair.

2 Planning your writing You will write your own folktale. Use the story map to help you prepare. Here are three story ideas. You can also develop your own idea.

A. The tiger wants to eat the monkey, but something happens. / The monkey helps the tiger. / They become friends.

B. The fox sees lots of animals he can eat. / Each animal that he tries to eat tells him a story, and he forgets that he is hungry. / The animals cook rice and eggs for the fox to eat.

C. The swan is sad because she has a broken feather and will not leave the house. / Other animals ask where the swan is. / They visit the swan. / They don't notice the broken feather. / The swan leaves the house with her new friends.

> **HELP writing**
>
> **Make your writing interesting**
> Use adverbs in your writing to make it more interesting and informative for your reader. Which of the following sentences helps you better imagine the scene?
> a. The girl hung up the phone.
> b. The girl angrily hung up the phone.
>
> 请注意运用副词让文章更生动

Title	Setting
Characters	
Event 1	Event 2
Event 3	Event 4
Moral	

3 Writing Write your folktale. Remember to:

- include reporting verbs (*explained, suggested, said, asked,* etc.)
- include simple past and past continuous verbs
- include sequence words (*First, Then, After that,* etc.)
- include adverbs
- check for correct spelling and punctuation

Unit 9

TEST

Test-taking strategy

Short answer questions   Some exams include short answer questions. "Fill in the blank" and "completion" questions are examples of short answer questions. You must write the answer rather than just choose an answer from three or four options.

Look at the example below. Use these steps to help you write the correct answer.

1. Read the question carefully. Make sure you understand what it asks for.
2. Find the answer in the sentence or paragraph. Highlight it.
3. Write your answer. Then read it over to be sure it makes sense.
4. Check your spelling and capitalization.

> **Example**
> Answer the question.
> The zoo has all types of animals: mammals, amphibians, reptiles, birds, and fish.
> 1. In the sentence, a synonym for warm-blooded animals is _____ .
>   You write: **mammals**   A synonym has the same meaning as another word.

PRACTICE

Read the paragraph and answer the questions.

> Folktales are traditional stories that have been handed down from one generation to the next. The characters in many folktales are animals that have human qualities. Folktales usually contain a message about what is right and wrong. This message is called a moral. Different cultures have different folktales, but some folktales appear in many different cultures.

1. Traditional stories are called _____ .
2. A synonym for a message about right and wrong is _____ .
3. Many folktales use _____ to tell the story.
4. The animals in folktales have _____ .

Unit 9

UNIT SUMMARY

Nouns
amphibian
animal
beak
bird
Brahmin
buffalo
eagle
feather
fish
folktale
fox
frog
iguana
jackal
mammal
monkey
pet rabbit
reptile
salmon
snake
swan
tiger
tortoise
tuna

Adjectives
cold-blooded
generous
hospitable
kind
selfish
ungrateful
warm-blooded

Verbs and verb phrases
ask
beg
classify
complain
explain
lay
promise
reply
say
suggest

Adverbs
angrily
happily
luckily
nervously
proudly
quietly
selfishly
stubbornly

Expressions
No way!
You're kidding!

Ask for more information about a story
But what about...
Really? Why did you do that?
So what did you do?
What do you mean?
What happened?

10 ▸ Home, sweet home

In this unit you...
- talk about homes, rooms, and furniture
- discuss renting an apartment
- describe the position of things in a room
- respond to suggestions

Grammar
- *should* for advice and the imperative for instructions
- *could* and *might* for possibility

START

Apartment for rent

1 Read the ad for an apartment for rent. Circle the floor plan it describes.

SoHo
索霍区(伦敦一地区)
natural light
自然光

A    B    C

FOR RENT
A beautiful apartment on a quiet street in SoHo. Top floor with lots of natural light and a sunny balcony. Kitchen-living area, one bedroom, and one bathroom. Ideal for young couple.

2 Match the words to the numbers on the floor plan of the apartment below. Then listen and check.
10_01

bedside table
床头柜

kitchen sink
厨房洗涤池

bathroom sink
浴室水槽

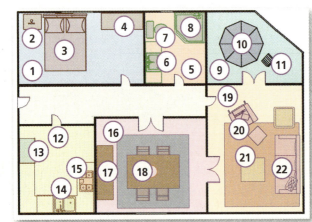

a. __1__ bedroom   l. ___ buffet
b. ___ kitchen   m. ___ coffee table
c. ___ refrigerator   n. ___ dining room
d. ___ shower   o. ___ bedside table
e. ___ bathroom   p. ___ armchair
f. ___ table and chairs q. ___ balcony
g. ___ sofa   r. ___ kitchen sink
h. ___ deck chair   s. ___ toilet
i. ___ living room   t. ___ stove
j. ___ bed   u. ___ bathroom sink
k. ___ dresser   v. ___ umbrella

Talk about it!

3 With a partner, ask and answer these questions about where you live.

1. Where do you live?
2. Do you live in a house or an apartment?
3. How many bedrooms does it have?
4. What other rooms does it have?
5. Does it have a balcony? A garage?
6. What's your favorite room? Why?

Unit 10

LISTENING

I'm calling about the apartment

1 Before listening Think about apartment features—the location, the rooms, and what's in the rooms. What are the most important features for you?

2 Listening Listen to a phone conversation between Tim and Mary about an apartment for rent. Complete these sentences with the correct information.

1. _____ is the owner of the apartment.
2. _____ might want to rent the apartment.
3. The apartment has _____ bedroom(s).
4. The apartment was _____ recently.
5. _____ Street is the closest subway station.

> **HELP listening**
>
> Listen for specific information
>
> Read any descriptions or questions about a listening passage *before* you listen. In fact, read them two or three times. This will help you focus on the information that you need most.

请注意听前读题

3 Listening Listen again and number the topics from 1 to 6 in the order that Tim and Mary speak about them.

____ the number of bedrooms   _1_ the apartment building
____ how to get to the apartment   ____ when to meet at the apartment
____ the condition of the apartment ____ the neighborhood

4 After listening Circle the correct answer to complete Mary's statements about the apartment. Check your answers with a partner.

1. It's on the (top) / first floor of a building in SoHo.
2. It's on a noisy / quiet street.
3. There are no / a few stores close to the building.
4. It's about five / fifteen minutes from the subway.
5. It doesn't have / has a lot of natural light.
6. It has / doesn't have a balcony.
7. The apartment has / doesn't have furniture.
8. There is / isn't a lot of space.

Talk about it!

5 Work with a partner. Role-play a conversation between a person renting an apartment and a person looking for an apartment. Include the following information in your discussion:

- location in the town / city
- location in the building
- number and names of rooms
- number of bedrooms
- what's nearby
- meeting time and place

115

Unit 10

VOCABULARY

What's in the living room?

> **ENGLISH express**
>
> Things you put in a room, like chairs, tables, and sofas are called furniture. Furniture is a noncount noun.
>
> There is a lot of furniture in my living room.
>
> 请注意 furniture 的含义和用法

1 Match the furniture words to the numbers in the picture of the living room. Then listen and check.

10_03

a. __5__ ceiling
b. _____ floor
c. _____ sofa
d. _____ shelves
e. _____ window
f. _____ door
g. _____ lamp
h. _____ picture
i. _____ rug
j. _____ wall
k. _____ coffee table
l. _____ armchair

2 Read the paragraph about where things are located in the room. Then use the underlined prepositions to complete the sentences below.

> There's a sofa <u>in the middle of</u> the room. There's a picture <u>above</u> the shelves. The lamp is <u>between</u> the door and the big picture. The coffee table is <u>in front of</u> the sofa. The armchair is <u>next to</u> the sofa. The bottle of water is <u>on top of</u> the coffee table. There's a window with a nice view <u>across from</u> the sofa. The shelves are <u>behind</u> the sofa.

1. The coffee table is _____ the rug.
2. The rug is _____ the room.
3. The ceiling is _____ the floor.
4. There's a wall _____ the armchair.
5. The coffee table is _____ the armchair.
6. The sofa is _____ the shelves and the coffee table.
7. _____ the sofa, there's a window.
8. The lamp is _____ the door.

> **culture matters**
>
> Different countries have different customs for when you enter a house. In many English-speaking countries, you wipe your shoes on a mat before you enter. In Japan, you take off your shoes.
> • What is the custom in your country?
>
> 请注意各国进屋时的不同习惯

Talk about it!

3 Work with a partner. Think of the items in a room in your home. Describe the room to your partner. Use exercise 2 as a model. Your partner draws the floor plan. Check your partner's work.

Unit 10

GRAMMAR

Should for advice and the imperative for instructions

ALSO GO TO Grammar Takeaway PAGE 203

the imperative
祈使句

1 Read the sentences. Then circle the correct words to complete the rules.

| advice | You should take the subway. It's faster. You shouldn't come by bus. |
| instructions | Take the subway to Prince Street station. Don't take the bus. |

Rules: • To give advice, we use the imperative / *should* + base form of the verb.
• To give instructions, we use the imperative / *should* + base form of the verb.

2 Help your friend decorate his new apartment. Write sentences giving advice and instructions.

Put the refrigerator in the kitchen, next to the stove. You shouldn't put the rug on the balcony.

_____
_____
_____
_____
_____
_____
_____

3 Match the questions and the answers.

1. Where should I put this picture? __c__
2. Do you think I should put my bed here? _____
3. When should I buy a refrigerator? _____
4. Do you think they should buy or rent an apartment? _____
5. Which table is best for the living room? _____
6. Does Wendy think we should buy a new lamp? _____

a. Right away! There isn't one in the apartment.
b. Probably rent one. They don't earn enough to buy one.
c. Put it over there, near the window.
d. Maybe this one. It's bigger than the other one.
e. Yes, she does. This one is broken.
f. Yes, this is a good place for it.

Talk about it!

4 Work with a partner. Ask for and give advice. You can discuss any topic.

A: My shoes are old. Do you think I should get some new ones?
B: Absolutely! You should buy some new ones today. Go after class.

ENGLISH express

To ask for advice, we often use *Do you think* + *should*.
Do you think I should paint this room red?

请注意"征求建议"的表达方式

WORKBOOK PAGE 71-72

117

Unit 10

READING

> **HELP reading**
>
> **Identify cause and effect**
> A *cause* is why something happens. An *effect* is what happens because of the cause. Cause and effect show relationships between events or situations. Look for cause and effect relationships as you read to help you understand better.
>
> 请注意阅读时查找因果关系

Feng Shui

1 Before reading Do you spend a lot of time decorating your room or home? Why or why not?

2 Reading 10_04 Read the introduction to a magazine article about Feng Shui and answer the questions.

1. What is Feng Shui?
2. How does Feng Shui work?

3 Reading 10_04 Now read the rest of the article and match the titles to the paragraphs.

Bedroom   Kitchen   Living room

4 After reading Based on the ideas in the article, choose the picture that best represents the ideal organization for each room. Check your answers with a partner.

have an effect on
对……有影响；
对……起作用

1. kitchen

2. bedroom

3. living room

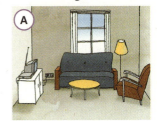 

MAKING A HOUSE INTO A HOME

This month's "House and Home" looks at Feng Shui, the 3,000 year-old Chinese art of living harmoniously in our homes.

Have you ever gone into a neighbor's house and felt immediately "at home"? Or walked into an office or building and felt uncomfortable, but you didn't know why? Feng Shui could be affecting you.

The Chinese believe all things contain energy. Feng Shui, meaning wind and water, is the art of organizing buildings to use this energy positively. It can have an effect on our homes, relationships, and work. Use our guide to improve your home—and life!

1 _____

This room contains two conflicting elements—fire and water. Because of this, the stove and the sink shouldn't be close together. Don't put the stove in a corner or in front of a large window. Ideally, the stove also won't be across from the door.

118

Unit 10

5 After reading With a partner, ask and answer these questions.

1. What do you think about Feng Shui? What ideas in the article do you agree or disagree with? Why?
2. Who do you know that would probably agree or disagree with the ideas of Feng Shui? Why?
3. Would you consider changing a room to improve its energy? Why or why not?
4. Have you ever changed the organization of your room or home? If so, why did you change it?

Talk about it!

6 Discuss your ideal room with a partner. What are your priorities? Put the different factors in order from 1 (the most important) to 8 (the least important). Compare and explain your lists.

_____ size   _____ window
_____ color   _____ view
_____ furniture   _____ natural light
_____ decoration   _____ position in the house / apartment

> **ENGLISH express**
>
> The modals **could** and **might** are used to say that something is possible.
>
> Feng Shui **could** / **might** be affecting you. = It's possible that Feng Shui is affecting you.

请注意 could 和 might 的含义

The room should be rectangular or square. Irregular shapes have a negative
25 effect on the flow of energy. A spacious room with good light is perfect.

2 _____

Don't put objects that reflect across from the bed—this includes mirrors and TVs. The bed shouldn't face the
30 door. Put it diagonally across the room. If you live in a house on two floors, this room shouldn't be above the garage or the kitchen. Don't put any plants here. Don't put the bed next to a
35 window or your spirit might leave the house while you're asleep!

3 _____

This room is important because it's where we entertain guests and friends. Lots of light, space, and natural colors
40 are best. Don't fill it with too much furniture. Don't put the room near the front door of the house. Again, as with the bedroom, no mirrors!

rectangular
矩形的

diagonally
斜对地；对角地

PROJECT

Design a floor plan of your ideal apartment or house. Use the plans you have seen in this unit to help you. Present the plan to your classmates and explain why it is ideal for you. Use *could* and *might* to talk about different possibilities.

I could have a TV in the living room.
I might put a hot tub on the balcony.

Unit 10

SONG

Close the door

baseball cap
棒球帽

| clock |
| books |
| baseball cap |
| cup |
| clothes |
| telephone |
| DVDs |
| snack |
| sweatshirt |
| MP3 |

1 Before listening Work with a partner. Choose an item from the list. Say where you usually find it but not what it is. Your partner guesses the item.

A: I have one on the table beside my bed.
B: Is it a clock?

2 Before listening Work in pairs. Use words in exercise 1 to complete the song.

3 Listening Listen to the song and check your answers to exercise 2.
10_05

Close the door

On the table there's a (1) _____ .
I can't remember when it stopped.
Dusty (2) _____ beside the bed.
Half of them you never read.
5 Your (3) _____ behind the door.
A pile of (4) _____ in the middle of the floor.
The closet's standing open wide,
Nothing left of yours inside.

Chorus
I should be cleaning
10 That dirty old blue (5) _____ .
The one you left next to the (6) _____
The day you said you were leaving home.
From floor to ceiling,
I should be sweeping up.
15 I should be putting all those things away,
Close the door on yesterday.

A memory here, a memory there,
On the shelves, at the top of the stairs,
In the drawers, behind the chair,
The things you left are everywhere.
The coffee table can't be seen.
It's covered by your (7) _____ .
In the fridge your favorite (8) _____ .
It doesn't mean you're coming back.

Chorus
25 I'll take your (9) _____ off the chair,
Make a space and sit down there.
Put on your favorite (10) _____ ,
Imagine you're still here with me.

Chorus

sweep up
扫除；打扫

4 Listening Listen to the song again. Which sentence describes the song best?
10_05
  a. You forgot to clean your room again.
  b. You've left home and I need to clean.
  c. It's my turn to clean the apartment.

5 After listening We often avoid repeating words by using substitute words, like *it*, *one*, or *there*. Match the words from the song with the things they substitute.

substitute words
代词

  a. it (line 2) __clock__
  b. them (line 4) _____
  c. the one (line 11) _____
  d. it (line 22) _____
  e. it (line 24) _____
  f. there (line 26) _____ .

Talk about it!

6 In groups, discuss these questions.
  1. Who is *you* in the song? Where do you think this person is now?
  2. Who is the singer of the song? How do you think the singer feels?
  3. Do you know anyone who has left home? Why did he / she leave?
  4. What is the ideal age to leave home? Explain.
  5. What are the advantages and disadvantages of living at home, compared to not living at home?

PRONUNCIATION

Vowel sounds /ʊ/ *wood*, /uː/ *you*, and /ɔː/ *for*

1 Listen to the examples of the three vowel sounds. Then put the words into three groups.
10_06

| blue | ~~could~~ | door | floor | good | new | put | room | store | should | two | your |

/ʊ/ wood	/uː/ you	/ɔː/ for
could		

2 Listen and check your answers. Then add at least three more words to each column.
10_07

Unit 10

CONVERSATION

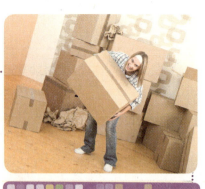

Responding to suggestions

1. In general, do you like your friends to give you suggestions about decorating, activities, hair, etc.? Why or why not? Who gives you good suggestions?

2. Eve is moving into a new apartment. Her friend, Min, is giving her suggestions. Read their conversation. Notice the words in purple.

   Min: I think you should put this chair in the living room.
   Eve: Maybe, but I'm not sure. I'd rather not put it there.
   Min: Then why don't you put it in your bedroom? Then you can read in your room.
   Eve: Hmm... I didn't think of that. Yes... That's a good idea.
   Min: And then you could use this lamp when you want to read.
   Eve: I see what you mean, but I'd prefer a new lamp.
   Min: But you don't have the money to buy another lamp.
   Eve: I suppose you're right.

CONVERSATION STRATEGY

Be polite when responding

When responding negatively to a suggestion, be polite. Use a positive expression first, followed by but.

I see what you mean, but I have another idea.

请注意如何礼貌地拒绝对方的建议

3. Write the positive and negative responses from the conversation in the chart.

positive responses	negative responses
Maybe	

Talk about it!

4. Work with a partner. Give suggestions on different topics, such as room decorating, activities, clothes, job, school, etc. Respond positively or negatively.

   A: You should get a haircut.
   B: Thanks, but I'm pretty happy with my hair right now.

Tell me more!

Visit the Takeaway English Online Learning Center at http://olcs.mcgraw-hill-education.com/takeaway/

 Check out the *Takeaway TV* video.

 Improve your English with the online activities.

Unit 10

WRITING

Writing an advice letter

1 Before writing Read the email and look at the picture of the office. What is the writer's problem?

> **HELP writing**
> **Write an effective response**
> When someone writes for advice, they want an answer to their problem. Make sure you understand all of the writer's concerns when you respond. Offer clear advice or a suggestion where the answer might be found.
>
> 请注意如何针对性地提出建议

Dear Interiors Magazine,

I read your article about Feng Shui, "Making a House into a Home." This is very interesting. Are there similar ideas about improving offices? I have included a picture of my office. Can you help me make it more comfortable?

Regards,

Patricia Pitt

2 Planning your writing Use the Problem-Solution Chart to list problems in Ms. Pitt's office. Use the Feng Shui tips to identify solutions to the problems.

> **Feng Shui tips for the workplace...**
> - Your workplace can affect how you feel, how you work, and the success of your business.
> - Don't sit with your back to the door.
> - Make a nice space for people to wait in when they come to see you.
> - Try to organize the office so you can see out of the window.
> - Put up relaxing pictures of mountains and rivers to look at.
> - Don't fill the office with a lot of furniture or unnecessary objects.

problem	solution
nothing on walls to look at	hang pictures of beautiful scenery

3 Writing Answer Ms. Pitt's email and give her advice about how to organize her office. Use imperative forms, *should* + verb, *could*, and *might*. For example: Move the desk... You should have... You could put... It might be a good idea to...

Begin like this:

Dear Ms. Pitt,

Thank you for writing to us about your problem. Yes, there are Feng Shui ideas about improving offices.

Unit 10

TEST

Test-taking strategy

Listening comprehension questions On some exams you hear a listening passage only one time. Listen carefully and take notes to help you answer the questions.

Use these steps to help you answer listening comprehension questions.

1. Read the directions and the questions carefully before you listen.
2. Have paper and pen ready to take notes.
3. Write down key words or information while you listen, for example, *amazing, going strong, have ½ her energy*.

For example, you hear this listening passage.

> My grandmother is amazing. She's almost 90 years old and she's still going strong. She loves to spend time with her fourteen grandchildren and four great-grandchildren. I hope I have half her energy when I'm her age.

You see this test question.

> *Example*
> **Listen. A woman is talking about her grandmother. Choose the correct answer. You will hear the listening only one time.**
> 1. How does the writer feel about her grandmother?
>   A. She wants to be like her when she is her age.   This is the correct answer.
>   B. She wants to have grandchildren also.   This is not a feeling about her grandmother.
>   C. She is strong and energetic.   This doesn't describe the writer's feelings.

PRACTICE

Listen to a man talking about his neighbors. Choose the correct answer. Mark the letter on the Answer Sheet. You will hear the listening only one time.

1. The man's neighbors are driving him _____ .
   A. to the manager
   B. crazy
   C. to the apartment
2. What do the neighbor's children do?
   A. jump on the floor
   B. cry all the time
   C. talk on the phone
3. What does the man decide to do?
   A. talk to the neighbors
   B. turn on his TV
   C. talk to the manager

Answer Sheet
Mark the letter.
1. A B C
2. A B C
3. A B C

Unit 10

UNIT SUMMARY

Nouns
apartment
armchair
balcony
bathroom
bathroom sink
bed
bedroom
bedside table
buffet
ceiling
chair
coffee table
deck chair
dining room
door
dresser
feature
floor
floor plan
furniture
kitchen
kitchen sink
lamp
living room
neighborhood
picture
refrigerator
rug
shelves
shower
sofa
stove
subway station
table
toilet
top floor
umbrella
wall
window

Verb
rent

Modals
could
might
should

Prepositions
above
across from
behind
between
in front of
in the middle of
next to
on top of

Expressions
Do you think + should…
for rent

Respond to suggestions
I didn't think of that.
I see what you mean…
I suppose you're right.
I'd prefer…
I'd rather not…
I'm not sure…
Maybe…
That's a great idea.

Review 2

VOCABULARY

Put the words and phrases into five groups. Then compare your answers with a partner. Together, add words and phrases of your own.

a sink	fluently	an eagle	elderly	a teenager	shelves	middle-aged
a buffalo	a suit	pick up	slang	a fox	get by	a monkey
a skirt	baggy	the ceiling	tight	the floor	a kid	

clothes	rooms	languages	age groups	animals
	a sink			

A: I think "slang" goes under "rooms".

B: Are you sure? I think it goes under "languages". Remember? "Slang" means *informal words*.

A: Oh, yeah. You're right.

GRAMMAR

Circle the correct answer to complete each sentence.

1. You had been here before, _____ you?
   - **A** hadn't
   - **B** didn't
   - **C** have
   - **D** had

2. I usually _____ in the evening for an hour before I go to bed.
   - **A** am studying
   - **B** study
   - **C** studies
   - **D** studied

3. She _____ when the teacher explained the assignment.
   - **A** wasn't listening
   - **B** no was listening
   - **C** not was listening
   - **D** not listened

4. I finished work and _____ home.
   - **A** walking
   - **B** was walking
   - **C** walked
   - **D** walk

5. I've lived in Singapore _____ 1998.
   - **A** for
   - **B** during
   - **C** since
   - **D** while

Review 2

LISTENING

1 You will hear a question and three responses. Circle the letter of the best response to each question. Then listen again and check your answers.

10_R2_01

1. A B C
2. A B C
3. A B C
4. A B C
5. A B C

CONVERSATION

1 Draw your family tree. Include as many members of your family as possible. Then work with a partner. Ask and answer questions about your family trees.

A: Who's Hana?

B: That's my mother. She's married to Kwan, my father. And Shin is my brother.

A: How old is Shin?

B: He's 17. He's five years younger than me.

2 With a partner, talk about the clothes you and your family wear.

A: What clothes does your mom usually wear during the week?

B: Well, she wears formal clothes to work, but she wears jeans and t-shirts on weekends.

A: My mom wears formal clothes on Saturday and Sunday too!

B: Really? Well, my Aunt Valerie also wears formal clothes on weekends.

3 With a partner, talk about something you did with your family. Use the simple past and past continuous. When you are listening, remember to show that you are interested.

A: Last weekend, my family and I celebrated my grandmother's birthday. It was raining, but we had a great time.

B: How old was she?

A: 95.

B: Wow! 95! How many people came to the party?

127

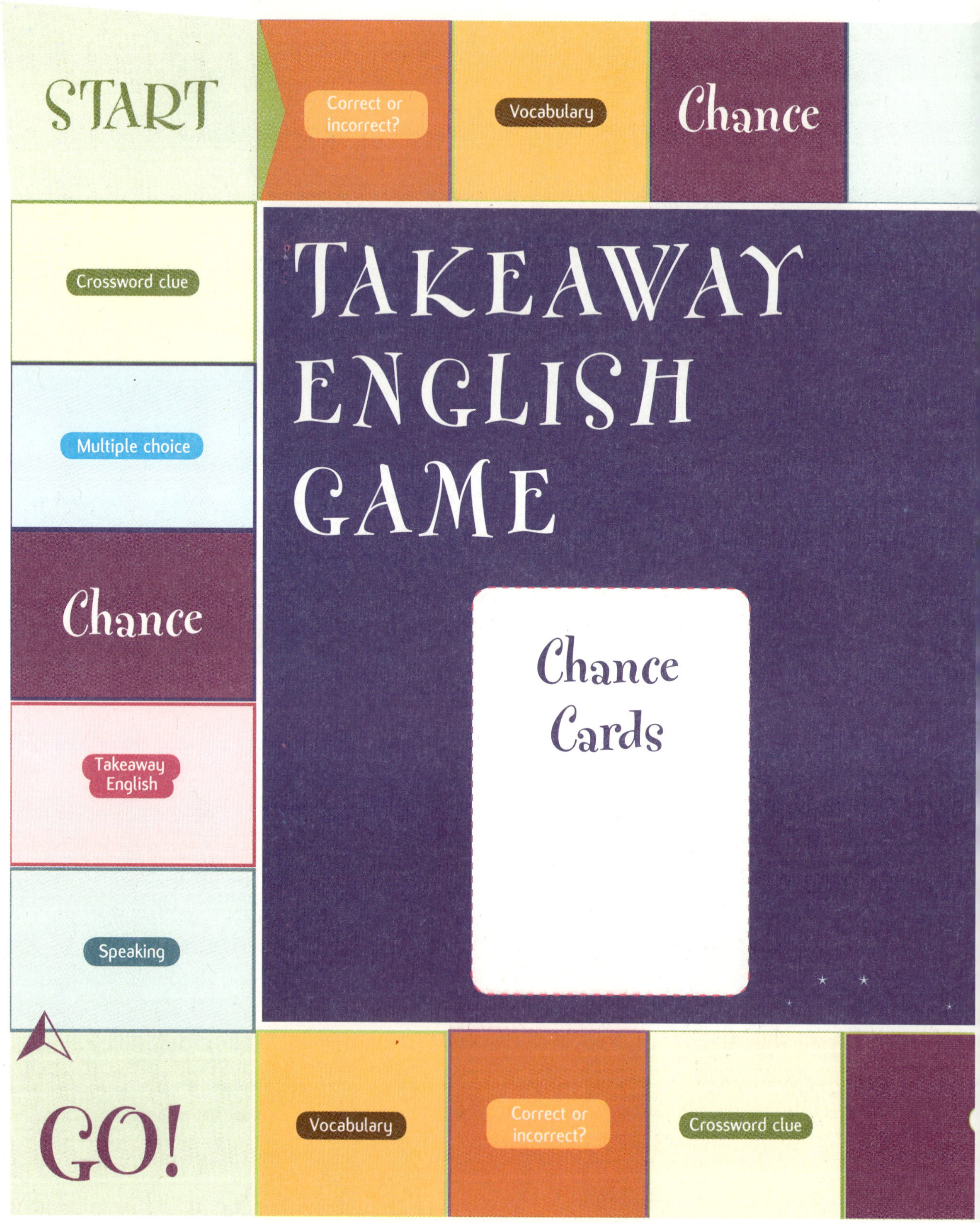

Review 2

TAKEAWAY ENGLISH GAME

START → Correct or incorrect? → Vocabulary → Chance

Crossword clue

Multiple choice

Chance

Takeaway English

Speaking

GO! → Vocabulary → Correct or incorrect? → Crossword clue

Chance Cards

Review 2

| Speaking | Takeaway English | Multiple choice | Spell it | **GO!** |

| Crossword clue |
| Correct or incorrect? |
| **Chance** |
| Vocabulary |
| Speaking |

PLAY THE TAKEAWAY ENGLISH GAME.

YOU WILL NEED

- A DIE
- SOME SMALL COINS OR GAME PIECES.
- THE CHANCE CARDS
- 2 or 3 players or teams
- 1 question reader (with "Questions and Answers" page)

HOW TO PLAY
Throw the die and move your game piece.
The question reader asks you a question.
Answer the question.
If you land on a Chance square, pick a Chance card.
If you land on a Go! square, take another turn.

SCORE
1 point for a correct answer

TO WIN THE GAME
The first player or team to get 20 points wins the game.

After each game, a different person is the question reader.

| Spell it | Chance | Multiple choice | Takeaway English | **GO!** |

11 ▶ Doing it for charity

In this unit you...
- talk about charity events
- discuss staying in shape
- talk about geographical features
- show support and offer help

Grammar
- future with *will*, *be going to*, and simple present

START

Charity events

1 A charity is an organization that helps people or animals, protects the environment, or helps with other important causes. What charities do you know about?

2 Read and listen to the newspaper stories about charity events. Match the stories to the pictures.
11_01

1

A HAIRCUT FOR CANCER
A 16-year-old girl has decided to donate all her hair to leukemia patients. Emma Cole will give her knee-length hair to the Leukemia Foundation to make wigs for leukemia patients. Leukemia patients often lose their hair during treatment for their illness.

2

SWIM TO THE STATUE
Daniel Garcia and Carla Chin hope to donate money to a group that organizes learn-to-swim programs in New York City. In May, they will swim from Battery Park to the Statue of Liberty with 200 other volunteers who give their time to the programs. They have each signed up more than 50 sponsors who will give them money if they complete the swim.

3

WALK FOR WORK
Andy Hopkins is raising money for a charity that helps set up work projects in southern Africa. He got many sponsors who will give him money for every mile he walks. He starts his trek across the hot, dry Kalahari Desert in Botswana and South Africa next June.

cancer 癌症
knee-length hair 长及膝部的头发
Leukemia Foundation 白血病基金会
make wigs 做假发

the Statue of Liberty 自由女神像
trek 艰苦跋涉
sign up 签定
Kalahari Desert 卡拉哈里沙漠
Botswana 博茨瓦纳

3 Find the purple words below in the stories. Use the context of these words to help you understand the meaning. Then match them to the definitions.

1. To donate money is ___b___
2. Raising money is _____
3. Sponsors are _____
4. Volunteers are _____

a. people who work without receiving money.
b. to give money to a person or an organization.
c. people or businesses that give money for an event.
d. collecting money for a special reason.

Talk about it!

4 With a partner, ask and answer these questions.

1. Would you participate in any of these charity events? Why or why not?
2. Which charities do you think are most important—those that deal with children, with health issues, with education, or with animals? Why?

participate in 参加; 参与
deal with 涉及; 处理

Unit 11

LISTENING

A walk for charity

1 Before listening Who are some famous people involved in charity work? What is their charity? Does being famous make it easier to raise money for a charity? Why or why not?

be involved in
参与……
raise money
募资

2 Listening Listen to the radio interview. Which person from the stories on page 130 is being interviewed? _____
11_02

3 Listening Listen again and number the pictures in the order that they are mentioned.
11_02

　　work out　　　　　　　a compass　　　　　take an exercise class

HELP listening

Identify sequence
Identifying the sequence of events in a listening can improve your overall understanding. Pay attention to question / answer exchanges and sequence words (*first, next*). You can practice this skill by taking brief notes while you listen.

请注意听时记录事件发生的顺序

4 After listening Circle the correct words to complete these sentences.

1. Andy (feels positive about) / doesn't want to go on the trek.
2. He was in good / bad physical condition.
3. He isn't doing any special training / is doing a lot of exercise.
4. He will walk for about a week / a month.
5. The charity helps homeless / poor people.

ENGLISH express

Use *expect* + *infinitive* for events in the future that will probably happen.
　Andy expects to finish in a month.
Use *hope* + *infinitive* for events in the future that we would like to happen.
　Daniel and Carla hope to donate money to a charity organization.

请注意 expect 和 hope 的不同含义

physical condition
身体状况

Talk about it!

5 With a partner, ask and answer these questions.

1. Have you ever taken part in a sponsored event (walk / run / swim, etc.) to raise money for a charity? What kind of an event was it?

   A: Have you ever taken part in a sponsored event for charity?
   B: No, I haven't. Have you?
   A: Yes, I have. I went on a 6-kilometer run to raise money for the homeless.

2. Do you think that charities are a good idea? Why or why not?
3. Do you think that all the charity money goes to the people who need it? Explain.

sponsored event
赞助活动

131

Unit 11

stay in shape
保持身材

work out
锻炼

be out of shape
身材走样

VOCABULARY

What do you do and where do you go to stay in shape?

1 Do you think that you get enough exercise? Why or why not?

2 Match the expressions in the box to the categories. Then listen and check.
11_03

| 1. to train | 3. to be in good shape | 5. to go trekking | 7. to be in bad shape |
| 2. to work out | 4. to be out of shape | 6. to stay in shape | 8. to go running |

a. to be in bad physical condition: __4__, ____
b. to be in good physical condition: ____, ____
c. to exercise: ____, ____, ____, ____

geographical
features
地理特征

3 Match the place names to the pictures. Then listen and check. Which geographical features can you find in your country?
11_04

1. __D__ a valley
2. ____ a beach
3. ____ an ocean
4. ____ a lake
5. ____ an island
6. ____ a desert
7. ____ a mountain
8. ____ a river

4 What activities can or can't you do in each place in exercise 3?

You can go running on a beach.
You can't go skiing on a beach.

Talk about it!

5 With a partner, complete the questions with words from the box. Then ask and answer the questions.

| trek | exercise | shape | ~~climbed~~ | work out | oceans |

1. Have you ever __climbed__ a high mountain? Which one?
2. Do you think that young people _____ enough these days? Explain.
3. Is it important to stay in good _____? Why?
4. Would you like to _____ across the Kalahari Desert? Why or why not?
5. Are there any rivers, lakes, or _____ near here where you can swim?
6. Do you think that some people _____ too much? Explain.

Unit 11

GRAMMAR

Future forms: *will*, *be going to*, simple present

ALSO GO TO
Grammar Takeaway
PAGE 204

1. The future is uncertain, but we can make plans and predictions. What are you going to do tonight? Tomorrow? Next week? Next year?

2. Look at the chart. Both *will* and *be going to* are used to talk about future plans and predictions.

	will	be going to
affirmative	I'm really tired. I think I'll go to bed. (I will = I'll)	We're going to meet at 7 o'clock.
negative	I won't be late. I promise! (will not = won't)	There's not enough time. He's not going to finish.
question	Will you lend me $5?	Are you going to get in shape?

ENGLISH express

The simple present can be used to talk about future scheduled events or timetables.

We leave on June 15th.

请注意如何用一般现在时表达将来发生的事情

Are these sentences predictions, plans or scheduled events? Check (✔) the correct answers.

1. The train leaves at 6 p.m. ☐ prediction ☐ plan ✔ scheduled event
2. It'll be really hot. ☐ prediction ☐ plan ☐ scheduled event
3. I'm going to start exercising a lot. ☐ prediction ☐ plan ☐ scheduled event
4. We're not going to work out today. ☐ prediction ☐ plan ☐ scheduled event
5. How long will the trek take? ☐ prediction ☐ plan ☐ scheduled event
6. They arrive on May 1st. ☐ prediction ☐ plan ☐ scheduled event

Talk about it!

3. Ask and answer these questions with a partner. Think of your own questions. Use your imagination!

1. What are you going to do on your next vacation?
2. How will the world be different in 100 years?
3. How will your life be different in 20 years?
   - **A:** How will your life be different in 20 years?
   - **B:** Well, I think I'll be married and I'll probably have kids. How about you?
   - **A:** Me? I'm not going to get married. That's for sure. I'm going to travel all over the world.

for sure
肯定

Unit 11

READING

A blog about a charity event

1 Before reading What is a blog? Do you read blogs? Which ones? Do you write blogs?

2 Before reading Look at the pictures in the blog. What sponsored event are Daniel and Carla preparing for?

> **HELP reading**
>
> Understand the writer's purpose
>
> It is important to understand not only the details of what you are reading, but the author's purpose as well. Ask yourself questions while you read. Is the author trying to teach me something or persuade me?
>
> 请注意理解作者的写作意图

3 Reading Read Daniel and Carla's blog. Match these titles to the paragraphs.

- What are we going to do?
- ~~Who are we?~~
- Preparations
- Where are we going?

4 After reading Circle *True* or *False*.

1. Daniel and Carla learned to swim when they were very young. — True (False)
2. They are going to swim in a lake. — True False
3. Manhattan is an island. — True False
4. Local schools and colleges will sponsor Daniel and Carla. — True False
5. The foundation helps people learn to swim. — True False
6. Daniel and Carla are going to train three times a week. — True False

Daniel and Carla's

1 _Who are we?_

Our names are Daniel and Carla. We're both college students. We live in East Harlem, a neighborhood in New York City. It's important to know how to swim, and it's fun too. We learned to swim when we were about 12 and 13. We learned in a special learn-to-swim program that was free and open to the public. Before, we were afraid of the water. But now we're great swimmers! We wanted to do something to help other young people who can't swim.

2 _____

We're going to raise some money to donate to the Manhattan Island Foundation. The foundation organizes swimming events around Manhattan and supports public learn-to-swim programs in New York City. In May, we're going to swim from Battery Park to the Statue of Liberty. This is about 1 mile (1.5 kilometers), and it will take less than 45 minutes. We're going to swim with about 200 other people! We hope that local stores and businesses will sponsor us, and we're going to donate this money to the Manhattan Island Foundation. We already have $800! Some people say we're crazy, but they still give us money. Some of them are coming to watch us swim too.

Unit 11

Blog!

3 _____

Battery Park is at the bottom of the island of Manhattan. We're going to swim straight out to the Statue of Liberty, passing Ellis Island on the way. We're going to come back to Battery Park on the ferry!

4 _____

We're going to train twice a week from now until the day of the challenge because we need to be in great shape. We'll swim about 1.5 miles (2.5 kilometers) each day. Before we can do the swim, we need a certificate from the Foundation. To get the certificate, we have to complete a 1-mile (1.5-kilometer) swim in a swimming pool in less than 45 minutes.

Talk about it!

5 With a partner, choose a charity event that you are going to take part in. You can choose an event from the unit, a local event, or you can invent a new charity event. Make notes.

- What are you going to do?
  _____
- Why are you going to do it?
  _____
- When are you going to do it?
  _____
- What charity are you helping?
  _____
- What preparations will you make?
  _____
- How long will it take?
  _____
- What things will you take?
  _____

at the bottom of
在……底部

on the ferry
乘渡船

Use your notes to tell the class what you are going to do. Take a class vote to decide which event is the most interesting.

We're going to rollerblade across Mexico. We're going to do this because...

rollerblade
滑旱冰

in great shape
身材很棒

certificate
证书

PROJECT

Work with a group. There are many important causes that could benefit from a charity. Set up your own charity. What cause will your charity benefit? What is the name of your charity? How will you raise money? How will you spend the money? Be creative. Prepare a brochure about your charity to present to your classmates. Decide who has the best idea for a new charity.

Unit 11

CULTURE

Charities around the world

1 Before reading Why do you think people give their time and money to charities? With so many charities to choose from, how do people select one?

2 Reading 11_06 How do you think the pictures are connected with charities? Read and match the texts with the pictures.

have no access to
无法得到

water filter
滤水器
provide sb. with sth.
为某人提供……

make a donation
捐赠
parachute jump
跳伞

the rescue center
救护中心
refuge
收容所

sightseeing
观光
Zambia
赞比亚
left over
剩余的
run a lab
开实验室
Tanzania
坦桑尼亚
deadly
致命的
unexploded
land mines
未爆破的地雷
detect
探测
less likely
可能性小
tropical diseases
热带病

1. **C** Too many people die every year because they have no access to clean drinking water. Your donations can help buy water filters that provide people in Haiti with clean water at home.

2. ☐ Did you know that there are 26,000 trees in Central Park in New York City? Help us maintain them by adopting a tree in the U.S.A. and making a donation to the park.

3. ☐ Do a sponsored parachute jump in Ireland and raise money for cancer research. You don't need any experience because we provide all the necessary training.

4. ☐ **El Refugio del Burrito** has 68 donkeys and mules in its care. Every animal that arrives at the rescue center is given a life of loving, expert care, and attention. Adopt a donkey at this refuge in the south of Spain and your donations will help us continue our work.

5. ☐ How are you going to spend the summer after you graduate? Young adults and students can volunteer to teach English in Chile. Don't expect to earn much money, but you will have a great time and maybe you'll even learn some Spanish!

6. ☐ Are you looking for a vacation that includes more than just sightseeing? Then become part of a group of volunteers who work to repair dry stone walls in the English countryside.

7. ☐ Give money to buy seeds for families in Zambia. We provide families with the means to grow their own food. We hope that they will have enough to eat and enough left over to sell.

8. ☐ For the past seven years, Bart Warner has been running a unique lab in Tanzania, where he trains rats to find deadly unexploded land mines. Although dogs have traditionally been used to help humans detect mines, rats are lighter, cheaper to maintain, and less likely to get tropical diseases. Send donations to help Bart train the life-saving rats.

136

Unit 11

culture matters

In many English-speaking countries, young people sometimes have a "gap year" between finishing high school and going to college. Popular gap year activities are volunteer work in foreign countries or traveling abroad.

- What do young people do after they finish high school in your country?

请注意了解西方国家的 gap year

3 Reading Read the texts again.
11_06 Which charity / charities...

1. ask for money?   1, _____
2. ask for volunteers?   _____
3. help people?   _____
4. help animals?   _____
5. don't help people or animals?   _____

4 After reading Circle *True* or *False* for each statement.

1. Clean drinking water is always available in Haiti.   True   (False)
2. There are about 26,000 trees in the U.S.A.   True   False
3. Training is given to volunteers who do parachute jumps in Ireland.   True   False
4. The refuge in Spain takes care of donkeys and mules.   True   False
5. Sightseeing is included for dry stone wall volunteers in England.   True   False
6. You won't earn lots of money as a volunteer teacher in Chile.   True   False
7. A Zambian organization helps families produce food and make money.   True   False
8. Bart Warner uses dogs to detect mines.   True   False

Talk about it!

5 With a partner, discuss these questions.

1. Which charities do people donate money to in your country?
2. Which of the charities on page 136 do you think are the most / least worthy?

   A: I really think Bart Warner's charity is the most worthy.

   B: I couldn't agree more. Helping destroy land mines is so important.

PRONUNCIATION

Pronouncing contractions

1 Listen to five sentences with
11_07 contractions. Write the sentences. Then listen again and practice saying the sentences.

2 Make the sentences in exercise 1
11_08 negative. Then listen again and check your answers. Practice saying the sentences.

affirmative	negative
1. It'll be very hot.	1. It won't be very hot.
_____	_____
_____	_____
_____	_____
_____	_____

Unit 11

CONVERSATION

Showing support and offering help

1 Listen to Karla and Jake's conversation and answer the questions.

1. Whose idea was it to have a charity event?
2. What will the event raise money for?
3. What will Jake do?
4. What will Karla do?

have a charity event
办一个慈善活动

2 Complete Karla and Jake's conversation with expressions from the box. Then listen again to check your answers.

| What can I do? | I couldn't agree more. | How can I help? |
| Count me in! | I'll do anything I can. | ~~I hear you!~~ |

count sb. in
算上某人

stray dogs
流浪狗

CONVERSATION STRATEGY

Use contractions
When you use contractions (I'll, I've, it's, I'm, they'll) when speaking, you sound more like a native speaker.
请注意口语中使用缩略形式

Karla: You know, I've noticed more and more stray dogs lately.
Jake: (1) ___I hear you!___ It's so sad.
Karla: It is sad. We need to help the animal shelter.
Jake: (2) _____ No dog should be on the streets.
Karla: I'm going to organize a car wash to raise money for the shelter.
Jake: Great idea! (3) _____ (4) _____
Karla: Well, you could help me get volunteers from school to wash the cars.
Jake: No problem. (5) _____
Karla: (6) _____
Jake: You could go to some local businesses and see if they'll sponsor us. You know, with soap and other supplies.
Karla: Exactly! Maybe they'll donate some money too.
Jake: This is going to be great!

Talk about it!

3 Work with a partner. Share other ideas for charity events. Use the expressions you have learned to show support and offer help.

A: We really need to do something about the river. It's so dirty.
B: I hear you! But what can we do?

Tell me more!

Visit the Takeaway English Online Learning Center at http://olcs.mcgraw-hill-education.com/takeaway/

 Check out the *Takeaway TV* video.

 Improve your English with the online activities.

WRITING

Writing a blog to promote a charity event

1 Writing model Look at Daniel and Carla's blog on pages 134-135. What headings did they use in their blog? What information did they provide?

2 Before writing What plan did Daniel and Carla make before writing their blog? Complete the plan with their notes.

> **HELP writing**
>
> Make a plan
> Make a plan with notes before you write. This means that when you start writing, you already have your ideas organized and you can concentrate on your English.

请注意写作前计划好内容

#1 Who are we?	#2	#3	#4
• names: Daniel and Carla • college students • live in East Harlem			

3 Planning your writing You will write a blog to promote your own charity event. Use the graphic organizer to help you plan your writing. Think of a title for each paragraph and what information should be included. Some things to think about:

Who are you? What charity are you helping? What are you going to do? When? Are you looking for sponsors? What is your goal? What preparations will you make?

#1	#2	#3	#4

4 Writing Use your notes to write a blog promoting your charity event. Write four paragraphs. Give each paragraph a heading. Include pictures if you like.

Unit 11

TEST

Test-taking strategy

Choose the correct verb tense or form   For some test questions it's important to pay attention to the verb tense or form. Does the answer to the question require a verb in the future? Or does it require a verb in the simple present?

Look at the example below. Use these steps to help you choose the correct verb tense or form.

1. Look for words or phrases that show the verb tense or form. For example, *tomorrow* and *later* indicate future; *now* or a scheduled time or date indicate simple present.
2. What is the tense or form of the verb in the question?
3. Is the auxiliary verb *be* or *will*?
4. Pay attention to irregular verbs.

Example
Choose the correct answer.

1. **Ken:** Will you come with us to the soccer match tomorrow?
   Tom: Yes! Of course, I ____ with you.
   - **A.** come — This is the simple present of *come*.
   - **B.** will come — This is the correct answer. The question uses *will*. It requires a future answer.
   - **C.** coming — The *ing* form cannot be used without a form of the verb *be*.
   - **D.** came — This is the simple past of *come*.

PRACTICE

Choose the correct answer. Mark the letter on the Answer Sheet.

1. What are you doing later?
   - **A.** I went to the market.
   - **B.** I'm going to go to the market.
   - **C.** I go to the market.

2. Will you work out today?
   - **A.** Yes, I will.
   - **B.** Yes, I did.
   - **C.** Yes, I am.

3. When are you going to New York?
   - **A.** My train has left at 6.
   - **B.** My train leaves at 6.
   - **C.** My train left at 6.

4. Will you ____ with me to the beach?
   - **A.** going to come
   - **B.** went
   - **C.** come

Answer Sheet
Mark the letter.

	A	B	C
1.	A	B	C
2.	A	B	C
3.	A	B	C
4.	A	B	C

Unit 11

UNIT SUMMARY

Nouns
beach
cause
charity
desert
island
lake
mountain
ocean
organization
river
sponsor
trek
valley
volunteer
walk

Adjectives
homeless
poor

Verbs and verb phrases
be in bad shape
be in good shape
be out of shape
donate (money)
expect + infinitive
go running
go trekking
hope + infinitive
raise money
stay in shape
train
work out

Expression
be in good/bad physical condition

Show support and offer help
Count me in!
How can I help?
I couldn't agree more.
I hear you!
I'll do anything I can.
What can I do?

12 ▶ How do you stay healthy?

In this unit you...
- identify parts of the human body
- give physical exercise instructions
- describe pain and health problems
- have a conversation with your doctor

Grammar
- modal verb review

START

The human body

1. When you meet someone new, what do you notice first about the person's appearance?

2. Label the picture with the words. Then listen and check.
   12_01

   | nose   ear   mouth   ~~eye~~   cheek   chin   neck |

3. Listen to the names of the parts of the body in the photos. Then read the descriptions and identify the correct body parts.
   12_02

   a. You have ten. We use them to pick things up. __fingers__
   b. You have two. They are between your shoulders and your wrists. _____
   c. You have two. You stand on them and put shoes on them. _____
   d. You have one. It makes noises when you are hungry. _____
   e. You have two. You use them to see. _____
   f. You have two. You can carry things with them. _____

Talk about it!

4. Work with a group. Take turns making statements using words for parts of the body.

   A: People have eyes of different color.
   B: I broke my ankle when I was 12 years old.
   C: Sometimes my sister goes to a palm reader.

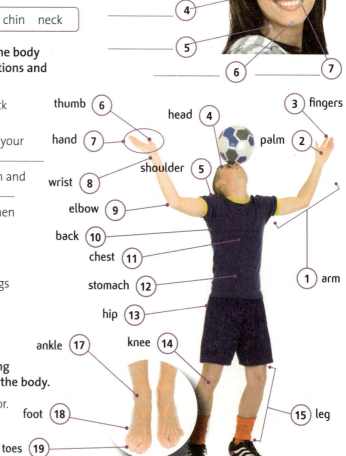

142

Unit 12

LISTENING

Let's exercise!

1 Before listening What are some of the ways that you exercise? Do you play sports? Do you go to the gym? What is the best way to stay in shape?

2 Listening Match the instructions to the correct pictures. Then listen and check.
12_03

HELP listening

Understand instructions
Understanding the instructions someone gives you is an important skill. If you can see the person, pay attention to his / her gestures (such as pointing). Listen for important words. The usual word order for instructions is: verb + object + prepositional phrase. Raise your leg up.

请注意听清指令

a. _6_ Turn your head to the left.
b. ___ Touch your right shoulder with your left hand.
c. ___ Raise your arms over your head.
d. ___ Stretch your arms and bend your wrists up and down.
e. ___ Bend over at the waist and touch your toes.
f. ___ Lower your head and look at your feet.

bend wrists
弯手腕
bend over at the waist
弯腰

3 Listening Now listen to some people talking. What is the relationship between the people? Check (✓) the correct box.
12_04

☐ doctor / patients ☐ instructor / students ☐ boss / employees

4 Listening Listen again. As you listen, act out the instructions.
12_04

5 After listening Match the two sentence parts.

1. The class _e_
2. The exercises help people ___
3. The instructor explains ___
4. The first exercise stretches ___
5. The second exercise stretches ___

a. who work with computers.
b. the arms and wrists.
c. the arms, shoulders, and upper back.
d. two exercises.
e. is doing stretching exercises.

stretching exercises
伸展运动

Talk about it!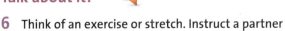

6 Think of an exercise or stretch. Instruct a partner on how to do it.

A: OK, sit on the floor with your hands on top of your knees.
B: Like this?
A: Yes, exactly. Then...

CONVERSATION STRATEGY

Check instructions
Use Like this? to check that you are doing something correctly.

请注意如何询问自己的动作是否正确

Unit 12

VOCABULARY

Where does it hurt?

1. Does any part of your body hurt right now? What part(s)?

2. Match the sentences to the pictures. Then listen and check.
   12_05

   a. __7__ My right elbow hurts.
   b. ____ I have a pain in my wrist.
   c. ____ I have a sore neck.
   d. ____ I hurt my left knee.
   e. ____ My right ankle is sore.
   f. ____ My back aches.
   g. ____ I have a stomachache.
   h. ____ I have a bad headache.

have a sore neck
脖子痛

stomachache
肚子痛; 胃痛

ENGLISH express

We use the verb *hurt* in two ways.

My left knee hurts.
I hurt my left knee.

请注意 hurt 的两种用法

3. Complete the sentences with *hurt*, *sore*, *ache*, or *pain*. Sometimes more than one answer is possible.

   1. I have a __pain__ in my ankle.
   2. He _____ his back.
   3. Her left arm is really _____ .
   4. My stomach really _____ .
   5. He has a _____ in his chest.
   6. She has a _____ thumb.
   7. I have a terrible head_____ .
   8. My neck and shoulders _____ .

Talk about it!

4. With a partner, make up a mini-conversation for each picture in exercise 2.

   A: What's the matter?
   B: I have a sore neck.
   A: What happened?
   B: I think I slept badly last night.
   A: Oh, no! Why don't you get a massage?

CONVERSATION STRATEGY

Express sympathy

You can use *Oh, no!* to express sympathy.
A: I'm really tired.
B: Oh, no! Did you get any sleep last night?

请注意如何表达同情之意

WORKBOOK PAGE 90

Unit 12

GRAMMAR
Modal verb review

ALSO GO TO
Grammar Takeaway
PAGE 205

physically fit
体格健康

sit-up
仰卧起坐
push-up
俯卧撑

1 How physically fit are you?
What can you do? What can't you do?

*I'm pretty fit. I can do lots of sit-ups,
but I can't do a lot of push-ups.*

2 Underline the modal verbs in sentences 1–4. Then match each sentence to an explanation.

1. Can you touch your toes? __c__
2. She might be tired or she could be sick. ___
3. Exercise can make you feel good. ___
4. You shouldn't work so much. ___

a. This is possible.
b. This is my advice.
c. Are you able to do this?
d. This is sometimes true.

This is always true.	It is healthy to exercise every day.
This is sometimes true.	Working at a computer can cause health problems.
This is possible.	We could go / might go to the gym this weekend. We might not go to the gym this weekend.

3 Circle the correct words to complete the sentences.

1. Eating fruits and vegetables is / can be good for you.
2. Working very hard makes / can make you sick.
3. Traveling by plane is / can be frightening.
4. Oranges contain / can contain a lot of vitamin C.

4 Rewrite the sentences using *might, could, can*, or the simple present so that the second sentence has the same meaning as the first.

1. It's possible that she isn't here. **She might not be here.**
2. It's sometimes true that eating badly causes heart disease. _____
3. It's possible that I will join a new gym this year. _____
4. It's sometimes true that yoga cures back problems. _____
5. It's true that smoking causes health problems. _____
6. It's possible that exercise will make you live longer. _____

Talk about it!

5 Work with a partner. Give advice on how to stay healthy. Explain why.

A: You should drink orange juice every day.
B: Why do you say that?
A: Well, oranges have a lot of vitamin C, and that can help prevent colds.

WORKBOOK PAGE 91-92

Unit 12

READING

HELP reading

Scan for specific information
It isn't always necessary to read every word of a text to find the information you are looking for. Look over a text for specific information without worrying about understanding every word or phrase.

请注意查读的技巧

health advice column
健康指导专栏

A health advice column

1 Before reading Who do you ask for health advice? Your friends? Your family? Your doctor? What are some other ways that people get health advice?

2 Reading Read four questions from the advice column of a health magazine. Then read some answers. Which two questions are answered?
12_06

YOUR HEALTH QUESTIONS ANSWERED!

HEALTH QUESTIONS

A When I use my computer, I often get a terrible headache. Can you give me some advice?

B My daughter spends lots of time working on the computer and she also spends time playing computer games. I'm worried that this might not be very good for her. What should I do?

RSI
重复性劳损

C For my job, I do a lot of work on the computer and I also spend time at home surfing the Internet. Recently, I've started to get pain in my wrist when I use the computer. A friend thinks I could have RSI. What is it? Do I have RSI?

D Could you suggest some exercises for people like me who spend a lot of time on the computer?

HEALTH ADVICE

Answer 1

Yes, there is lots you can do. Here is one for the neck and another for the shoulders and back. For the first one, stand or sit with your arms by your sides and look straight ahead. Slowly bend your head to the left towards your shoulder. Go as far as you can and hold the position for five seconds. Do this exercise five times on both sides. For the arms and shoulders, bend your left arm and hold your left elbow with your right arm. Gently push your left arm over your right shoulder. Repeat five times with each arm. Do these exercises a few times every day.

hold the position
保持这种姿势

Answer 2

Not necessarily. RSI—repetitive strain injury—can occur by repeating the same physical movements over and over again. It can be a problem for musicians, people who play sports, and those who use computers a lot, for example. You could be experiencing the first symptoms. Here are a few tips.

- You should always keep your wrists straight and flat—never bend them in any direction. Move the hands from the arms, not from the wrists. You can adjust your chair and keyboard to do this. Also remember to take lots of breaks to give your body a chance to rest.

straight and flat
平直的
alternate
交替
symptom
症状

- Using the mouse can also cause problems. Alternate hands sometimes with the mouse and learn how to use more of the keyboard controls instead of the mouse. If the symptoms persist, you should see a doctor.

3 **Reading**   Read the advice column again. Circle *True* or *False* for each statement below.

1. RSI means Repetitive Strain Injury.   (True)   False
2. RSI is caused by doing too much heavy, physical work.   True   False
3. RSI isn't only a problem for people who work with computers.   True   False
4. It's bad to bend your wrists when you type.   True   False
5. It's a good idea to change hands when using the mouse.   True   False
6. The writer suggests going to see a doctor immediately.   True   False

4 After reading   Instruct a partner on how to do the two exercises described in Answer 1 of the advice column. Are you a good instructor? Is your partner a good student?

Talk about it!

5   Conduct this class survey about computer use. Talk to several classmates and take notes. Summarize your findings and report back to the class.

Most of the people I talked to use the computer more than 3 hours a day.

Survey: Using computers

1. Do you use the computer every day?
   If so, how many hours?
2. When you use the computer, do you have problems with any part of your body?
   If so, which part(s)?
3. Do you do any exercise for your problems? If so, what do you do?
4. Do you use any special equipment when you work on the computer to help prevent injuries? If so, what equipment?

PROJECT

Work with a group to write your own health advice column for a magazine. Think of three questions and write answers. Add illustrations to go with the information.

Unit 12

SONG

What can this be?

1 Before listening When was the last time you were sick? What did you have? What were your symptoms?

2 Before listening Match the sentences to the pictures.

a. __3__ Her mouth is dry.   d. _____ Her legs are weak.
b. _____ Her hands are shaking.   e. _____ Her body's aching.
c. _____ Her stomach is churning. f. _____ Her head is burning.

churn
翻滚；搅动

3 Listening What do you think the diagnosis is for the woman's symptoms in exercise 2?
12_07 Listen to the song to check.

have the flu
得了流感

1. She has the flu. _____   2. She is in love. _____   3. She is angry. _____

4 Before listening Like poetry, songs often use words that rhyme.
Put the rhyming words into three groups.

| ~~be~~ | eyes | me | guy | weak | do | lies | speak | dry | flu |

/iː/ see	/aɪ/ my	/uː/ to
be		

5 Listening Complete the song with the words from exercise 4. You can use the
12_07 words more than once. Then listen and check.

6 After listening Look at the underlined phrases in the song. Match them to
these meanings.

1. I ask myself   __I gotta wonder__
2. I feel different   _____
3. if your heart begins to beat quickly   _____
4. What is my problem?   _____
5. like I can't stand up   _____

148

What can this be?

Ooh, eeh!
What can this (1) _be_ ?
Some strange thing's come over (2) _____ .
All I gotta do is see your (3) _____
'Cause they don't look away
And they don't tell (4) _____ .

Chorus

I gotta wonder why my heart's like thunder,
What you're doing to me makes me
    weak in the knees.
I'm still surprised when I look in your (5) _____
'Cause they don't look away
And they don't tell (6) _____ .
Don't look away
And they don't tell (7) _____ .

Ooh, eeh!
What's wrong with (8) _____ ?
When all of you is all I (9) _____ .
And when I look into your (10) _____ ,
I can't look away
And I can't tell (11) _____ .

Chorus

My hands are shaking,
My stomach is churning,
My body's aching,
And my head is burning.
I can hardly (12) _____ .
My mouth is (13) _____ .
My legs are (14) _____
When I look in your eye.

I went to the doctor
See what he could (15) _____ .
He said: It might be pneumonia,
Could be the (16) _____ .
But if your heart starts racing when you look in his eye,
It might just (17) _____ .
You're in love with that (18) _____ .

Chorus

Talk about it!

7 With a partner, discuss these questions.

1. Why do you think love is such a popular topic for songs?
2. What's your favorite love song? What is it about?
3. Do you think it's common to feel like the person in this song? Why or why not?
4. What do you think is causing the girl's symptoms? Is it physical or mental or both? Explain.

PRONUNCIATION

Sentence stress

 When we speak, some words are pronounced more strongly than others. Listen to the sentences. Underline the stressed words. Then listen again and repeat.

1. Yesterday I had a sore throat.
2. What's wrong with me?
3. Can you touch your toes?
4. She might be tired.
5. It's possible she went to the gym.

pneumonia
肺炎

Unit 12

CONVERSATION

Seeing the doctor

antibiotics 抗生素
painkiller 止痛药
asthma 哮喘
arthritis 关节炎
runny nose 流鼻涕
fluid 流质; 液体

1 Put the health-related words in the three categories. Then listen and check.

antibiotics	sore throat	a cold	knee pain	painkiller	cough
asthma	the flu	can't sleep	arthritis	fever	drink fluids
medicine	stress	rest	runny nose	difficulty breathing	

symptom	diagnosis	treatment
sore throat,	a cold,	antibiotics,

2 Complete the conversation with expressions from the box. Then listen and check.

Doctor: Hello. (**1**) _How can I help you_ ?
Patient: (**2**) _____ . I have a sore throat, and I feel really tired.
Doctor: (**3**) _____ ?
Patient: Well, I took two painkillers for my throat.
Doctor: OK. (**4**) _____ ?
Patient: Yes, I have a runny nose and a cough.
Doctor: And (**5**) _____ ?
Patient: No, my temperature is normal.
(**6**) _____ the flu?
Doctor: No. I think you just have a cold.
Patient: What should I do? Should I take antibiotics?
Doctor: No, not for a cold. (**7**) _____ . And drink lots of fluids.
Patient: Anything else?
Doctor: (**8**) _____ in a few days or if you have a fever, come back and see me.

> I don't feel well.
> Do you think I could have...?
> Are you running a fever?
> If you don't feel better...
> Are you taking any medication?
> Do you have any other symptoms?
> Try to get some rest.
> How can I help you?

CONVERSATION STRATEGY

Get all the information
When talking to your doctor, be sure you know everything that you need to know and do. Ask the question: Anything else?

请注意看病时问清所有问题

Talk about it!

3 Work with a partner. One of you is the patient, the other is the doctor. Role-play a conversation like the one in exercise 2.

Tell me more!

Visit the Takeaway English Online Learning Center at http://olcs.mcgraw-hill-education.com/takeaway/

 Check out the *Takeaway TV* video.

 Improve your English with the online activities.

Unit 12

WRITING

Writing an article giving advice

1 Before writing   What are some physical problems that you have experienced while traveling? Have you gotten sick from food or water? Have you experienced jet lag? What did you do to solve the problem?

jet lag
时差反应

2 Writing model   Read this letter from Gillian Hudson to the advice section of *Healthy Life* magazine. Underline the physical problems she mentions.

> Dear Healthy Life,
>
> I am an international business manager. As part of my job, I fly all over the world and I spend a lot of time in airports and sitting on planes. During long flights, I often get aches and pains in my back, shoulders, and legs.
>
> Spending lots of time on planes and in airports also makes me feel tired and lethargic. This is a real problem for me because I often arrive in foreign countries and have to go directly to important meetings. As you can imagine, I often have a terrible headache and it's difficult to do business!
>
> Could you give me some advice on how to survive the problems of long-distance travel—both in the airport and on the plane? Could you also suggest any exercises that I can do to help my tired, sore body?
>
> Thank you very much,
> Gillian Hudson

lethargic
无精打采的; 昏睡的

HELP writing

Use graphic organizers
Remember to use graphic organizers when preparing to write. Graphic organizers can help you come up with ideas, organize your thoughts, and improve the structure of your writing.

请注意借助组织图写作

3 Planning your writing   Use the Problem-Solution Chart to list the symptoms and problems Gillian experiences while traveling. Identify possible solutions.

problem	solution
aches and pains in the back, shoulders, legs	get up and walk around the plane

4 Writing   Write a reply to Gillian and give her advice on how to survive the problems of long-distance travel. Use modals to suggest different possibilities.

Useful expressions and ideas

Sitting still for long periods can be uncomfortable.
Also remember that…
You should do these exercises regularly.
Bend your right arm and touch your shoulder.
One problem might be that…
Finally, don't forget that…

Unit 12

TEST

Test-taking strategy

Compare and contrast Some test questions ask you to compare and contrast two people, places, or things.

Look at the example below. Use these steps to help you answer compare and contrast questions.

1. Compare means to notice how two things are alike.
2. Look for comparison words such as *both*, *too*, *same*, *like*, *also*, *each*.
3. Contrast means to notice how two things are different.
4. Look for contrast words such as *different*, *however*, *but*, *on the other hand*.

Example
Read the paragraph and answer the questions.

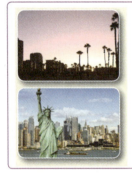

I have visited both Los Angeles and New York in the United States. Each city is located next to an ocean, but they are very different. Los Angeles is spread out. It feels open. New York is on an island. It feels crowded. Los Angeles is very large, and New York is too, but the people are not the same. I think the people in Los Angeles are easygoing. In New York, they are very stressed.

spread out
分散

1. Name two ways mentioned in the paragraph that New York and Los Angeles are alike.
   _____   _____

   Both cities are in the United States. Both cities are located next to an ocean. The words *both* and *each* indicate things that are alike.

PRACTICE

Read the paragraph above again and answer the questions.

1. Name two ways that New York and Los Angeles are different.
   _____   _____

2. How does the paragraph contrast the people in New York and Los Angeles?
   _____   _____

3. Based on the paragraph, do you think Los Angeles and New York are more similar or more different?
   _____

Unit 12

UNIT SUMMARY

Nouns
ankle
antibiotics
arm
arthritis
asthma
back
cheek
chest
chin
cold
cough
ear
elbow
eye
fever
finger
flu
fluid
foot
hand
head
headache
heel
hip
knee
leg
medicine
mouth
neck
nose pain
painkiller
palm
rest
shoulder
sore throat
stomach
stomachache
stress
thumb
toe
wrist

Adjectives
dry
runny
sore
weak

Verbs and verb phrases
ache
bend over
breathe
burn
churn
cough
drink
hurt
lower
raise
rest
shake
stretch
touch
turn

Expressions
I gotta wonder…
If your heart starts racing…
Like this?
Oh, no!
Some strange thing's come over me.
weak in the knees
What's wrong with me?

See the doctor
Anything else?
Are you running a fever?
Are you taking any medication?
Do you have any other symptoms?
Do you think I could have…
How can I help you?
I don't feel well.
If you don't feel better…
Try to get some rest.

13 ▸ Space travel

In this unit you...
- talk about the Moon
- discuss space travel
- use expressions for checking into a hotel

Grammar
- *would* for hypothetical situations

START

Fly me to the Moon

1 What do you know about the Moon? Circle your answers. Then listen and check.
13_01

1. When was the first Moon landing?
   a. July 20th, 1959   b. July 20th, 1969   c. July 20th, 1979
2. Who was the first man on the Moon?
   a. Neil Armstrong   b. Buzz Aldrin   c. Michael Collins
3. Gravity on the Moon is about ____ of gravity on Earth.
   a. 17%   b. 37%   c. 57%
4. How far away is the Moon?
   a. approximately 2,389 miles (3,844 kilometers)
   b. approximately 23,886 miles (38,440 kilometers)
   c. approximately 238,857 miles (384,403 kilometers)
5. What's the weather like on the Moon?
   a. similar to Earth's weather   b. cold and stormy   c. it's very cold but there's no weather

gravity 重力

2 Have these space events *already happened* or *not happened yet*?

1. People have walked on the Moon. **This has already happened.**
2. Scientists have a permanent station on the Moon.
3. Scientists have discovered water on the Moon.
4. Tourists have traveled into space.
5. Tourists have traveled to the Moon.

permanent station 永久空间站

Talk about it!

3 Work with a partner. Discuss this question:
Should scientists build a permanent station on the Moon?

A: I think scientists should build a permanent station on the Moon. We can learn a lot about space by studying the Moon.

B: I disagree. We should spend the money on something else.

Unit 13

LISTENING

A vacation on the Moon

1 Before listening   What is the most unusual place you have ever been to on vacation? What was it like?

2 Listening   Listen to Marta, Earl, and Vanessa. Who says that they would like to go on vacation to the Moon?

13_02

☐ Marta   ☐ Earl   ☐ Vanessa

3 Listening   Listen again and complete the sentences. Check your answers with a partner.

13_02

1. Marta: I _____ _____ the Moon would be a very nice place.
2. Marta: I _____ it would be very cold there.
3. Earl: I _____ once you're there on the Moon it could be interesting.
4. Vanessa: I _____ I'd find the trip there quite frightening.
5. Vanessa: And I _____ that a hotel on the Moon would be... like... a five-star hotel.

HELP listening

Understand hesitations
In natural speech, hesitations are common. Sounds like *um* and *uh* usually mean the speaker is trying to think about what to say.

A: Would you like to, *uh*, go out with me?
B: *Um*, I'm not sure. Can I think about it?

请注意如何表达迟疑

ENGLISH express

Use **I guess** and **I imagine** to say you think something is likely or probable.

I guess it could be interesting.
I imagine it would be cold.

请注意如何表达猜测

five-star hotel
五星级饭店

4 After listening   Who said what? Check (✔) the person's name.

	Marta	Earl	Vanessa
1. It would be very cold.	✔		
2. You can do things that you can't do on Earth.			
3. There would be great views of Earth.			
4. I prefer nature to the Moon.			
5. I'd like to get away from the effects of gravity.			
6. You can't go home when you want to.			

Talk about it!

5 Work with a partner. Ask and answer these questions. Use *guess* and *imagine*.

1. Would you like to travel in space? Why or why not?
2. Would you like to get away from the effects of gravity? What could you do?
3. What exciting or adventurous thing would you like to do in your life? Why?

adventurous
冒险的

155

Unit 13

VOCABULARY
Build your vocabulary!

1 In order to learn English, it's important to discover the meanings of new words on your own. For example, if you know the verb *excite*, then you can guess the meaning of the noun *excitement*.

Complete the table of verbs and nouns. Then listen.

What endings are added to the verbs to make nouns? _____

	verb	noun
1.	amaze	amazement
2.	improve	
3.		arrangement
4.	announce	
5.		imagination
6.		existence
7.		preference
8.		discovery

2 Complete each sentence with the correct form of the word in parentheses.

in theory
理论上

1. The ____existence____ of life on other planets is possible, in theory. (exist)
2. Do you think life _____ on other planets? (exist)
3. Scientists have _____ water on the Moon. (discover)
4. The _____ of water makes travel to the Moon more possible. (discover)
5. Which vacation do you like the most? Do you have a _____? (prefer)
6. Marta _____ a beach vacation. (prefer)
7. Have there been any _____ in space rockets? (improve)
8. It takes a lot of _____ to picture what a Moon vacation would be like. (imagine)

Talk about it!

3 With a partner, ask and answer these questions.

1. Do you believe in the existence of life on other planets? Why or why not?
   - **A:** Do you believe in the existence of life on other planets?
   - **B:** Well, I guess there could be some form of life somewhere. What about you?
   - **A:** No, I don't think so. Not in our solar system. I imagine we would see signs, if there were.

solar system
太阳系

2. What are some recent improvements in air travel?
3. Do you think the discovery of water on the Moon is important? Why?
4. What kind of vacations do you prefer—relaxing or adventurous? Explain why.

Unit 13

GRAMMAR

Would for hypothetical situations

ALSO GO TO Grammar Takeaway PAGE 206

hypothetical situation
假设情况

1 Do these sentences describe real or hypothetical (guessed or assumed) situations?

1. It will be very cold this weekend. — ✓ real — ☐ hypothetical
2. It would be very cold on the Moon. — ☐ real — ☐ hypothetical
3. She would go to Rome if she had the money. — ☐ real — ☐ hypothetical
4. You'd have to wear warm clothes in Antarctica. — ☐ real — ☐ hypothetical
5. You'll have to study science to be an astronaut. — ☐ real — ☐ hypothetical

Antarctica
南极洲

2 Look at the chart. Then circle the correct word to complete each sentence below.

real	hypothetical
I **will** (I'll) visit Mexico City next month. I **won't** be home until July.	I **would** (I'd) love to visit Alaska some day. I **wouldn't** travel to the Moon. I'd be too afraid. **Would** you like to go into space?

go into space
去太空

1. Will / **(Would)** you travel in space?
2. Will / Would you like to live in a different country?
3. If you have time this weekend, will / would you go to the science museum?
4. Do you think the weather will / would be good tomorrow?
5. Will / Would you be able to finish all the exercises in the workbook?
6. What will / would you do if you had more free time?

3 Answer the questions with real and hypothetical information. Use the example answers for ideas.

1. What is one thing you will do? — *I will go to the beach this summer.*
2. What is one thing you won't do? — *I won't be late to school tomorrow.*
3. What is one thing you would do? — *I would go to Spain if I had more money.*
4. What is one thing you wouldn't do? — *I would not buy that smartphone.*

smartphone
智能手机

Talk about it!

4 Work with a partner. Ask and answer the questions from exercise 2.

A: Would you travel in space?
B: I'm not sure. I think I wouldn't. How about you?
A: I definitely would. The idea is so exciting.
B: You're more adventurous than I am.

Unit 13

READING

> **HELP reading**
>
> **Skim for the main idea**
> Skimming is a good strategy when you only need very general information about a text. It is done much faster than normal reading. For example, you might only read the first sentence of every paragraph.
>
> 请注意略读的技巧

What about the Moon?

1 Before reading Do you think that people will live on the Moon in your lifetime? Why or why not?

in your lifetime 在你有生之年

2 Before reading Skim the news article very quickly and circle the best title.

A. Living on the Moon   B. Hotels on the Moon   C. First city on the Moon

3 Reading Now read the article slowly. Then match the companies to the hotels they plan to build.

- Nishimatsu
- Shimuzu
- Hilton

 A  B  C

Escargot City 蜗牛城
Hilton 希尔顿
snail 蜗牛

Would you like a honeymoon on the Moon? This might be possible one day:
5 Hilton International, the international hotel company, has announced plans to build the first hotel
10 on the Moon. The announcement follows the discovery of water, which has greatly increased the possibility of colonizing the Moon.

The Lunar Hilton would have five thousand
15 rooms and many facilities, including restaurants, a church, and even a beach. Food would come from farms on the Moon's surface, and the ice discovered at the Moon's poles could be used for water. The hotel would be powered by
20 solar panels.

Two Japanese companies have also expressed interest in this development in the space race. Shimuzu is planning an orbiting 64-room space hotel by 2020 and a hotel on the Moon's
25 surface. Nishimatsu Construction Company also has plans for a Moon resort, called Escargot City—a reference to the shape of the ten towers they plan to build ("escargot" means *snail* in French).

30 So what does the Moon offer tourists who would like to experience a lunar vacation? After completing the journey, guests could enjoy a variety of activities from golf and tennis to excursions in special Moon buses. They would
35 first have to get used to wearing special boots because there is very little gravity on the Moon.

The Hilton has already been in contact with NASA about transportation of passengers and building materials, but scientists have
40 reacted with surprise and disbelief. They have mentioned both the incredible expense and the dangers of space travel. However, tourists looking for a room with a really special view would love it. Also, honeymoon couples,
45 wanting to give a new meaning to the word, might find the Moon a perfect destination.

excursion 短程旅行
colonize 开拓领地
lunar 月球的

pole 极地
incredible expense 巨额的花销
solar panel 太阳能电池板
space race 太空竞赛
orbiting 轨道式的; 盘旋式的

Unit 13

4 **Reading** Read the article again. Circle *True* or *False* for each statement below.

13_04

1. Scientists discovered water on the Moon, and then the Hilton announced its plans. (True) False
2. The Lunar Hilton plans to send food from Earth for the hotel. True False
3. Energy for the Lunar Hilton would come from the sun. True False
4. Both of Shimuzu's hotels will be on the Moon. True False
5. There will be lots of things for hotel guests to do. True False
6. Scientists' reactions to the plans aren't very positive. True False

5 **After reading** Match the underlined words in the article to the definitions.

1. the place you go to when you are traveling — destination
2. when you go one day to see something special — _____
3. a person who stays in a hotel — _____
4. the process of going from one place to another — _____
5. a person in a bus, train, plane, etc. — _____
6. a place for people on vacation — _____
7. a person traveling on vacation — _____
8. what you can see from your window — _____

Talk about it!

6 With a partner, make a list of other vocabulary associated with hotels. Then discuss the questions below.

1. What are the best hotels in your city?
2. What hotel amenities do you think are important for a hotel to have?
3. What are the most popular vacation destinations in your country?
4. What famous hotels in other countries would you like to stay in? Why?

minibar
room service
key

amenity
便利设施

PROJECT

Design a fantasy hotel. Where would it be? What kind of facilities would it have? Use your imagination! Make a poster with a drawing of the hotel, a map of the facilities, and a list of amenities. Present your hotel to your classmates. Decide which fantasy hotel most students would like to visit.

fantasy
梦幻; 奇幻

Unit 13

CULTURE

Space food

1 Before reading Look at the pictures. Circle the names of the foods that you think astronauts eat in space.

1. herbal tea
2. pills
3. crackers
4. food in tubes
5. spicy food
6. nuts
7. mangoes

2 Reading 13_05 Read the article and match these titles with the paragraphs. Then check your answers to exercise 1.

Space food in the past ~~New menus in space~~
A specialist's opinion   What the astronauts say

3 Reading 13_05 Read the article again. Complete the table with space foods from different countries.

Korea	cinnamon tea,
China	
Malaysia	
Russia	

4 After reading Match the underlined words in the text with the correct definitions.

1. a type of metal — aluminum
2. with no bacteria — _____
3. modern — _____
4. cut into small pieces — _____
5. different people like different things — _____
6. put in sauce for some time — _____
7. not spicy — _____

herbal tea 花草茶
cracker 饼干
cutlery 餐具
spicy food 辣的食物
spacecraft 宇宙飞船
cater to 满足……口味
cinnamon 肉桂
pickled dish 腌菜
bacteria-free 无菌的
suck out of 从……中吸出
aluminum tube 铝管
cosmonaut （俄）航天员 （相当于astronaut)
be jealous of 妒忌
new-fangled 新奇的

SPACE spiced up

Without refrigeration, hot water, or cutlery, eating in space in the past was not exactly fun. But space food has become a lot more interesting. Nowadays, space food doesn't have to be dry or eaten from a tube. Water, which is generated from spacecrafts, is added just before eating. Food containers are attached by Velcro to tables with built-in food heaters, and astronauts eat with spoons. As well as being tastier, space menus now cater to different nationalities, cultures, and religions. Space food has come a long way!

1. New menus in space

South Korea's first astronaut, Yi So-Yeon, has brought spicy Asian food to the International Space Station (ISS). Cinnamon tea, noodles, and South Korea's beloved pickled dish, *kimchi*, all developed by a Korean institute to be bacteria-free so that refrigeration isn't necessary, are now on the menu for the team of international astronauts at the ISS.

2. _____

Astronauts in previous decades complained about being hungry. To eat, they had to suck food out of small aluminum tubes and plastic bags. Former Russian cosmonaut Pavel Vinogradov spent a total of 380 days in space, mostly in the 1990s. He admits to being a little jealous of the new-fangled space food. "The food now is completely different. We didn't complain then, but we always wanted a little bit more."

Unit 13

FOOD

3. _____

With a growing number of countries producing astronauts, space food is becoming more cosmopolitan. When
40 the first Chinese astronaut, Yang Liwei, flew into space in 2003, he brought with him Chinese herbal tea, shredded pork with garlic, and marinated Kung Pao chicken to make him feel at home.
45 Malaysia's first astronaut, Sheikh Muszaphar Shukor, celebrated the end of the Muslim holy month of Ramadan in 2007 by offering the ISS crew typical food from his country, including
50 mangoes and Malaysian-style satay. Muszaphar said ahead of the launch that the food was milder than usual. It was not very spicy so that the Russians would be able to eat it. "We really liked the
55 Malaysian food. My favorite was dried mango," U.S. astronaut Peggy Whitson said after a recent space expedition. "Today, we can choose the food that we want," the Russian mission commander
60 Sergei Volkov told reporters at a press conference. "The specialists try and make it as close to real food as possible."

4. _____

Tatyana Gavruchenko is a space food specialist at the Birulevsky Research
65 Institute in Russia. The institute produces around 200 food items, including traditional Russian and Central Asian dishes. She says that the Americans like the soups and crackers produced by the
70 Russians, but that everyone's favorite is white cheese with nuts. Tatyana says that Russian space food is delicious. "I think the Russian food is better, but to each his own—it also depends on
75 habits and traditions," she said.

5 After reading Answer the questions with the names from the article. Who...

1. brought spicy Asian food to the ISS?
   <u>Yi So-Yeon from South Korea</u>

2. wasn't happy with space food in the 1990s?
   _____

3. took pork and chicken into space?
   _____

4. altered a traditional dish for his Russian colleagues?
   _____

5. really liked the Malaysian food?
   _____

6. prefers Russian food?
   _____

Talk about it!

6 With a partner, discuss these questions.

1. What foods have you tried from the countries in exercise 3? What did you think about them?
2. Which space foods mentioned in the text would you like to try? Why?
3. What foods from your country would you recommend for astronauts to eat in space? Why?

PRONUNCIATION

Contracted *would*

1 In spoken English, *would* is often contracted.
13_06

| I'd go. | She'd come. | It'd be cold. |

Listen. Check (✔) the sentences that contain the contracted form of *would*.

1. ✔   3. ☐   5. ☐   7. ☐
2. ☐   4. ☐   6. ☐   8. ☐

2 Listen and write the four sentences with the
13_07 contracted form of *would*.

_____
_____
_____
_____

cosmopolitan
世界性的

shredded pork
肉丝
marinated
卤制的

Malaysian-style satay
马来西亚风味沙嗲

space expedition
太空探险
mission commander
任务指挥官

white cheese with nuts
带坚果的白奶酪

161

Unit 13

CONVERSATION

Checking into a hotel

1 Listen to a conversation at a hotel reception desk. What is the guest's reservation?
☐ a single room for one night   ☐ a single room for three nights

2 Complete the conversation with expressions from the box. Then listen again to check your answers.

> Your name, please?
> A single room for three nights?
> And could you fill out this form, please?
> I'll need a picture ID and a credit card, please.
> Here's your key and a map of the hotel.
> ~~How can I help you?~~
> I'm checking in.
> I made the reservation online.

CONVERSATION STRATEGY
Check understanding
To check that you understood what someone said to you, repeat or summarize what they said. For example, a hotel clerk might repeat your name to confirm that he / she heard it correctly.

请注意如何确认信息

Hotel clerk: Welcome to the Riverside Hotel! (1) _How can I help you?_
Guest: Good afternoon. (2) _____ .
Hotel clerk: (3) _____ ?
Guest: Taylor. Tom Taylor. (4) _____ .
Hotel clerk: Oh, yes, here it is, Mr. Taylor. (5) _____ ?
Guest: Yes, that's correct.
Hotel clerk: (6) _____ .
Guest: Certainly. Here you go.
Hotel clerk: Thank you. (7) _____ ?
Guest: Sure. Do you have a pen?
Hotel clerk: Certainly. And (8) _____ . It's room 301, on the third floor.
Guest: Thanks very much.

Talk about it!

3 Work with a partner. Take turns playing a hotel clerk and a guest. Use the conversation in exercise 2 as a model. Also give information about the hotel facilities.

Tell me more!

Visit the Takeaway English Online Learning Center at http://olcs.mcgraw-hill-education.com/takeaway/

 Check out the *Takeaway TV* video.

 Improve your English with the online activities.

Unit 13

WRITING

Writing an email to request hotel information

1 Before writing Have you ever written an email requesting information? Who did you write to? Did you use an informal or formal writing style?

HELP writing

Write a professional email
A professional or business email is not the same as an email you send to a friend. Write a meaningful subject line. Keep the content focused and specific. Use a formal style. End the email in a professional and polite manner.

请注意如何撰写专业的电子邮件

2 Writing model Complete the email with the words from the box.

| would | leave | activities | will | ~~reservation~~ | resort | amenities |

To: info@hoteloceanside.com
Subject: new reservation request

Dear Hotel Oceanside:

I would like to make a (1) __reservation__ at your hotel for four people for six nights. We are traveling from Tokyo, Japan, and we (2) _____ arrive on July 8th in the afternoon. We will (3) _____ the morning of July 14th. We (4) _____ like two rooms with two beds in each room.

We are interested in going scuba diving and fishing. Would it be possible to make reservations for these (5) _____ from your (6) _____? We'd also like to know more about the (7) _____ and recreation activities you offer.
I look forward to hearing from you.

Sincerely,
Kenji Kudo

scuba diving
深水潜水
make reservations
预订

3 Planning your writing Use the Lakeside Resort reservation form below to help you plan an email. Note any special requests you have.

LAKESIDE RESORT
Name (last, first):
City / Country of origin:
Check in:
Check out:
Room type:
Special requests:

4 Writing Write an email to the Lakeside Resort in Canada. Include all necessary information. Use the reservation form from exercise 3 and the email from exercise 2 to help you.

Unit 13

TEST

Test-taking strategy

Vocabulary questions: Select meaning by word Tests may ask you vocabulary questions in two different ways—"select meaning by word" and "select word by meaning". Here we will practice "select meaning by word". For these items, you see a word and select the meaning.

Look at the example below. Use these steps to help you answer "select meaning by word" vocabulary questions.

1. Try to determine what part of speech the target word is.
2. If you can't decide what part of speech the word is, determine what part of speech it is *not*.
3. Based on your analysis, eliminate answers.
4. From the remaining answers, choose the best answer.

> *Example*
> Choose the correct answer.
> 1. **existence** Most words that end in *ence* are nouns (such as *difference*).
>   - ~~A.~~ *adj*. relating to the sky, heavenly   *Existence* is not an adjective.
>   - ~~B.~~ *v*. to forgive or excuse   *Existence* is not a verb.
>   - C. *n*. the fact or state of being   This is the correct answer. *Existence* is a noun.
>   - ~~D.~~ *adj*. hating or distrusting people   *Existence* is not an adjective.

PRACTICE

Choose the correct answer. Mark the letter on the Answer Sheet.

1. **preference**
   - A. *n*. liking or favoring one thing over another
   - B. *v*. to conceal or hide the truth   *(conceal the truth 隐瞒真相)*
   - C. *adj*. sickly or unwell
   - D. *n*. a false or untrue statement

2. **amazing**
   - A. *v*. to cut with a sharp instrument
   - B. *v*. to cause wonder or surprise
   - C. *n*. a criminal
   - D. *adj*. causing wonder or surprise

3. **discover**
   - A. *adj*. sad or sentimental to the point of tears
   - B. *n*. a group of people with similar interests
   - C. *v*. to see, learn of, or find out for the first time
   - D. *n*. a general agreement or understanding

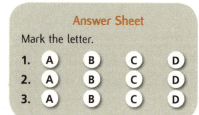

Answer Sheet
Mark the letter.
1. A B C D
2. A B C D
3. A B C D

Unit 13

UNIT SUMMARY

Nouns
aluminum
amazement
announcement
arrangement
cracker
destination
discovery
excitement
excursion
existence
gravity
guest
imagination
improvement
journey
landing
mango
nut
passenger
pill
preference
resort
scientist
solar system
station
tourist
tube
view

Adjectives
adventurous
bacteria-free
herbal
marinated
mild
new-fangled
permanent
shredded
spicy

Verbs and verb phrases
amaze
announce
arrange
discover
excite
exist
imagine
improve
prefer

Expression
I guess…
I imagine…
to each his own
uh
um

Check into a hotel
A single room for three nights?
And could you fill out this form, please?
Here's your key and a map of the hotel.
How can I help you?
I made the reservation online.
I'll need a picture ID and a credit card, please.
I'm checking in.
Your name, please?

14 What have you been doing?

In this unit you...
- talk about the average person
- discuss losing, wasting, spending, and passing time
- describe approximate and precise times
- apologize and accept apologies

Grammar
- present perfect continuous

START

The average American

1 What do you know about the people in your country? Make some statements that you think are true for the average person.

the average person 一般人

The average person in my country works 40 hours a week and sleeps eight hours a night.

2 Read the facts about the average American. With a partner, guess the missing numbers. Then listen and check.
14_01

on average 平均

1. People in the U.S., on average, live for _____ years.
   A) 68   B) 78   C) 87
2. They spend _____ years of their life watching TV.
   A) 2   B) 5   C) 8
3. They have _____ children and _____ grandchildren.
   A) 2 / 4   B) 3 / 5   C) 4 / 6
4. They walk _____ miles in their lifetime.
   A) 1,359   B) 13,594   C) 135,940
5. The average American will eat _____ eggs.
   A) 61   B) 1,610   C) 16,100
6. He or she spends _____ years on the telephone.
   A) one and a half   B) two and a half   C) three and a half
7. He or she works continuously for _____ years.
   A) 16   B) 26   C) 56

continuously 连续地

Talk about it!

3 With a partner, discuss these questions.
1. Which fact about Americans surprised you the most / the least? Why?
2. Which facts do you think are similar / different for people in your country?

   A: What surprised me the most is how much time Americans spend watching TV.
   B: I know. It's amazing, and...

Unit 14

LISTENING

How long does it take?

1 Before listening   What is your typical day like? What do you do in the morning? How much TV do you watch? What do you like to do in your free time?

2 Before listening   Look at the pictures. Who is...

a. **2** going to work?   d. ☐ watching TV?
b. ☐ waiting in line?   e. ☐ getting ready in the morning?
c. ☐ shopping?

HELP listening

Take notes
Take notes as you listen. It's not necessary to write complete words. For example, write **40 mins** instead of **forty minutes**. This way, you can quickly note important information.

请注意听力练习时要记笔记

wait in line
排队等候

3 Listening   Listen. Which two people from exercise 2 are talking? _____
14_02

4 Listening   Listen again and complete the chart.
14_02

	speaker 1	speaker 2
1. How long does it take you to get ready in the morning?		
2. How long does it take you to go to work?		
3. How much time do you spend watching TV every day?		
4. How much time do you spend shopping for food in one day?		
5. How do you pass the time when you are waiting in line?		

5 After listening   With a partner, ask and answer the questions in exercise 4. Are your answers similar to speaker 1 or speaker 2?

Talk about it!

6 With a partner, prepare a conversation for one of the other three pictures in exercise 2. Role-play your conversation for the class.

Unit 14

VOCABULARY

Time flies!

1 In one week, what activity do you spend most of your time doing?

2 Write the correct time-related verb—lose, waste, spend, or pass—to complete each sentence. Use the correct verb tense.

1. Every spring, we change the clock and we ____lose____ an hour.
2. I don't _____ a lot of time watching the news.
3. Sometimes I read a magazine to _____ the time.
4. Liza's parents say she _____ too much time watching TV.
5. Last summer we _____ ten days in Hawaii.
6. I _____ five hours flying from New York to London.
7. The project failed. Sam feels like he _____ two months on it.
8. I didn't mind the flight. The time _____ quickly.

culture matters

In many countries, such as in the U.S., people lose an hour when the clocks change in the spring. They gain an hour when the clocks change again in the fall.
- Is this the same in your country?

请注意不同的时制

3 What time is it? Check (✓) the phrases that describe each clock. Then listen and check.
14_03

1

2

3

☐ It's approximately 9 o'clock.	☐ It's approximately 2 o'clock.	☐ It's approximately 10 o'clock.
☐ It's past 9 o'clock.	☐ It's past 2 o'clock.	☐ It's past 10 o'clock.
☐ It's about 9 o'clock.	☐ It's about 2 o'clock.	☐ It's about 10 o'clock.
☐ It's almost 9 o'clock.	☐ It's almost 2 o'clock.	☐ It's almost 10 o'clock.
☐ It's exactly 9 o'clock.	☐ It's exactly 2 o'clock.	☐ It's exactly 10 o'clock.
☐ It's just before 9 o'clock.	☐ It's just before 2 o'clock.	☐ It's just before 10 o'clock.
☐ It's just after 9 o'clock.	☐ It's just after 2 o'clock.	☐ It's just after 10 o'clock.
☐ It's precisely 9 o'clock.	☐ It's precisely 2 o'clock.	☐ It's precisely 10 o'clock.
☐ It's not quite 9 o'clock.	☐ It's not quite 2 o'clock.	☐ It's not quite 10 o'clock.

precisely
准确地

Talk about it!

4 With a partner, ask and answer these questions.

1. What time is it? Give the time in at least two different ways.
2. How much time do you spend sleeping (studying, watching TV, etc.) each day / week?
3. How many hours a day do you think you waste? How?
4. What do you think is the best way to pass the time when waiting in line?

GRAMMAR

Present perfect continuous

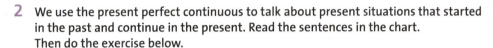

1. It's Saturday afternoon. What are you doing?
   How long have you been doing it?

   I'm shopping at the mall. I've been shopping for three hours!

2. We use the present perfect continuous to talk about present situations that started in the past and continue in the present. Read the sentences in the chart. Then do the exercise below.

   > I have been walking for 20 minutes. I have been walking since 11 o'clock.
   > (I started walking 20 minutes ago with Dave, at 11 o'clock, and I'm still walking.)
   > Dave has been walking for 20 minutes too.

   Look at the pictures, and circle the correct sentence.

   1. a. She waits for the bus.
      b. She's waiting for the bus.
   2. a. "How long have you been waiting?"
      b. "How long are you waiting?"
   3. a. "I've waited for half an hour."
      b. "I've been waiting for half an hour."

3. Write the correct question or answer for the situations below.

   1. Q: How long has Jackie been studying English? (two years)
      A: <u>Jackie's been studying English for two years.</u>
   2. Q: How _____ ?
      A: Ed's been working on this exercise for five minutes.
   3. Q: _____ ?
      A: They've been using this book since October.
   4. Q: How long has he been living here? (2008)
      A: _____ .
   5. Q: How long have you been working on this exercise?
      A: _____ .

Talk about it!

4. Work with a partner. Talk about how you have been spending your time. Ask and answer five present perfect continuous questions.

   A: How long have you been studying English?
   B: I've been studying English for approximately three years. How about you?

Unit 14

READING

HELP reading

Ask and answer questions
Before reading, look at the title, visuals, etc. What is the reading about? What questions do you have? Look for the answers while reading. Were your questions answered?

请注意带着问题进行阅读

Have you been waiting long?

1 Before reading Approximately how much time do you spend each day doing these activities?

1. standing in line   **15 minutes**
2. waiting for a bus or train
3. looking for something you have lost
4. stuck in a traffic jam
5. shopping
6. waiting for the check in a restaurant

a pair of scissors 一把剪刀
stuck 被堵住
traffic jam 交通阻塞

2 Reading 14_04 Read the news article and decide if you waste more or less time than the average person in the U.S. Explain your answer to a partner.

3 Reading 14_04 Read the article again. Circle the correct words to complete each sentence below.

account for 占用

1. People in the U.S. waste more than (1 hour) / 1½ hours / 2 hours a day doing nothing.
2. They spend over ¼ hour / ½ hour / 1 hour a week waiting for public transportation.
3. They waste 1 hour / 1½ hours / 2 hours a week looking for things.
4. They spend 1 hour / 1½ hours / 2 hours a week stuck in traffic jams.
5. They waste 1 hour / 1½ hours / 2 hours a week standing in lines.
6. All in all, they lose approximately 2½ / 7½ / 24 hours of time a week.
7. This adds up to about 2½ / 3½ / 12 years of an average American's lifetime.
8. This compares to 8 / 18 / 80 years spent watching TV.

bureaucracy 繁文缛节

add up to 合计达

Wasting Time

When was the last time you wasted half the morning looking for your glasses, or a pair of scissors, or the car keys? How much time do you spend standing in lines
5 or stuck in traffic jams? How long did you spend waiting for the check the last time you went to a restaurant?

A recent survey in the U.S. found that American people waste over an hour a day
10 simply doing nothing. For example, they spend over half an hour a week waiting for public transportation, and almost one and a half hours a week looking for things at home. Traffic jams account for another
15 hour and a half of wasted time each week. People spend over an hour a week shopping unsuccessfully, and over two hours is wasted standing in lines in banks or stores, waiting to be served, or dealing with needless
20 bureaucracy.

Unit 14

This adds up to seven hours and 24 minutes of lost time each week, or roughly two and a half years of the average American's life. Add this to the eight years they spend watching TV, and the fifteen plus years they spend sleeping, and you wonder how they get any work done at all!

The survey also shows that young people waste twice as much time as older people, and that men waste more time than women. People in Los Angeles suffer most from traffic jams and slow public transportation—on average, it takes them six hours a week to get nowhere.

How can you reduce time-wasting? The survey analysts recommend careful planning. For example, deciding what you want to buy before you go shopping, and shopping after work instead of on weekends. Living near your place of work is another obvious solution. Wearing your glasses around your neck is another.

4 After reading With a partner, discuss these questions.

1. Do you think that watching TV is a waste of time? Explain.
2. Do you think it's true that men waste more time than women? Why or why not?
3. When was the last time you wasted a lot of time standing in line or waiting for something? What happened?
4. Do you think that people in your country waste time in the same way as people in the U.S.? Explain.

Talk about it!

5 Work in a small group. Write questions with *How long do you...? How many hours do you...? How much time do you...?* Ask students in your group the questions.

Question ideas:

- sleep / a night?
- waste / being stuck in traffic / every day?
- spend / a day / watching TV?
- take / to have breakfast?
- spend / talking on the phone / every day?
- spend / doing housework?
- take / to get to school?
- spend / reading every day?

A: How much time do you spend talking on the phone every day?

B: I spend only a few minutes talking, but I spend a couple of hours texting.

6 Tell the class about your results.

Three people spend more than nine hours sleeping every night.
Approximately half spend...

PROJECT

Work with a group. Survey 10–20 people as to what they waste time doing. Make a list of the top 10 time-wasters. Next to each time-waster, write at least one recommendation for avoiding this problem. The end of the reading mentions a couple of ways to reduce time-wasting. Present your report to the class.

roughly
大概

twice as much time as
两倍的时间
suffer from
忍受

analyst
分析师

recommendation
建议
a couple of
几个

Unit 14

SONG

Passing the time

1 Before listening Not everyone agrees on what activities are time-wasters. What are some examples of what one person might consider wasting time, and another might consider spending time well?

2 Listening Listen to the song. Complete the song with the following words.
14_05

Verse 1:

fine / corner / you / wasting my time / on / blue

Verse 2:

you / people / world / hour / time

Verse 3:

you / money / not / time

3 Listening Listen to the song again. Underline these expressions as you listen. Then match them with the definitions below.
14_05

1. __d__ I'm not blue
2. _____ I take no notice
3. _____ to stroll by
4. _____ How do you do?
5. _____ in a hurry

a. I don't think it's important
b. to walk slowly past
c. How are you?
d. I'm not sad
e. going quickly to arrive on time

take no notice
不理会; 没注意
stroll by
漫步于……

Passing the time

I'm standing ①__on__ the
②_____.
Life sure is ③_____.
Some people say
That I'm ④_____.
I take no notice,
I'm not ⑤_____,
Passing the time
Thinking about ⑥_____.

I've been watching the ⑦_____
For an ⑧_____ or two.
No need to do nothing,
I've nothing to do.
⑨_____ stroll by
With a "How do you do?"
Passing the ⑩_____
Thinking about ⑪_____.

People in a hurry,
I'm ⑫_____ that way inclined.
They like spending ⑬_____,
I like spending ⑭_____
Thinking about ⑮_____.

Unit 14

4 After listening Discuss these questions with a partner.

1. Who is *you* in the song?
2. How does the singer feel?
3. Do you like the song? Why or why not?
4. Do you know other songs about wasting, spending, or passing time? What are they?

5 After listening With a partner, change the six words from verse 1 to make it your own. (1) and (2) are done for you as examples only. Choose your own words. Be creative! Use the correct part of speech for each word. When you are finished, read your verse to the class.

I'm standing (**1**) ____in____ the (**2**) ____garden____ .
Life sure is (**3**) _____ .
Some people say
That I'm (**4**) _____ .
I take no notice,
I'm not (**5**) _____ ,
Passing the time
Thinking about (**6**) _____ .

1 = preposition ____in____
2 = a place ____garden____
3 = adjective _____
4 = present continuous _____
5 = adjective _____
6 = noun / pronoun _____

Talk about it!

6 Put the activities in order from 1 to 8; 1 = the biggest waste of time and 8 = NOT a waste of time. Then discuss your list with a partner.

____ watching TV
____ texting with friends
____ playing video games
____ lying on the beach
____ surfing the Internet
____ doing puzzles, Sudoku, etc.
____ window-shopping
____ daydreaming

do puzzles
玩拼图游戏
do Sudoku
玩数独游戏

A: I think daydreaming is the biggest waste of time.
B: I don't think daydreaming is a waste of time. It's creative and it's a good way to relax.

PRONUNCIATION

Understanding numbers and times

1 Listen and circle the numbers and times you hear.
14_06

A.	2½	2:30	2¼	2:15
B.	7:50	7:15	715	750
C.	5:30	5:13	5⅓	530
D.	905	950	9:05	9:50

2 Listen and repeat all the numbers and times.
14_07

173

Unit 14

CONVERSATION

Apologizing and accepting an apology

1 In what situations do you apologize? Is it something you like to do? Why or why not?

2 14_08 Listen to the conversation. What's the man's excuse for being late?

3 14_08 Complete the conversation with expressions from the box. Not all expressions are used. Then listen again to check your answers.

Eric:	Hi!
Rita:	Finally! I didn't think you were coming!
Eric:	(1) _I'm sorry_ I'm late, but there were no taxis.
Rita:	(2) _____ . (3) _____ to all of us. How long did it take you to find one?
Eric:	Almost 30 minutes! Then we got stuck in traffic. How long have you been waiting?
Rita:	About 45 minutes.
Eric:	(4) _____ that I kept you waiting.
Rita:	(5) _____ . (6) _____ this time. But you're buying dinner!

CONVERSATION STRATEGY

Admit responsibility
When you apologize, admit responsibility and explain what happened.

I'm sorry that I didn't come, but my I missed my train.

请注意如何真诚地道歉

Apologizing
I apologize...
Excuse me, but...
Forgive me...
~~I'm sorry...~~
I really am sorry...
It's my fault.

Accepting an apology
Don't worry about it.
No problem.
It happens...
I forgive you...

Talk about it!

4 Work with a partner. Think of a situation where you have done something wrong. Apologize and hope your partner accepts your apology.

A: I apologize for missing your party.
B: You always miss my parties. What's your excuse this time?

Tell me more!

Visit the Takeaway English Online Learning Center at http://olcs.mcgraw-hill-education.com/takeaway/

 Check out the *Takeaway TV* video.

 Improve your English with the online activities.

Unit 14

WRITING

Writing a survey report

1 Before writing Have you ever written a report in English? In your own language? What was the report about? Was it a success? Why or why not?

HELP writing

Organize parts of a report
A good report will have four basic parts. A clear title that lets the reader know what to expect. An introduction that lays out the question(s) and how the information was gathered. A body of information that gives and explains the results. And finally, a conclusion that summarizes the results and makes recommendations.

请注意报告的四个基本部分

write a survey report
撰写调查报告
lay out
列出

2 Writing model Read a survey report. Match the titles with the paragraphs. Then put the paragraphs in order.

> introduction   survey results   ~~conclusion~~

3 A. _conclusion_

To sum up, I recommend that the people in my group need to spend less time watching TV and they should spend more time sleeping.

B. _____

We asked 10 people aged 19 to 22 some questions to find out how they spend their time.

C. _____

Our survey shows that most people in the group sleep seven hours a night and roughly half of the group spends three hours a day watching TV. Four people said...

3 Planning your writing Use a graphic organizer like the one here to organize your notes from your group survey in exercise 5 on page 171. Refer to the paragraphs in exercise 2 as a guide.

Title	
Introduction	
Survey results	
Conclusions	

4 Writing Now write a report on how the people in your English group spend / waste their time. Include some recommendations for reducing time-wasting.

175

Unit 14

TEST

Test-taking strategy

Use context clues to answer questions When answering questions during a test, there will be some words that you do not know. Context clues can help you guess the meaning.

Look at the example below. Use these steps to help you answer questions.

1. When you see a new word, decide if you need to know the word to understand the meaning of the sentence or paragraph.
2. If yes, use context clues to help discover the meaning.
3. Context clues can come before or after the new word. They include definitions, synonyms, antonyms, examples, and explanations.

synonym
同义词
antonym
反义词

Daylight Savings
Time
夏时制

Example
What is the meaning of the underlined phrase in this sentence? Choose the correct answer.

1. Daylight Savings Time, which is gaining or losing an hour on the clock in the spring or fall, occurs in most countries.

    ~~A.~~ a type of clock   Daylight Savings Time is not a clock.

    ~~B.~~ the start of a season   Daylight Savings Time does not mark the beginning of a season.

    ~~C.~~ the time in one country   Daylight Savings Time occurs in most countries.

    D. a change in time   This is the correct answer. A context clue (definition) immediately follows the phrase.

PRACTICE

Read the paragraph below. Choose the correct answer. Mark the letter on the Answer Sheet.

> When you add time to your life each day, you can reduce stress and increase happiness. One way to add time is to use public transportation: buses, trains, or even ferries. If you're not stuck in your car in a traffic jam, you are adding to your time instead of wasting it. That allows you to use that time to do other things while someone else does the driving.

1. What is an example of public transportation?

    A. happiness
    B. a ferry
    C. a traffic jam
    D. stress

2. What is an antonym for *add*?

    A. waste
    B. reduce
    C. allow
    D. save

Answer Sheet
Mark the letter.
1. A   B   C   D
2. A   B   C   D

UNIT SUMMARY

Noun
lifetime

Adjective
average

Verbs and verb phrases
lose
pass
spend
waste

Adverbs
about
almost
approximately
exactly
just after
just before
not quite
precisely

Preposition
past

Expressions
How do you do?
I take no notice.
I'm not blue.
in a hurry
stroll by

Apologize
Excuse me, but…
Forgive me…
I apologize…
I really am sorry…
I'm sorry…
It's not my fault.

Accept an apology
Don't worry about it.
I forgive you…
It happens…
No problem.

15 ▶ Great adventures

In this unit you...
- talk about explorers and expeditions
- discuss camping trips and equipment
- shop for camping equipment

Grammar
- passive voice

START

Famous expeditions

1 How many famous explorers can you name? What famous explorers are from your country?

2 Read short biographies of three explorers. Which explorer disappeared on his expedition?
15_01

> **Marco Polo (1254–1324)**, the son of a merchant, was born in Venice. With his uncle and father, he left home in 1271 and traveled overland to China—a route that became known as the "Silk Road." He finally returned to Italy 25 years later.
>
> **David Livingstone (1813–1873)**, a Scottish explorer and doctor, explored much of central Africa. In 1866, he set out to look for the source of the Nile River. He never came back. During his travels, Livingstone visited many places where no European had been before.
>
> **Christopher Columbus (1451–1506)** wanted to discover a new route to India. He believed the quickest route was to sail west from Europe. He set sail in 1492 and arrived in the area now known as the Americas on October 12th. He thought he had arrived in India.

Marco Polo
马可·波罗
travel overland
走陆路

David Livingstone
戴维·利文斯通
set out
出发；动身
the Nile River
尼罗河
Christopher Columbus
克利斯多弗·哥伦布
set sail
启航

3 Match the three explorers to their expedition maps.

1. ☐ David Livingstone   2. ☐ Marco Polo   3. ☐ Christopher Columbus

Talk about it!

4 Think of one of the explorers you named in exercise 1. Tell a partner as much about his or her story as you can.

A: Have you ever heard of Zheng He?
B: No, I haven't.

A: Well, he was a Chinese explorer who led an expedition in the 1400s to...

expedition
探险队

Unit 15

LISTENING

Expedition to Lhasa

1 Before listening What do you know about Tibet? Where is it? What famous mountain is located there?

2 Listening Listen to the story about an expedition to Lhasa, Tibet. Circle the correct answers to the questions.
15_02

1. Where did Alexandra David-Néel come from?
   - A Tibet
   - **B France**
   - C Asia

2. When was she born?
   - A 1868
   - B 1924
   - C 1969

3. Who traveled with David-Néel?
   - A her son
   - B her husband
   - C her sister

4. How did they travel?
   - A by day
   - B by night
   - C both day and night

5. What kind of storm allowed them to enter the city?
   - A rain
   - B snow
   - C sand

3 After listening Put these events from the story in the correct order from 1 to 6. Compare your answers with a partner.

___ They visited the Potala Palace.
___ David-Néel was ordered to leave Tibet four times.
_1_ David-Néel received some money.
___ She decided to try to travel to Lhasa again with her son.
___ A sandstorm allowed them to enter the city.
___ She decided to go to Tibet.

HELP listening

Focus on what you understand
When listening, don't focus on what you *don't* understand. It's OK to *not* understand everything. Focus on what you *do* understand!

请注意听时聚焦能听懂的内容

Lhasa
拉萨
Tibet
西藏

Potala Palace

CONVERSATION STRATEGY

Show interest
To keep your listener interested when you're telling a story, ask questions like, *And guess what happened then?* or, *Have you heard of...*

请注意如何激发听者的兴趣

the Potala Palace
布达拉宫（拉萨）

sandstorm
沙尘暴

Talk about it!

4 With a partner, ask and answer these questions.

1. What are some of the challenges for a woman traveling alone today? Was it more or less difficult for women to travel alone in the past? Why?

2. Who would you travel with if you were going on an adventure vacation? Why?

3. In your opinion, was travel more or less exciting in the past? Explain.

Unit 15

VOCABULARY

Equipment for a camping trip

1. Have you ever gone camping? Where? What are some great places to go camping in your country?

2. Read the text and match the equipment mentioned to the pictures. Then listen and check.
15_03

essentials
必需品

sleeping bag
睡袋

hiking boots
登山鞋
waterproof
防水的
first aid kit
急救药箱
sewing kit
针线包

Essentials for a Camping Trip

If you're going on a camping trip, here's a guide for several things you're going to need.

Most important is a good tent (1) __I__ . You'll also need a sleeping bag (2) _____ and a sleeping pad (3) _____ to put under the sleeping bag because it can get very cold at night. Hot food and drinks are another great way to keep warm. For this, you'll need a stove (4) _____ for cooking and some pots and pans (5) _____ for heating food and water. Don't forget to take matches (6) _____ to light the stove. If you're going to be hiking a lot, you'll certainly need a good pair of hiking boots (7) _____ . A waterproof jacket (8) _____ will also be very important when the weather is bad.

What about emergencies? A first aid kit (9) _____ is very important for injuries or sickness. And a sewing kit (10) _____ can be used to repair clothes. Many problems are caused by getting lost, so take a map (11) _____ and a compass (12) _____ . Also bring a whistle (13) _____ . In an emergency, blow it six times.

And finally, you need a good backpack (14) _____ to carry all of this in!

3. Imagine you are going camping in the mountains for a week. You can take only EIGHT of the items of equipment. Make a list of the eight items you choose.

Talk about it!

4. With a partner, compare your lists. You now need to make a list of eight items that you both agree on.

   A: OK. The first thing on my list is the map, because it's really important not to get lost.
   B: I agree with that.
   A: Next I have...

ENGLISH *express*

get lost = the process of losing your way

be lost = the state of not knowing where you are

I got completely lost in the woods.
I'm completely lost. Where's the trail?

请注意 get lost 与 be lost 的区别

WORKBOOK PAGE 111

GRAMMAR

Passive voice

ALSO GO TO
Grammar Takeaway
PAGE 208

1 Look at the pictures. Circle the sentence that describes each picture.

1. A) The woman was kissed by the baby.
   B) The woman kissed the baby.
2. A) A man was bitten by a dog.
   B) A man bit a dog.
3. A) The girl was eaten by the fish.
   B) The girl ate the fish.

2 The sentences in exercise 1 are examples of active and passive voice.
Which sentences are active? _____ Which sentences are passive? _____

In active voice sentences, the subject (the woman) does the action.	In passive voice sentences, the subject (the baby) receives the action. subject + *be* + main verb (past participle)
The woman kissed the baby.	The baby was kissed by the woman.

3 The following sentences are written in the active voice. Rewrite the sentences in the passive voice. Pay attention to the verb tense in the active voice when forming the passive voice.

1. Many tourists visit Lhasa.   **Lhasa is visited by many tourists.**
2. All campers need a first aid kit.
3. A sandstorm hit the city.
4. Marco Polo traveled the "Silk Road".
5. Unprepared campers have caused many problems.
6. Lightning starts many fires.

Talk about it!

4 With a partner, ask and answer the questions.
Answer in the passive voice.

1. Who founded Microsoft?
   A: Who founded Microsoft?
   B: I think Microsoft was founded by Bill Gates.
2. Who invented the light bulb?
3. Who developed the theory of relativity ($E = mc^2$)?
4. Which countries make up North America?
5. Who taught you English?
6. Who has influenced you the most in your life?

light bulb
电灯泡
the theory of relativity
相对论

Unit 15

READING

HELP reading

Predict

Before you read something, look at the title of what you're about to read, look at any pictures, and think of what you already know about the subject. This can help you prepare for the reading and predict what it will be about.

请注意借助标题和图片预测文章大意

Adventures in Africa

1 Before reading What do you know about Africa and the animals that live there?

2 Before reading Look at the pictures. With a partner, predict the correct order of the events shown. Do you think the story has a happy ending?

3 Reading Read the story. Which of your predictions were correct?

Livingstone and the lion

David Livingstone was a Scottish missionary and explorer. He was born in 1813 and died in 1873. He led many expeditions in Africa, searching for the source of the Nile River. He was unusual for a Western explorer because he traveled lightly, without a lot of equipment and supplies. He treated the native people with
5 respect and traded with them.

On his third expedition into the African interior in 1843, Livingstone discovered the Mabotsa Valley. It was so beautiful that he decided to stay for a while and explore the region. There was, however, one big problem—lions. This was a region famous for the ferocity of its lions. Humans were frequently attacked by these wild animals. Livingstone decided to try to solve the problem. He had heard that if you kill one lion, the rest of the lions leave
10 the area. So he set off with a native friend, Mebalwe, to kill a lion.

After walking for several hours, Livingstone and Mebalwe found the trail of a lion. They crept quietly through the bush until they saw it. Livingstone took his gun and he shot the lion. But while he was preparing to fire the gun again, he was attacked by the lion. Mebalwe picked up the gun, but when the lion saw the movement it attacked him as well. Fortunately, before it could kill Mebalwe, the lion died from the first gun shot that Livingstone had
15 fired. Livingstone's arm was very badly injured. He couldn't use it properly for the rest of his life.

This story does have a happy ending, however. After shooting the lion, Livingstone went back to the village of Kuruman, where his arm was treated and he was able to recover. He spent a lot of time here with an English woman, Mary Moffatt. They were married in 1844 and they went back to the Mabotsa Valley to live.

Scottish missionary
苏格兰传教士

the African interior
非洲内部
the Mabotsa Valley
玛波塔撒山谷

set off
出发
native friend
当地朋友

Unit 15

4 Reading Read the story again. Circle *True* or *False* for each statement below.

1. The story is about Livingstone's first expedition to Africa. — True (False)
2. Livingstone wanted to kill the lion to make the other lions leave the valley. — True False
3. The lion was shot once by Livingstone. — True False
4. Mebalwe also fired the gun at the lion. — True False
5. Livingstone made a complete recovery from the lion attack. — True False
6. Livingstone never returned to the Mabotsa Valley. — True False

5 After reading Write the underlined words in the story next to the definitions below.

1. the track or smell of a person or animal ___trail___
2. the fierce and violent nature of an animal, thing, or person _____
3. a person who does religious work in a foreign country _____
4. the inside part of a thing or place _____
5. to become well again _____
6. started a journey _____
7. a part of a country _____
8. the beginning of a river _____

fierce
凶猛的
violent
暴力的

6 After reading Circle five examples of the passive voice in the story.

Talk about it!

7 With a partner, ask and answer these questions.

1. What do you think about Livingstone's decision to kill the lion?
   A: I think Livingstone had no choice but to kill the lion.
   B: I'm not sure I agree with you. He could have...
2. What do you think about killing lions nowadays?
3. What wild animals are there in your country? Do you think people should be allowed to hunt them? Why or why not?

PROJECT

Do some research on a wild animal in Africa that is in danger of becoming extinct. Learn as much as you can about the animal and why it is in danger of disappearing. Prepare an illustrated poster that includes information about the animal (description, habitat, life span, etc.) as well as what is being done to protect it. Present your poster to the class.

Unit 15

CULTURE

Excursions and transportation around the world

1 Before reading Think about any famous excursions (trips for fun) or transportation in your country. Why are they famous? What have been your personal experiences with them?

2 Before reading Match the famous excursions and transportation to the pictures.

1. Nile River cruise ___E___
2. the Inca Trail _____
3. the Silk Road _____
4. San Francisco cable cars _____
5. the Way of St. James _____
6. Venetian gondolas _____
7. the Trans-Siberian Railway _____
8. Grand Canyon donkey ride _____

Nile River cruise 尼罗河邮轮
the Inca Trail 印加古道
cable car 缆车
Venetian gondolas 威尼斯贡多拉游船
Trans-Siberian 穿越西伯利亚的
Grand Canyon （美）大峡谷

3 Reading Read the article to see where the excursions and transportation are located.

See for yourself!

in part 在某种程度上

Machu Picchu 马丘比丘 （古城，位于秘鲁中部偏南）
lay eyes on 看到
take a cruise 乘坐邮轮

Every year millions of people travel on famous routes and take transportation that is well-known the world over. Even if you've never been to Italy, who hasn't heard of the Venetian gondolas? So what is the attraction of using transportation that
5 could be slow, uncomfortable, or expensive? Maybe, in part, to just be able to say you did it.

It would be a lot faster and easier to fly from St. Petersburg to Vladivostok in Russia than take the Trans-Siberian Railway; but then you wouldn't see the expanse of Russia, Mongolia, and
10 China outside your window.

The Inca Trail is traveled by so many people that the Peruvian government has been forced to limit the number of people allowed access. Why bother with such a well-traveled path? Well, for starters, who would want to miss walking through a
15 cloud forest or seeing the glorious ruins of Machu Picchu?

San Francisco, California, in the United States has underground trains, modern buses, and taxis at the wave of a hand. Why would anyone want to take old, very loud, very slow cable cars? Certainly not for the comfort! But would you really be able
20 to say that you left your heart in San Francisco if you didn't?

The history of Egypt is known by people all over the world. Why spend all that money and time taking a cruise on the Nile River? There are plenty of picture books at your local library. Maybe it has something to do with the magic of seeing the temples at
25 Luxor from the ancient waterway that made this great civilization possible.

People have been traveling the Silk Road between China and Europe for thousands of years. Little has changed since caravans carried silk and other valuable products to different trading cities.
30 Is there anything new to be learned? Perhaps the answer to that question lies in riding a camel of your own or watching the sun set over the Gobi Desert.

The Way of St. James is the pilgrimage to the cathedral of Santiago de Compostela in northwestern Spain. People have
35 been making this journey for more than a thousand years. People continue to do so today on foot, by bicycle, and even on horseback. Hasn't this route been traveled enough times already? Not if you haven't traveled hard to lay eyes on the cathedral yourself.

40 The Grand Canyon in Arizona in the United States has many beautiful hotels overlooking the scenery. Why would anyone travel by donkey down dangerous trails into the canyon to camp? Maybe it has something do with waking up in your tent, deep down in the canyon, next to the river that carved this
45 wonder of nature over millions of years.

What about you? Which excursion would you choose?

Unit 15

4 After reading Use the underlined words in the text to complete the sentences.

1. Modern day ___caravans___ of camels still travel across the Sahara desert to conduct trade.
2. Some sensitive wildlife areas have limited tourist _____ to protect the animals.
3. There are numerous _____ to follow on the Way of St. James, but they all end at Santiago de Compostela.
4. Petra is an _____ city in the country of Jordan.
5. Millions of people travel to Alaska each year to see the breathtaking _____ .
6. It is almost impossible to truly understand the immense _____ of the interior of Australia until you have seen it yourself.
7. Muslims from all over the world make a _____ to the holy city of Mecca each year.
8. The Inca _____ developed around 1200 in what is today the country of Peru.

caravans of camels
骆驼商队
conduct trade
做生意

breathtaking
令人惊叹的

Petra

the holy city of Mecca
麦加圣城

Talk about it!

5 Work with a partner. Ask and answer these questions.

1. What message do you think the writer is trying to give in the text? Does the title convey that message?
2. Do you agree with the writer? Why or why not?
3. How would you answer the final question in the article: Which excursion would you choose?

PRONUNCIATION

The sound /ɜː/

1 Say the word *learn* aloud. The letters *ear* have the /ɜː/ sound. Listen and
15_06 underline the /ɜː/ sound in these words.

1. certainly   3. emergency   5. journey
2. circle   4. first aid kit 6. return

2 Say the words aloud. Circle the word that does NOT have the sound /ɜː/.
15_07 Then listen to all the words and check for the correct answers.

1.	turn	Tuesday	Thursday
2.	girl	third	their
3.	there	were	verb
4.	word	world	more

185

Unit 15

camping equipment
露营设备

CONVERSATION

Shopping for camping equipment

1 What are some questions you need to ask a salesperson when shopping for camping equipment?

2 Listen to the conversation. What three adjectives are used to describe the tent?
15_08
_____ _____ _____

3 Complete the conversation with expressions from the box.
15_08 Then listen again to check your answers.

Salesperson:	Hello. (1) _How can I help you_?
Customer:	Hi. (2) _____ a tent.
Salesperson:	OK. (3) _____ tent are you looking for?
Customer:	Well, I'm not really sure. (4) _____ lightweight, waterproof, and big enough for two people.
Salesperson:	OK. (5) _____ ? It's a two-person tent. It's very lightweight, and completely waterproof.
Customer:	Yeah… (6) _____ . How much is it?
Salesperson:	Ninety-five dollars.
Customer:	(7) _____ . I'll take it.
Salesperson:	Great. (8) _____

> ~~How can I help you?~~
> What kind of…?
> What about this one?
> Sounds good.
> It has to be…
> I'm looking for…
> That looks good.
> Let me ring you up.

lightweight
重量轻的

CONVERSATION STRATEGY

Give feedback

When you're shopping it's important to give feedback to the salesperson.

That looks good. = You like what you are being shown.

That sounds good. = You like the person's suggestion.

请注意购物时反馈信息给销售人员

Talk about it!

4 With a partner, practice shopping for other camping equipment.

A: Hello. How can I help you?
B: Hi. I'm looking for a new sleeping bag.
A: How cold will it be where you're going camping?

ENGLISH express

When a salesperson says **Let me ring you up**, he / she is offering to complete the sale at the cash register. In the old days, cash registers used to make a ringing sound.

请注意销售人员如何表达"请去付款"

Tell me more!

Visit the Takeaway English Online Learning Center at http://olcs.mcgraw-hill-education.com/takeaway/

 Check out the *Takeaway TV* video.

 Improve your English with the online activities.

Unit 15

WRITING

Writing a blog about a trip

1 Before writing   Look at the pictures. Where do you think the person's vacation was? Does it look like a trip that you would enjoy? Why or why not?

2 Writing model   Use the phrases to complete a blogger's story of a recent trip.

| one afternoon | We were met there by | It was really | After that |
| The next morning | ~~This was the best vacation~~ | I think I'll go | |

(1) _This was the best vacation_ I've ever had. We had to fly into Melbourne, and we were then taken by boat to Hobart, Tasmania. (2) _____ our guide, Fred, who was just fantastic. He took us to our campsite, showed us how to put the tents up, and then we all went off for a walk on the beach. It was so beautiful. (3) _____ , we got up early and we were taken by bus to the beginning of a four-day walk across Cradle Mountain. (4) _____ hard walking, but so much fun—and awesomely beautiful. Sometimes it got pretty difficult and scary. We were taught how to climb rock, but I didn't really like it. (5) _____ , we had a couple of days to rest, which was great—just hanging out at the beach or having coffee in town. I went horseback riding on the beach (6) _____ . I loved it, even though the horse didn't always do what I wanted! And then, suddenly, it was time to come home again. Tasmania is a fantastic place for a vacation, so (7) _____ back there next year.

put the tents up
搭帐篷

awesomely
棒极了

3 Planning your writing   You will write a similar blog about a vacation or trip that you have taken. Use a story map to organize your notes.

Title:		
Where:		When:
Major characters:		Minor characters:
Plot / Problem:		
Event 1:	Event 2:	Event 3:
Outcome / Conclusion:		

4 Writing   Use the notes from your story map and the phrases from exercise 2 to help you structure your blog. Include a photograph if you can.

HELP writing

Use the active vs. passive voice in writing
Writers should, in general, use the active voice rather than the passive. It's a more powerful and direct form of expression.

请注意写作时多用主动语态

187

Unit 15

TEST

Test-taking strategy

Vocabulary questions: Select word by meaning Tests may ask you vocabulary questions in two different ways—"select meaning by word" and "select word by meaning". Here we will practice "select word by meaning". For these items, you see a meaning and select the word.

Look at the example below. Use these steps to help you answer "select word by meaning" vocabulary questions.

1. Try to determine the part of speech for the answer choices.
2. If you can't decide what part of speech the answers are, try to determine what parts of speech they are *not*.
3. Based on your analysis, eliminate answers.
4. From the remaining answers, choose the best answer.
5. Guess if necessary.

> **Example**
> **Choose the correct answer.**
> 1. *n.* the fact or state of being
>   - A. amazing — *Amazing is an adjective.*
>   - B. discover — *Discover is a verb.*
>   - C. existence — This is the correct answer. This word is probably a noun.
>   - D. announcement — This word is most likely a noun. But it is not the correct answer.

PRACTICE

Choose the correct answer. Mark the letter on the Answer Sheet.

1. *n.* area located well inland from the border or coast of a country
   - A. extinct
   - B. fearless
   - C. interior
   - D. expedition

2. *adj.* savagely wild or fierce
   - A. ferocious
   - B. missionary
   - C. equip
   - D. region

3. *v.* to begin to move, start a journey
   - A. emergency
   - B. set off
   - C. violent
   - D. extinct

4. *v.* to regain one's health or strength
   - A. recover
   - B. source
   - C. route
   - D. famous

Answer Sheet
Mark the letter.
1. A B C D
2. A B C D
3. A B C D
4. A B C D

Unit 15

UNIT SUMMARY

Noun
access
backpack
biography
cable car
camping
caravan
civilization
compass
cruise
donkey ride
emergency
equipment
expanse
expedition
explorer
ferocity
first aid kit
gondola
hiking boots
injury
interior
map
match
merchant
missionary
pan
pilgrimage
pot
region
route
sandstorm
scenery
sewing kit
sickness
silk
sleeping bag
sleeping pad
source
storm
stove
tent
trail
waterproof jacket
whistle

Adjective
ancient

Verbs and verb phrases
be lost
blow
disappear
get lost
heat
hike
keep warm
light
recover
repair
sail
set off
set sail

Expressions
And guess what happened then?
Have you heard of…

Shop for camping equipment
How can I help you?
I'm looking for…
It has to be…
Let me ring you up.
Sounds good.
That looks good.
That sounds good.
What about this one?
What kind of…

Review 3

VOCABULARY

1 Which word or phrase is different? With a partner, explain how it is different.

1.	donate	raise	sponsor	(spend)
2.	train	be out of shape	do exercise	work out
3.	river	mountain	ocean	lake
4.	neck	ankle	elbow	knee
5.	sleeping bag	tent	backpack	sleeping mat
6.	bend	stretch	turn	ache
7.	gravity	space	astronaut	mission
8.	about	exactly	almost	approximately

A: I think "spend" is different because it's not about giving money to charity.
B: Yes, I agree.

2 With your partner, write four more "which one is different" lists. Use words from Units 1 to 10. Exchange lists with another pair.

1. faded, checkered, baggy, striped

3 Put the words in the box in three groups. Then think of three more words for each group.

arm	key	knee	tent	reservation
guest	sleeping bag	stove	leg	palm

parts of the body	camping equipment	hotels
arm		

4 With a partner, ask and answer these questions about camping equipment. Explain your choices.

1. What two items can be used to find your way in the jungle?
2. What three items can be used to cook a meal?
3. What three items would be used at bedtime?
4. What two items would be useful in an emergency?

Review 3

GRAMMAR

1 Circle the correct answer to complete each sentence.

1. _____ to a new beach resort next year.
   - A) I go
   - B) I went
   - **C) I'm going**
   - D) I will

2. What do you do to stay _____ shape?
   - A) on
   - B) in
   - C) at
   - D) with

3. We _____ to the beach this weekend.
   - A) might go
   - B) are
   - C) can to go
   - D) could to go

4. I _____ my back.
   - A) pain
   - B) sore
   - C) hurt
   - D) ache

5. _____ you go to the Moon if you had enough money?
   - A) Will
   - B) Can
   - C) May
   - D) Would

6. Scientists have _____ water on the Moon.
   - A) discover
   - B) discovering
   - C) discovery
   - D) discovered

7. How long does it _____ you to get ready in the morning?
   - A) takes
   - B) spend
   - C) take
   - D) took

8. How long have you _____ ?
   - A) be waiting
   - B) waited
   - C) waiting
   - D) been waiting

9. _____ fly to the Moon if it weren't too expensive.
   - A) I'll
   - B) I'm
   - C) I've
   - D) I'd

10. This resort _____ in 1865.
    - A) constructed
    - B) is constructed
    - C) was constructed
    - D) had constructed

11. I _____ the key to my hotel room yesterday.
    - A) give
    - B) gave
    - C) have given
    - D) was given

12. We didn't have a map, so we _____ .
    - A) got lost
    - B) were lost
    - C) had lost
    - D) are lost

2 Complete the following paragraph with the correct form of the verb in parentheses.

Sir Alexander Fleming (**1**) ___discovered___ (discover) the miracle drug penicillin in 1928. The drug is made from penicillin mold. Before that time, millions of people (**2**) _____ (die) from bacterial infections. His discovery (**3**) _____ (change) the course of human history. Fleming (**4**) _____ (award) a Nobel prize in 1945 for his achievement.

Review 3

TAKEAWAY ENGLISH

1 Complete these mini-conversations with the phrases from the box.

| I hear you | I forgive you | Are you taking any medication |
| That sounds good | I'm checking in | I'm looking for |

1. **A:** Good afternoon. How can I help you?
   B: Hello. _____ .
   A: Very good. What's the name, please?

2. **A:** I've been sick in bed for three days.
   B: That's too bad. _____ ?
   A: Yes, but it doesn't seem to be helping.

3. **A:** Hello. Can I help you?
   B: Yes, please. _____ a new winter coat.
   A: No problem. Do you know what size you are?

4. **A:** I'm so sorry that I forgot your birthday.
   B: Well, I was angry before, but _____ .
   A: Thank you! Will you let me buy you dinner?

5. **A:** There just seem to be so many problems in the world.
   B: _____ . Do you think there's anything we can do?
   A: I really don't know.

6. **A:** I think we should try the new Chinese restaurant.
   B: _____ . I'm starving!
   A: Me too. Let's go.

2 Check your answers to exercise 1 with a partner. Then discuss these questions about each conversation.

1. Who do you think is talking?
2. Where are they?
3. What are they doing?

A: Who do you think is talking in the first conversation?
B: I think it's someone checking in for a flight at the airport.
A: That's possible, or it could be someone checking into a hotel.

READING

1 Reading Read the article and match the headings with the paragraphs.

| Repair | Assembly | Exercise | Supply |

ASTRONAUTS IN SPACE

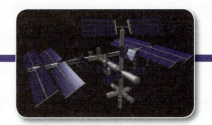

Just like people on Earth, astronauts have different jobs in space. Some astronauts fly the spacecraft. Other astronauts work with the equipment that's launched into space, for instance they conduct scientific experiments or replace parts of satellites. Astronauts' tasks can be divided into four main areas.

1 _____ Astronauts work mostly with the transportation of equipment, new modules, and food supplies for the International Space Station.

2 _____ On the space station, astronauts spend much of their time keeping the station in good condition, both inside and outside. Almost daily, some astronauts take space walks to maintain the station.

3 _____ First and foremost, the station itself must be assembled. New modules arrive regularly, and the task of attaching them to the station take a long time.

4 _____ Weightlessness requires astronauts to spend a considerable amount of time keeping in shape. Astronauts work out every day. Astronauts on a spacecraft exercise half an hour a day. But astronauts on the space station have to spend two hours a day exercising to stay healthy.

So, astronauts are usually very busy. But if they find themselves with nothing to do, they can pass the time just looking out the window. What a view!

2 Reading Read the article again. Circle the best answer for each question.

1. What is the main idea of the text?
   A All astronauts share certain responsibilities.
   B Spacecraft pilots have the most difficult jobs.
   C Astronauts specialize in separate areas of work.
   D Most astronauts dislike physical exercise.

2. Weightlessness is _____ gravity.
   A the increase of
   B the lack of
   C the decrease of
   D the importance of

3. According to the text, _____.
   A astronauts spend most of their time working
   B there aren't enough astronauts to get all the work done
   C astronauts spend all of their free time exercising
   D astronauts waste quite a bit of time looking out the window

3 After reading With a partner, discuss these questions.

1. What do you think you would like and dislike about working in space? Explain.
2. What do you think you would miss most about being on Earth? Explain.

Grammar Takeaway 1

ALSO GO TO:
Unit 1 Grammar
PAGE 5

Grammar Takeaway

Simple past

We use the simple past to talk about:
- completed actions in the past, often with a definite time. I **went** to the beach on Saturday afternoon.
- a series of completed actions in the past. She **came** home, **made** a cup of tea, and **read** the news.

simple past of regular verbs

affirmative	I / You / He / She / We / They **wanted** a new job.
negative	I / You / He / She / We / They **didn't want** a new job.
yes / no questions and answers	**Did** you **want** a new job? Yes, I **did**. / No, I **didn't**.
information questions	Why **did** you **want** a new job?

spelling rules for regular verbs

Add *ed* to the infinitive of most verbs	want = want**ed**
When the infinitive ends in *e*, add *d*	decide = decid**ed**
When the infinitive ends in *y*, change the *y* to *ied*	study = stud**ied**

simple past of *be*

Be is irregular in the simple past.

affirmative	I / He / She / It **was** sick last weekend.
negative	You / We / They **were** sick last weekend.
yes / no questions and answers	**Was** she sick? Yes, she **was**. / No, she **wasn't**. **Were** they sick? Yes, they **were**. / No, they **weren't**.
information questions	When **was** she sick?

simple past of other irregular verbs

affirmative	I / You / He / She / We / They **got** a new job.
negative	I / You / He / She / We / They **didn't get** a new job.
yes / no questions and answers	**Did** you **get** a new job? Yes, I **did**. / No, I **didn't**.
information questions	When **did** you **get** a new job?
common irregulars	become – became get – got see – saw

*See page 140 for a full list of irregular verbs in the simple past.

Grammar Takeaway 2

ALSO GO TO
Unit 2 Grammar
PAGE 17

Grammar Takeaway

Present perfect

We use the present perfect to talk about:
- things that happened at a non-specific time in the past.
  I've seen my favorite rock band in concert.
- things that started in the past and are still happening now.
  He's been a movie director for 10 years.

We form the present perfect with the present tense of *have* plus a past participle.

affirmative	I / You / We / They have been to Paris. He / She has been to Paris.
negative	I / You / We / They haven't been to Paris. He / She hasn't been to Paris.
yes / *no* questions and answers	Have you (ever) been to Paris? Yes, I have. / No, I haven't. Has he (ever) been to Paris? Yes, he has. / No, he hasn't.
Information questions and answers	How long have you collected sunglasses? I've collected sunglasses for many years. I've collected sunglasses since 1998.

For and *Since*

We use *for* and *since* with the present perfect to say when something started.
- Use *for* before periods of time.
  He's collected stamps for 12 years.
- Use *since* before a set time in the past.
  I've lived here since 2005.

Spelling rules for regular past participles

Add *ed* to the infinitive of most verbs	act = acted
When the infinitive ends in *e*, add *d*	decorate = decorated
When the infinitive ends in *y*, change the *y* to *ied*	try = tried

Common irregular past participles

be – been	eat – eaten	have – had	see – seen
become – become	find – found	know – known	sell – sold
buy – bought	get – gotten	make – made	take – taken
come – come	give – given	pay – paid	tell – told
do – done	go – gone	say – said	win – won

Grammar Takeaway 3

ALSO GO TO:
Unit 3 Grammar
PAGE 29

Grammar Takeaway

Past continuous

affirmative	I / He / She was sitting on the sofa last night. You / We / They were sitting on the sofa last night.	
negative	I / He / She wasn't sitting on the sofa last night. You / We / They weren't sitting on the sofa last night.	
yes / no questions and answers	Was he sitting on the sofa last night? Were they sitting on the sofa last night?	Yes, he was. / No, he wasn't. Yes, they were. / No, they weren't.
information questions and answers	Where were you sitting? What was he doing when he fell?	I was sitting on the sofa. He was walking across the bridge.

Past continuous versus simple past

We use the past continuous to describe:

- actions in progress in the past

    My sister and I were walking over an old bridge.

- a situation or scene in the past

    It wasn't snowing very hard that day.

We use the simple past to describe:

- completed actions in the past

    I fell into the water.

- states of being, such as feelings or knowledge

    He was embarrassed.
    I didn't know his name.

Grammar Takeaway

ALSO GO TO:
Unit 4 Grammar
PAGE 41

The passive voice

- We use the passive voice to emphasize the object and action. It is usually used when the person doing the action is unknown, obvious, or unimportant.

    Chocolate is made from the bean of the cacao tree. (person is unimportant)

    The mail is delivered in the morning. (no obvious person)

    My computer was stolen. (person is unknown)

- With passive forms we can use *by* + noun if we want to say who does the action.

    The picture was painted by a child.

- Passive forms are also used in written and formal English.

    The letter was sent to you on July 1. (formal, written English)

    "We sent you the letter on July 1." (informal, spoken English)

Passive forms

Sentences in the passive voice are formed using the auxiliary verb *be* + the past participle.

Passives can be used with any verb tense. The tense is indicated by the *be* verb form.

   Present: The mail is delivered every morning.

   Past: The letter was sent in July.

   Future: The post office will be closed tomorrow.

affirmative	Chocolate is made from cacao beans. Cacao beans are found in the fruit of the cacao tree.
negative	Chocolate sauce isn't made with water. Cacao trees aren't grown all over the world.

yes / no questions and answers	Is chocolate made from cacao beans?
	     Yes, it is. / No, it isn't.
	 Are cacao trees grown all over the world?
	     Yes, they are. / No, they aren't.

information questions	How is chocolate made? When was chocolate brought to Europe?

Grammar Takeaway 5

ALSO GO TO:
Unit 5 Grammar
PAGE 53

Grammar Takeaway

Object pronouns

Object pronouns are short words we use in place of object nouns.
Object nouns and pronouns receive the action of the verb.
They answer the questions "Who?" or "What?"

  I gave the man the money. (object noun—the man receives the money)
  I gave him the money. (object pronoun—*him* is used in place of *the man*. He receives the money.)

subject pronouns	I	you	she	he	it	we	you	they
object pronouns	me	you	her	him	it	us	you	them

Sentence patterns with object nouns and pronouns

Verbs that can have an object are called *transitive verbs*. All transitive verbs can follow the pattern: verb + noun + *to* / *for* + noun / pronoun.

I donated my old car to a charity.
We raised money for the charity.
She gave the food to me.

Some transitive verbs can also follow the pattern: verb + noun / pronoun + noun.

- *give, lend, pass, throw, show,* and *bring*

  Can you give me a hand?
  They lent the woman ten goats.

- verbs of communication, like *ask, tell, write,* and *read* (but not *say*)

  I asked the teacher a question.
  She read us a story.

- naming verbs like *name* and *call*

  We named our daughter Melissa.

- verbs about nominating, like *make, appoint,* and *elect*

  My boss made me sales manager.

Grammar Takeaway

ALSO GO TO:
Unit 6 Grammar
PAGE 69

Simple present versus present continuous

Use the simple present to talk about habits, routines, and facts—things that are often permanent.

Use the present continuous to talk about changing situations and developments—things that are often temporary.

simple present	present continuous
I speak a little Japanese.	I'm studying Japanese at night school.
Jill's sister lives in Italy.	Everyone is learning English these days.
I think Chinese is going to be an important language in the future.	We're thinking of having an online chat.

Stative verbs

Stative verbs (verbs that show a state, possession, thought, sense, or emotion) are not usually used in the continuous form.

These include:
be, have, own
hear, see, smell, taste
think, know, understand, believe, mean
love, like, hate, prefer, loathe

I have a car. NOT: I am having a car.
I believe you. NOT: I'm believing you.

Stative verbs like *have* and *be* can be used in the continuous in certain contexts.

She is having a difficult time.
He is being stubborn.

The verb *think* is stative when it means "believe", but not when it means "consider".

I'm thinking about studying a new language.

Say and *tell*

present	past
say	said
tell	told

Immediately after *tell*, we use an object pronoun (*me, you, her, him, it, us, them*).
 He told her that it was time to go.
 Tell them what time to be at the party.

After *say*, we don't usually use an object pronoun.
 Did you say something?
 Remember to say goodbye when you leave.

After *say*, we put *to* before the person or thing.
 That's what she said to John.

After both *say* and *tell*, we can put *that* or we can leave it out.
 He told her that it was time to go.
 He told her it was time to go.
 She said that she would do it.
 She said she would do it.

Grammar Takeaway 7

ALSO GO TO:
Unit 7 Grammar
PAGE 81

Grammar Takeaway

Verb patterns

The verbs *like, love, prefer, want,* and *hate* can all follow the pattern:

subject	verb	infinitive	adjective/noun
Some teenagers	like love prefer want hate	to be to look	cool. different.

Some teenagers like to be cool.
Some teenagers prefer to look different.
She wants to wear formal clothes.

We prefer to wear informal clothes.
They love to be well dressed.
Alex hates to look too casual.

Infinitive or verb-*ing*

- *Want* is usually followed by an infinitive.

  I want to buy some new clothes.
  Joanna wants to be fashionable.
  They want to look good.

- *Like, love, prefer,* and *hate* can be followed by verb-*ing* or infinitive.

  They don't like wearing the same clothes as their parents.
  They don't like to wear the same clothes as their parents.

  She loves wearing her big sister's clothes.
  She loves to wear her big sister's clothes.

  We prefer getting up early on the weekend.
  We prefer to get up early on the weekend.

Adjective order

When there is more than one adjective before a noun, they usually follow the order of opinion (attitude or judgment), size, age, color, type (or material) followed by the noun.

opinion	size	age	color	type	noun
pretty beautiful nice ugly	little long small short	 new old	pink gray white brown blue	leather baggy checkered striped	shoes pants t-shirt skirt tie

Grammar Takeaway

ALSO GO TO:
Unit 8 Grammar
PAGE 93

Present perfect

past ——————————(10 years ago)————————————————→ present
              I got married. I've been married for 10 years.

The present perfect is formed with the auxiliary verb *have* + past participle.

The present perfect is used to talk about:
- situations that started in the past and continue now: I've lived here for almost 10 years now.
- experiences at an indefinite time in the past: I've been to New York.

present perfect	
affirmative	I / You / We / They have lived here for 10 years. He / She has lived here for 10 years.
negative	I / You / We / They haven't lived here for 10 years. He / She hasn't lived here for 10 years.
questions	Have I / you / we / they lived here for a long time? Has he / she lived here for a long time?

For and since

for + a period of time — We've been here for 10 minutes.
since + a point in time — We've been here since 9:30.

Past perfect

past ——↑———————————————————↑—————— present
     Ed turned 18.   Ed got a job.
         Ed had turned 18 before he got a job.

The past perfect is used to talk about events and states that happened before another event in the past.

The past perfect is formed with the auxiliary verb *had* + past participle.
     I visited Mexico after I had studied Spanish. (= I studied Spanish, then I visited Mexico.)

Contractions: I had = I'd   you had = you'd   he had = he'd
                she had = she'd   we had = we'd   they had = they'd

past perfect	
affirmative	After they had turned 21, they got married.
negative	She hadn't studied English before she arrived in England.
question	What had you done before you got this job?

Grammar Takeaway 9

ALSO GO TO:
Unit 9 Grammar
PAGE 105

Grammar Takeaway

Simple past

We use the simple past to talk about:
- finished actions in the past, often with a definite time.
  I went to the beach on Saturday afternoon.
- a series of finished actions in the past.
  The kids arrived at school. The teacher read them a folktale. They begged for another one.

simple past			
affirmative	negative	question	answer
She insulted me.	She didn't insult me.	Did she insult you?	Yes, she did. / No, she didn't.

Past continuous

We use the past continuous:
- for actions in progress at a moment in the past.   The tigers were sleeping when I went to the zoo.
- in narratives to describe scenes in the past.   The swans were swimming and the monkeys were playing.

past continuous	
affirmative	negative
I / He / She was reading.	I / He / She wasn't reading.
You / We / They were reading.	You / We / They weren't reading.

questions and answers		
Was I / he / she reading?	Yes, I / he / she was.	No, I / he / she wasn't.
Were you / we / they reading?	Yes, you / we / they were.	No, you / we / they weren't.

Adverbs of manner

Adverbs of manner are used with verbs to describe *how* something happens.

They can be next to the verb or at the end of a sentence.
  He slowly opened the cage door.   OR   He opened the cage door slowly.

They cannot be placed between a verb and an object.   NOT: He opened slowly the cage door.

formation	kind	gentle	angry	shy	dramatic
	kindly	gently	angrily	shyly	dramatically

Grammar Takeaway

ALSO GO TO:
Unit 10 Grammar
PAGE 117

Imperatives

We use imperatives to give instructions, advice, or encouragement.
The imperative is the base form of the verb (the infinitive without *to*).

affirmative	negative
Put the picture here. It'll look good here. Look before you cross the street.	Don't have plants in the bedroom. Don't worry, be happy.

Advice

We use *should* + base form of the verb to give advice.

affirmative	negative	questions
She should paint this room a different color. (= It's a good idea.)	You shouldn't put the lamp so close to the TV. (= It's not a good idea.)	Should I paint the room blue? Do you think I should paint the room blue? What color do you think I should paint the room?

Possibility

We use *could* or *might* + infinitive to express possibility.

affirmative	negative	questions
Feng Shui could be affecting you. Your spirit might leave the house while you're asleep.	It might not affect everybody. NOT: It couldn't affect everybody.	Could this be the problem? Might this be the problem?

203

Grammar Takeaway

ALSO GO TO:
Unit 11 Grammar
PAGE 133

Future forms

Will + base form of the verb is used to:
- talk about a future fact or prediction.

  The weather forecast says it'll be really hot.
- write formally about the future.

  The swimmers will collect money from sponsors when they finish.

Sometimes you can use *will* or *be going to* for predictions.

I think it'll rain tonight.   OR   I think it's going to rain tonight.

Affirmative contractions: I will = I'll   he will = he'll   we will = we'll
                            you will = you'll   she will = she'll   they will = they'll

Negative contraction: will not = won't

will + base form of the verb	
affirmative	I'll / You'll / He'll / She'll / We'll / They'll live in a big house.
negative	I / You / He / She / We / They won't arrive today.
question	Will I / you / he / she / we / they call tomorrow?

Be going to + base form of the verb is used to talk about future plans.

We're going to take lots of water and a compass!

be going to + base form of the verb	
affirmative	I'm going to go swimming tonight. You're / We're / They're going to go swimming tonight. He's / She's going to go swimming tonight.
negative	I'm not going to go swimming tonight. You're / We're / They're not going to go swimming tonight. He's / She's not going to go swimming tonight.
question	Am I going to go swimming tonight? Are you / we / they going to go swimming tonight? Is he / she going to go swimming tonight?

The simple present is used to talk about scheduled events.

We leave on June 1st.

Grammar Takeaway 12

ALSO GO TO:
Unit 12 Grammar
PAGE 145

Grammar Takeaway

Modal verbs

Modal verbs are followed by the base form of a verb (except *ought*, which is followed by *to*).

They **might** be late for exercise class.

You **ought to** work out more. (ought to = should)

You **can** go to the gym Monday through Friday.

NOT: ~~You can to go to the gym Monday through Friday.~~

Do not add an *s* to a modal verb in the third person singular.

He **should** go to the doctor.

NOT: ~~He shoulds go to the doctor.~~

Modal verbs do not use the auxiliary *do* in the negative and question forms.

You **might not** have the flu.

He **wouldn't** say where it hurts.

Should I take antibiotics?

Can you tell me what to do for my cough?

NOT: ~~Do you tell me what to do for my cough?~~

Can, *could*, and *might* for possibility

can (sometimes or often true)

affirmative	negative
Exercising **can** help you lose weight.	You **can't** be 45! You look so young.
Using a keyboard **can** cause RSI.	The pain just **can't** get any worse!

might and *could* (possible)

affirmative	negative
I **might** go to the doctor tomorrow.	They **might not** go to the gym.
She **could** have asthma.	NOT: ~~They couldn't go to the gym.~~

Grammar Takeaway

ALSO GO TO:
Unit 13 Grammar
PAGE 157

Will versus would

Use *will* + verb to talk about future situations that are certain or real.
  I will stay in a hotel in Dublin.

Use *would* + verb to talk about hypothetical (not real) present or future situations.
  I would love to be a space tourist. (But I don't have the money.)

Would for hypothetical situations

Would is often used in sentences that describe hypothetical situations that depend on conditions. In these sentences, the word *if* introduces the condition.
The verb that describes the condition is in the past tense.

affirmative	negative	question
I would stay in a five-star hotel if I had more money.	I wouldn't stay in a youth hostel if I had more money.	Where would you stay if you had more money?

Contracted forms of *would*

In spoken English, *would* is often contracted.

  I'd go.
  You'd probably like it.
  He'd never do that.
  She'd come if she could.
  It'd be cold.
  We'd like to go.
  They'd prefer to go to the beach.

Grammar Takeaway

ALSO GO TO:
Unit 14 Grammar
PAGE 169

Present perfect continuous

The present perfect continuous is used to talk about present situations that started in the past and continue in the present.

I have been waiting for half an hour.
I have been waiting since 12 o'clock.

Contractions: I have = I've   he has = he's   we have = we've
               you have = you've   she has = she's   they have = they've

	present perfect continuous
affirmative	I / You / We / They have been reading. He / She has been reading.
negative	I / You / We / They haven't been reading. He / She hasn't been reading.
questions	Have I / you / we / they been reading? Has he / she been reading?
answers	Yes, I / you / we / they have. No, I / you / we / they haven't. Yes, he / she has. No, he / she hasn't.

Present perfect simple versus present perfect continuous

- The present perfect simple refers to more permanent situations.
   My parents have lived here all their lives.
- The present perfect continuous refers to more temporary actions and situations.
   I've been living in Jan's apartment for the last month.

Present perfect simple for results in the present

We also use the present perfect simple to describe completed actions in an unfinished period of time. Compare:

present perfect continuous	present perfect simple
I have been reading all afternoon. I have been writing songs since I was a teenager.	I have read 300 pages. I have written more than 500 songs.

Grammar Takeaway

ALSO GO TO:
Unit 15 Grammar
PAGE 181

Passive voice

Use the passive voice in a narrative (story) when you want to make the object of a sentence into the subject. Compare:

active voice	passive voice
Someone took John to the hotel.	John was taken to the hotel by someone.

Use the passive voice:
- when the agent (person or thing that does an action) is not known
- when the agent isn't important
- when the speaker is more interested in the object of the active sentence

agent is not known	My backpack was stolen last night.
agent is not important (the important thing is my bags!)	My bags were checked at the airport.
speaker is interested in the object (the important thing is the Inca Trail, not the people)	The Inca Trail is traveled by many people.

The passive is formed using the auxiliary verb *be* + the past participle.

present passive	A whistle is blown when a hiker is lost.
past passive	A whistle was blown by one of the climbers.

affirmative	My suitcase was checked at the airport.
negative	My suitcase was not checked at the airport.
question	Was your suitcase checked at the airport?

With passive forms, we can use *by* + noun if we want to say who does the action.
We were questioned by the immigration officer.

Irregular Verbs

Base form	Simple past
be	was / were
bring	brought
buy	bought
come	came
do	did
drink	drank
drive	drove
eat	ate
fall	fell
get	got
give	gave
go	went
hang	hung
have	had
hear	heard
know	knew
lie	lay
leave	left
make	made
meet	met
read	read
ride	rode
rise	rose
run	ran
say	said
see	saw
sell	sold
sing	sang
sit	sat
sleep	slept
speak	spoke
swim	swam
take	took
teach	taught
think	thought
wake up	woke up
wear	wore
write	wrote

Key to Phonetic Symbols

Vowels

Symbol	Sample word
/æ/	hat
/eɪ/	name
/ɑː/	father
/ɔː/	mall
/e/	get
/iː/	he
/ə/	about
/ɒ/	cross
/ɜː/	nurse
/ɪ/	gift
/aɪ/	line
/əʊ/	old
/uː/	do
/ʊ/	book
/ɔɪ/	boy
/aʊ/	town
/ʌ/	mother
/ɪə/	here
/eə/	pair
/ʊə/	tour

Consonants

Symbol	Sample word
/b/	bike
/d/	day
/dʒ/	just, age
/f/	fine
/g/	give
/h/	happy
/k/	car
/l/	let
/m/	make
/n/	no
/ŋ/	sing
/p/	pick
/r/	run
/s/	son
/ʃ/	shoe
/t/	ten
/tʃ/	watch
/θ/	thousand
/ð/	this
/v/	very
/w/	wife
/j/	yes
/z/	zero
/ʒ/	television

Vocabulary

NOTE:
The following list includes productive vocabulary in *Takeaway English 2*.

1 in 4 chance 1/4的机会
101 Dalmatians 《101只斑点狗》(电影名)

A

a couple of 几个
a feeling of admiration 崇拜感
a huge collection of 大量的收藏
a middle-aged person 中年人
a month-long trip 为期一个月的旅行
a pair of scissors 一把剪刀
a person in his/her twenties 20多岁的人
Abel Tasman University 亚伯塔斯曼大学
above / əˈbʌv / *prep.* 在……上面
accept/decline the offer 接受/拒绝请求
access / ˈækses / *n.* 进入
account for 占用
ache / eɪk / *v.* 疼痛
achieve success 取得成功;获得成功
acne / ˈækni / *n.* 痤疮; 粉刺
adapt to 使……适合
add up to 合计达
adopt / əˈdɒpt / *v.* 收养
adult / ˈædʌlt / *n.* 成年人
adventurous / ədˈventʃ(ə)rəs / *adj.* 爱冒险的
after a drawing 开奖后
aid organization 援助机构
aid / eɪd / *v.* 援助; 帮助
alternate / ˈɔːltəneɪt / *v.* 交替
aluminum / əˈluːmɪnəm / *n.* 铝
aluminum tube 铝管
amaze / əˈmeɪz / *v.* 使吃惊
amazement / əˈmeɪzm(ə)nt / *n.* 惊异
amenity / əˈmiːnɪti / *n.* 便利设施
amphibian / æmˈfɪbɪən / *n.* 两栖动物
an elderly person 上了年纪的人
an only child 独生子(女)
analyst / ˈænəlɪst / *n.* 分析师
ancient / ˈeɪnʃ(ə)nt / *adj.* 古代的

anecdote / ˈænɪkdəʊt / *n.* 趣闻; 轶事
Angola / æŋˈɡəʊlə / *n.* 安哥拉
angrily / ˈæŋɡrɪli / *adv.* 愤怒地
ankle / ˈæŋk(ə)l / *n.* 踝关节
announce / əˈnaʊns / *v.* 宣布
announcement / əˈnaʊnsm(ə)nt / *n.* 公告; 宣告
Antarctica / ænˈtɑːktɪkə / *n.* 南极洲
antibiotics / ˌæntɪbaɪˈɒtɪks / *n.* 抗生素
antioxidant / æntɪˈɒksɪd(ə)nt / *n.* 抗氧化剂
antique jewelry 古董珠宝
antonym / ˈæntəˌnɪm / *n.* 反义词
apart / əˈpɑːt / *adj.* 分离的
apartment / əˈpɑːtm(ə)nt / *n.* 公寓
apologize to sb. for sth. 为某事向某人道歉
Arabic / ˈærəbɪk / *n.* 阿拉伯语
armchair / ɑːmˈtʃeə / *n.* 扶手椅
arrange / əˈreɪn(d)ʒ / *v.* 安排
arrangement / əˈreɪn(d)ʒm(ə)nt / *n.* 安排; 布置
arthritis / ɑːˈθraɪtɪs / *n.* 关节炎
as well 也; 此外
aside from 除……以外
asthma / ˈæsmə / *n.* 哮喘
at the bottom of 在……的底部
at the reception 在接待处
average / ˈæv(ə)rɪdʒ / *adj.* 普通的; 平均的
awesomely / ˈɔːsəmli / *adv.* 棒极了
Aztec / ˈæztek / *n.* 阿兹特克人(墨西哥印第安人)

B

baby / ˈbeɪbi / *n.* 婴儿
back up 支持; 援助
backpack / ˈbækpæk / *n.* 双肩包
bacteria-free 无菌的
baggy / ˈbæɡi / *adj.* 宽松的
baggy sweater 宽松的毛衣
bake / beɪk / *v.* 烤; 烘焙
balcony / ˈbælkəni / *n.* 阳台
ban / bæn / *v.* 禁止

211

Vocabulary

ban from 禁止
base form 原形
baseball cap 棒球帽
basic / ˈbeɪsɪk / adj. 基础的
bathroom / ˈbɑːθruːm / n. 浴室
bathroom sink 浴室水槽
be a good driver 成为一位好司机
be alive 活着的; 健在的
be an adult 成人了
be apart 分别; 离别
be born 出生了
be dead 死了
be dedicated to 致力于
be divorced 离婚了
be employed 被雇佣了
be in bad shape 身材不好
be in good shape 身材很好
be in good/bad physical condition 身材状况良好/不好
be in touch 保持联系
be involved in 参与……
be jealous of 妒忌
be married 结婚了
be native to 原产于; 源于……的
be out of shape 身材走样
be pregnant 怀孕了
be sick 生病了
be similar to 类似的; 相同的
be supposed to 应该; 被期望
be thrilled with 非常兴奋; 极为激动
beach / biːtʃ / n. 海滩
beak / biːk / n. 喙
become trapped 被困住
bedside table 床头柜
beg / beg / v. 恳求
beige body 浅褐色身体
belt / belt / n. 腰带
bend over at the waist 弯腰
bend over 弯腰
bend wrists 弯手腕
Big Brothers and Big Sisters 兄姐会
big fan 铁粉
biography / baɪˈɒɡrəfi / n. 传记
black coffee 不加奶的咖啡; 清咖啡
blow / bləʊ / v. 风吹
boil / bɔɪl / v. 煮

bolded words 黑体字
boots / buːts / n. 靴子
Botswana / bɒˈtswɑːnə / n. 博茨瓦纳
Brahmin / ˈbrɑːmɪn / n. 婆罗门
brand-name clothes 品牌服装
break up 结束; 破碎
breathe / briːð / v. 呼吸
breathtaking / ˈbreθteɪkɪŋ / adj. 令人惊叹的
bright / braɪt / adj. 明亮的; 鲜艳的
Bristol / ˈbrɪstl / n. 布里斯托尔
broken / ˈbrəʊk(ə)n / adj. 破碎的; 坏掉的
broken Maori 蹩脚的毛利语
brother-in-law 姐/妹夫
brush one's hair 梳头发
buffalo / ˈbʌfələʊ / n. 水牛
bullet points 要点
bureaucracy / ˌbjʊ(ə)ˈrɒkrəsi / n. 繁文缛节
burn / bɜːn / v. 灼烧; (使)燃烧
Burundi / bʊˈruːndɪ / n. 布隆迪(非洲国家)
by hand 用手

C

cable car 缆车
cacao bean 可可豆
call the police 打电话报警
camping equipment 露营设备
camping / ˈkæmpɪŋ / n. 露营; 野营
cancer / ˈkænsə / n. 癌症
cappuccino / ˌkæpʊˈtʃiːnəʊ / n. 卡布奇诺; 热牛奶咖啡
car trunk 后备箱
caravan / ˈkærəvæn / n. (穿过沙漠地带的)旅行队
caravans of camels 骆驼商队
CARE 美国援外合作署
Cary Grant 加里·格兰特(美国演员)
cast...aside 把……丢在一边
casual / ˈkæʒjʊəl / adj. 非正式的
casual clothes 休闲装
cater to 满足……口味
cause / kɔːz / n. 原因
ceiling / ˈsiːlɪŋ / n. 天花板
certificate / səˈtɪfɪkət / n. 证书
charitable organization 慈善组织
charity / ˈtʃærɪti / n. 慈善
chat with an e-pal 和网友聊天
checkered / ˈtʃekəd / adj. 有方格的

Vocabulary

cheek / tʃiːk / n. 面颊
chest / tʃest / n. 胸部
chin / tʃɪn / n. 下巴
chocolate chip cookies 碎粒巧克力饼干
chocolate shake 巧克力奶昔
Christopher Columbus 克利斯多弗·哥伦布
church / tʃɜːtʃ / n. 教堂
churn / tʃɜːn / v. 翻滚；搅动
cinnamon / 'sɪnəmən / n. 肉桂
civil war 内战
civilization / ˌsɪvɪlaɪ'zeɪʃən / n. 文明
classify / 'klæsɪfaɪ / v. 分类
clean up 清理；大捞一笔
clearly / 'klɪəlɪ / adv. 清晰地
clover / 'kləʊvə / n. 三叶草
coffee table 咖啡台
coin / kɒɪn / n. 硬币；钱币
cold-blooded 冷血的
cold-blooded animal 冷血动物
collecting fever 收集热潮
colonize / 'kɒlənaɪz / v. 开拓领地
come to no good 失败；没有好结果
come to one's mind （突然）想起
commit crimes 犯罪；做坏事
common stimulant 常见刺激物
compass / 'kʌmpəs / n. 指南针
complain / kəm'pleɪn / v. 抱怨
conceal the truth 隐瞒真相
conduct survey 展开调查
conduct trade 做生意
connecting words 连接词
constant fear 持续的恐惧
continuously / kən'tɪnjʊəslɪ / adv. 连续地
Cooperative for American Relief to Everywhere 美国援外合作署
cope with 处理；应付
cosmonaut / 'kɒzmənɔːt / n. (俄)航天员(相当于astronaut)
cosmopolitan / ˌkɒzmə'pɒlɪt(ə)n / adj. 世界性的
cough / kɒf / n. 咳嗽 v. 咳嗽
count sb. in 算上某人
cracker / 'krækə / n. 饼干
crash into 撞到……上；闯入
cream / kriːm / n. 奶油
cruise / kruːz / n. 乘船游览
cultural traditions 文化传统

cut off 砍下；切断
cut / kʌt / v. 切
cutlery / 'kʌtlərɪ / n. 餐具

D

Dalmatian 达尔马提亚狗
daughter-in-law 儿媳妇
David Livingstone 戴维·利文斯通
Daylight Savings Time 夏时制
deadly / 'dedlɪ / adj. 致命的
deal with 涉及；处理
deck chair 躺椅
denim / 'denɪm / n. 斜纹粗棉布
denim jeans 斜纹布料的牛仔裤
desert / 'dezət / n. 沙漠
dessert recipe 甜点食谱
destination / ˌdestɪ'neɪʃ(ə)n / n. 目的地
detect / dɪ'tekt / v. 探测
diagonally / daɪ'æg(ə)nəlɪ / adv. 斜对地；对角地
dining room 餐厅
disabled / dɪs'eɪbld / adj. 残废的；有缺陷的
disappear / dɪsə'pɪə / v. 消失
discotheque / 'dɪskətek / n. 迪斯科舞厅
discover / dɪ'skʌvə / v. 发现；发觉
discovery / dɪ'skʌv(ə)rɪ / n. 发现
disease / dɪ'ziːz / n. 疾病
disguise oneself as 把某人伪装成……
do the backstroke 仰泳
do the illustrations 插图
Doctors Without Borders 无国界医生组织
do puzzles 玩拼图游戏
do Sudoku 玩数独游戏
donate / də(ʊ)'neɪt / v. 捐赠
donate (money) 捐款
donkey ride 骑驴
dress / dres / n. 连衣裙
dress smart 着装体面
dresser / 'dresə / n. 梳妆台
dressing room 更衣室；化妆室
drive through 开车穿过
driver's license 驾照

E

eagle / 'iːg(ə)l / n. 鹰
Earl Grey 伯爵茶

Vocabulary

earthquake / 'ɜːθkweɪk / n. 地震
East Harlem 东哈莱姆市
Egypt / 'iːdʒɪpt / n. 埃及
elbow / 'elbəʊ / n. 肘
elderly / 'eldəlɪ / adj. 上了年纪的
electronics equipment 电子设备
elementary level 初级阶段
Elvis / 'elvɪs / n. 埃尔维斯(猫王，美国著名摇滚明星)
embroider / ɪm'brɔɪdə / v. 刺绣；镶边
emergency / ɪ'mɜːdʒ(ə)nsɪ / n. 紧急情况
emergency provider 急救人员
epidemic of smallpox 天花的流行
equipment / ɪ'kwɪpm(ə)nt / n. 设备
Escargot City 蜗牛城
espresso / e'spresəʊ / n. 意大利式黑咖啡(用蒸汽加压煮出的)
essentials / ɪ'senʃəls / n. 必需品
event / ɪ'vent / n. 活动；项目
exactly / ɪɡ'zæk(t)lɪ / adv. 恰好地；正是
excite / ɪk'saɪt / v. 激起；刺激……
excitement / ɪk'saɪtmənt / n. 兴奋；刺激
exclamation points 感叹号
excursion / ɪk'skɜːʃ(ə)n / n. 短程旅行
exist / ɪɡ'zɪst / v. 存在
existence / ɪɡ'zɪst(ə)ns / n. 存在；生存
expanse / ɪk'spæns / n. 广阔
expedition / ekspɪ'dɪʃ(ə)n / n. 探险；探险队
explorer / ek'splɔːrə(r) / n. 探险家
extended family 大家庭
extra large 特大号
extra small 特小号

F

fable / 'feɪb(ə)l / n. 寓言；童話
facial expression 面部表情
faded / 'feɪdɪd / adj. 已褪色的
fairy tale 童话；神话故事
fall asleep 入睡；睡着
fall down 跌倒
fall in 跌入；投进
fall in love with 爱上
fall off 跌落
fall out of 从……掉出来
fall over 倒下；跌倒
family reunion 家庭团聚

fantasy / 'fæntəsɪ / n. 梦幻；奇幻
faraway kingdoms 遥远的王国
fashionable / 'fæʃ(ə)nəb(ə)l / adj. 流行的；时髦的
fashionista / 'fæʃənɪstə / n. 赶时髦的人
feather / 'feðə / n. 羽毛
feature / 'fiːtʃə / n. 特征
feel alone 感到孤独
feel like 感觉像是……
feel scared 感到害怕
ferocity / fə'rɒsɪtɪ / n. 凶猛；残忍
fever / 'fiːvə / n. 发烧
fierce / fɪəs / adj. 凶猛的
find out 找出
fire department 消防队
first aid kit 急救药箱
five-star hotel 五星级饭店
flea market 跳蚤市场
float up 飘起來
flood / flʌd / n. 洪水
floor plan 平面图
flu / fluː / n. 流感
fluent / 'fluːənt / adj. 流利的
fluently / 'fluːəntlɪ / adv. 流利地
fluid / 'fluːɪd / n. 流质；液体
flying high career 职位高升
focus on 集中(注意力、精力等)
folktale / 'fəʊkteɪl / n. 民间故事
for rent 供出租
for sure 肯定
four-leaf clover 四叶草；幸运草
Fred Flintstone 弗雷德·弗林斯特
free from 使摆脱；免于
frog / frɒɡ / n. 青蛙
fry / fraɪ / v. 油炸；油煎
furniture / 'fɜːnɪtʃə / n. 家具

G

generous / 'dʒen(ə)rəs / adj. 慷慨的
geographical features 地理特征
German / 'dʒɜːmən / n. 德语
Germany / 'dʒɜːmənɪ / n. 德国
get a driver's license 拿到驾照
get a flat tire 轮胎没气
get a job 找到工作
get better 变得更好

get by in 过得去
get dark 变黑
get/be divorced 离婚
get engaged 订婚
get ignored 被忽视
get in touch 取得联系
get in trouble 遇到麻烦
get lost 迷路
get/be pregnant 怀孕
get rich 变得富有
get scratched 有刮痕
get sick 生病
get the promotion 提拔；升职
get tired of 厌烦；对……感到厌倦
get worse 变糟
give aid 提供帮助
give sb. a hand 给予某人帮助
give up 放弃
go back 返回
go into space 去太空
go out of style 过时
go out 熄灭
go running 跑步
go trekking 长途跋涉
gold diggers 淘金者
gondola / 'gɒndələ / n. 长平底船
Grand Canyon （美）大峡谷
grandson / 'græn(d)sʌn / n. 孙子/外孙
gravity / 'grævɪtɪ / n. 重力；地心引力
guest / gest / n. 客人；宾客

H

hand down 传递
hang down 垂下
happen to sb. 某人发生……
have a charity event 办一个慈善活动
have a sore neck 脖子痛
have a winning ticket 中奖
have an effect on 对……有影响；对……起作用
have an online chat 在线聊天
have... in common 在……有共同之处
have no access to 无法得到
have the flu 得了流感
headache / 'hedeɪk / n. 头痛
health advice column 健康指导专栏
health issues 健康问题
heart attack 心脏病；心脏病发作
heat / hiːt / v. 加热
heel / hiːl / n. 脚后跟
herbal / 'hɜːb(ə)l / adj. 草药的
herbal tea 花草茶
hike / haɪk / v. 徒步旅行
hiking boots 登山鞋；旅行靴
Hilton / 'hɪltən / n. 希尔顿
hip / hɪp / n. 臀部
historical events 历史事件
hit the road 出发
hold hands 手拉手
hold the position 保持这种姿势
homeless / 'həʊmlɪs / adj. 无家可归的 n. 无家可归的人
honey / 'hʌnɪ / n. 蜂蜜
horseback riding 骑马
horseshoe / 'hɔːsʃuː / n. 马蹄铁
hospitable / hɒ'spɪtəb(ə)l / adj. 热情友好的
hot chocolate 热巧克力
hot climates 热带
house insulation 房屋隔热
housebound / 'haʊsbaʊnd / adj. 不能离家外出的
hunger / 'hʌŋgə / n. 饥饿
hungry / 'hʌŋgrɪ / adj. 饥饿的
hypothetical situation 假设情况

I

ice-cold 冰冷的
iguana / ɪ'gwɑːnə / n. 蜥蜴
imagination / ɪˌmædʒɪ'neɪʃ(ə)n / n. 想象力
imagine / ɪ'mædʒɪn / v. 想像；猜想
improve / ɪm'pruːv / v. 改善
improvement / ɪm'pruːvm(ə)nt / n. 改善
in a backpack 背包里面
in a coma 陷于昏迷状态
in a long time 长时间
in advance 率先；预先
in bold 黑体；粗体
in favor of 赞同；支持
in great shape 身材很棒
in need 在困难时；在灾难中
in part 在某种程度上
in the brochure 小册子里的
in theory 理论上

Vocabulary

in your lifetime 在你的有生之年
incredible expense 巨额的花销
informal *adj.* 非正式的
injury / 'ɪn(d)ʒ(ə)rɪ / *n.* 伤
instant message 即时信息
intensive course 精读课程
interior / ɪn'tɪə:rɪə / *n.* 内部
island / 'aɪlənd / *n.* 岛；岛屿

J

jackal / 'dʒækəl / *n.* 豺
jacket / 'dʒækɪt / *n.* 夹克
jeans / dʒi:nz / *n.* 牛仔裤
jet lag 时差反应
journey / 'dʒɜ:nɪ / *n.* 旅行；行程
jump out of 跳出
just after 刚在……以后
just before 刚在……之前

K

Kalahari Desert 卡拉哈里沙漠
karate / kə'rɑ:tɪ / *n.* 空手道
keep an eye on 照看；留意
keep one's promise 守信
keep warm 保温
kitchen / 'kɪtʃɪn / *n.* 厨房
kitchen sink 厨房洗涤池
knee / ni: / *n.* 膝盖
knee-length hair 长及膝部的头发

L

labor pain 分娩时的阵痛
ladder / 'lædə / *n.* 梯子；阶梯
lake / leɪk / *n.* 湖
lamp / læmp / *n.* 灯
landing / 'lændɪŋ / *n.* 登陆；着陆
large pumpkin 大南瓜
lay / leɪ / *v.* 产卵；下蛋
lay eyes on 看到
lay out 列出
lean on 倚；靠
leather / 'leðə / *adj.* 皮革的
leave behind 留下；遗落
left over 剩余的
lemon juice 柠檬汁

lend / lend / *v.* 贷；把……借给
less likely 可能性小
lethargic / lɪ'θɑ:dʒɪk / *adj.* 无精打采的；昏睡的
Leukemia Foundation 白血病基金会
Levi Strauss 李维斯·史特劳斯（Levi's 的创始人）
Lhasa / 'lɑ:sə / *n.* 拉萨
lifetime / 'laɪftaɪm / *n.* 终生；一生
light / laɪt / *v.* 点燃
light bulb 电灯泡
lightweight / 'laɪtweɪt / *adj.* 重量轻的
live music and dancing 现场歌舞表演
living room 起居室
logo / 'lɒgəʊ / *n.* 商标
look up 查找
lottery / 'lɒt(ə)rɪ / *n.* 彩票
lottery ticket 彩票；奖券
loudly / 'laʊdlɪ / *adv.* 大声地；响亮地
low education level 文化程度低
lower / 'ləʊə / *v.* 减轻
luckily / 'lʌkɪlɪ / *adv.* 幸运地
lunar / 'lu:nə / *adj.* 月球的

M

Machu Picchu 马丘比丘（古城，位于秘鲁中部偏南）
maiden name （女子的）婚前姓
main course 主菜
Main Street 大街
make a big difference 有很大影响；意义重大
make a donation 捐赠
make an agreement 达成协议；达成共识
make an offer 提出要求
make into movies 拍成电影
make reservations 预订
make wig 做假发
Malaysian-style satay 马来西亚风味沙嗲
mammal / 'mæm(ə)l / *n.* 哺乳动物
mango / 'mæŋgəʊ / *n.* 芒果
Manhattan Island 曼哈顿岛
manure / mə'njʊə / *n.* 肥料；粪肥
Marco Polo 马可·波罗
marinated / 'mærɪneɪtɪd / *adj.* 酱卤的
match up with 和……相配
Meals on Wheels 上门送餐服务
medical care 医疗护理
medical professionals 医学专家

medium / 'miːdɪəm / *n.* 中号
medium sweet 中等甜度
Mercedes Benz 梅赛德斯·奔驰
merchant / 'mɜːtʃ(ə)nt / *n.* 商人
Mesoamerica / ˌmesəʊə'merɪkə / *n.* 中美洲
Mesopotamia / ˌmesəpə'teɪmɪə / *n.* 美索不达米亚
microwave oven 微波炉
mild / maɪld / *adj.* 温和的
mirror / 'mɪrər / *n.* 镜子
mission commander 任务指挥官
missionary / 'mɪʃ(ə)n(ə)rɪ / *n.* 传教士
mix / mɪks / *v.* 配制; 使混和
mocha latte 摩卡拿铁
model airplane 模型飞机
musical procession 音乐队伍

N

native friend 当地朋友
native language 方言
natural disasters 自然灾害
natural light 自然光
natural resources 自然资源
naturally / 'nætʃ(ə)rəlɪ / *adv.* 自然地
neck / nek / *n.* 脖子
neighborhood / 'neɪbəˌhʊd / *n.* 邻居
neither...nor... 既不……也不
Nepal / nɪ'pɔːl / *n.* 尼泊尔
nervously / 'nɜːvəslɪ / *adv.* 紧张地
New Hampshire 新罕布什尔(美国州名)
new-fangled 新奇的
newlywed / 'njuːlɪwed / *n.* 新婚夫妇
next to 在……旁边
Nile River cruise 尼罗河邮轮
no word from home 没收到家信
nod / nɒd / *v.* 点头
normally / 'nɔːm(ə)lɪ / *adv.* 通常地
nose pain 鼻子酸痛
not quite 不完全地
nothing more than 仅仅; 只不过
nuclear family 小家庭
nut / nʌt / *n.* 坚果

O

object pronouns 人称代词宾格
ocean / 'əʊʃ(ə)n / *n.* 海洋

offer shade and shelter 遮阴和庇护
on a date 约会
on average 平均
on the ferry 乘渡船
on the ground 在地面上
on the tenth floor 在10楼
on the weekend 周末
on top of 在……顶上
on vacation 度假
orange juice 橘汁
orbiting / 'ɔːbɪtɪŋ / *adj.* 轨道式的; 盘旋式的
organization / ˌɔːgənaɪ'zeɪʃn / *n.* 组织
orphan / 'ɔːf(ə)n / *n.* 孤儿
orphaned / 'ɔːfənd / *adj.* 失去双亲的
ounce / aʊns / *n.* 盎司
Oxfam (Oxford Committee for Famine Relief) 牛津饥荒救济委员会

P

painkiller / 'peɪnkɪlə / *n.* 止痛药
palm / pɑːm / *n.* 手掌
pan / pæn / *n.* 平底锅
pants / pæn(t)s / *n.* 裤子
parachute jump 跳伞
part of speech 词性
participate in 参加; 参与
passenger / 'pæsɪndʒə / *n.* 旅客
permanent / 'pɜːm(ə)nənt / *adj.* 永久的
permanent station 永久空间站
pet rabbit 家兔
physical condition 身体状况
physically fit 体格健康
pick up 不费力地学会
pickled dish 腌菜
pilgrimage / 'pɪlgrɪmɪdʒ / *n.* 朝圣
pill / pɪl / *n.* 药丸
plain / pleɪn / *adj.* 朴素的; 简单的
plastic sandals 塑料凉鞋
plots of land 地块
pneumonia / njuː'məʊnɪə / *n.* 肺炎
pole / pəʊl / *n.* 极地
Portuguese explorers 葡萄牙探险家
Portuguese / ˌpɔːtjʊ'giːz / *n.* 葡萄牙语
pot / pɒt / *n.* 壶; 盆
pounce on 猛扑向; 突然袭击

Vocabulary

pour / pɔː(r) / v. 倾泻; 流出
precisely / prɪˈsaɪslɪ / adv. 精确地; 恰恰
prefer / prɪˈfɜː / v. 更喜欢; 宁愿
preference / ˈpref(ə)r(ə)ns / n. 偏爱
promise / ˈprɒmɪs / v. 许诺
pros and cons 利与弊; 支持与反对
proudly / ˈpraʊdlɪ / adv. 傲慢地; 自负地
provide sb. with sth. 为某人提供……
push-up 俯卧撑
put art on the walls 在墙上来点艺术
put on one's make-up 上妆
put on 穿上
put out 把……放好备用
put the tents up 搭帐篷

Q

quietly / ˈkwaɪətlɪ / adv. 安静地

R

raise / reɪz / v. 举起; 养育
raise money 募资
read over 仔细阅读; 再读一遍
recommendation / ˌrekəmenˈdeɪʃ(ə)n / n. 建议
recover / rɪˈkʌvə / v. 恢复
rectangular / rekˈtæŋɡjʊlə / adj. 矩形的
recycling / riːˈsaɪklɪŋ / v. (资源、垃圾等) 回收利用
refer to 指的是
refrigerator / rɪˈfrɪdʒəreɪtə / n. 冰箱
refuge / ˈrefjuːdʒ / n. 收容所
region / ˈriːdʒ(ə)n / n. 地区
relate to 涉及; 有关
religious ceremonies 宗教仪式
remarry / ˌriːˈmærɪ / v. 再婚
rent / rent / v. 出租
reply / rɪˈplaɪ / v. 回答
reptile / ˈreptaɪl / n. 爬行动物
rescue from 抢救; 营救
resort / rɪˈzɔːt / n. 度假胜地
ride a skateboard 滑滑板
rock band 摇滚乐团
role models 榜样
rollerblade / ˈrəʊləbleɪd / v. 滑旱冰
roughly / ˈrʌflɪ / adv. 大概
route / ruːt / n. 路线; 航线
PSI 重复性劳损

rug / rʌg / n. 地毯
run a lab 开实验室
run across 跑着穿过
run into 偶遇
runny / ˈrʌnɪ / adj. 流鼻涕的
runny nose 流鼻涕
Russia / ˈrʌʃə / n. 俄罗斯
Russian / ˈrʌʃ(ə)n / n. 俄语

S

sail / seɪl / v. 航行
salmon / ˈsæmən / n. 鲑鱼
sandstorm / ˈsæn(d)stɔːm / n. 沙尘暴
sauce / sɔːs / n. 汁/酱
scenery / ˈsiːn(ə)rɪ / n. 风景
scientific basis 科学基础
Scottish missionary 苏格兰传教士
scratch off 擦去; 刮掉
scuba diving 深水潜水
second-hand clothes 二手衣服
selfish / ˈselfɪʃ / adj. 自私的
selfishly / ˈselfɪʃlɪ / adv. 自私地
sensational / senˈseɪʃ(ə)n(ə)l / adj. 耸人听闻的
service trip 服务旅行
set off 出发
set out 出发; 动身
set sail 起航
settle down 定居
sewing kit 针线包
shake / ʃeɪk / v. 摇动
shelves / ʃelvz / n. 架子
shiny / ˈʃaɪnɪ / adj. 闪耀的
shirt / ʃɜːt / n. 衬衫;汗衫
shooting star 流星
shorts / ʃɔːts / n. 短裤
shoulder / ˈʃəʊldə / n. 肩膀
shower / ˈʃaʊə / n. 淋浴
shredded / ʃredɪd / adj. 切碎的
shredded pork 肉丝
sickness / ˈsɪknɪs / n. 疾病
sightseeing / ˈsaɪtsiːɪŋ / n. 观光
sign up 签定
silk / sɪlk / n. 丝绸
single parent family 单亲家庭
sit-up 仰卧起坐

Vocabulary

size / saɪz / n. 尺寸
slang / slæŋ / n. 俚语
slang words 俚语
sleeping bag 睡袋
sleeping pad 睡垫
slip on 滑倒
smartphone 智能手机
snail / sneɪl / n. 蜗牛
sneakers / 'sniːkəz / n. 球鞋；运动鞋
social class 社会地位
SoHo / 'səʊhəʊ / n. 索霍区(伦敦一地区)
solar panel 太阳能电池板
solar system 太阳系
some pieces of paper 几张纸
sore / sɔː / adj. 疼痛的
sore throat 嗓子痛
source / sɔːs / n. 水源
souvenir teaspoon 纪念品茶匙
space expedition 太空探险
space race 太空竞赛
spacecraft / 'speɪskrɑːft / n. 宇宙飞船
Spanish / 'spænɪʃ / n. 西班牙语
spare tire 备胎
spicy / 'spaɪsi / adj. 辛辣的
spicy food 辣的食物
sponsor / 'spɒnsə / n. 赞助商 v. 赞助；发起
sponsored event 赞助活动
sports memorabilia 体育纪念品
spread out 分散
spring break 春假
staatsloterij 国家彩票
stay in shape 保持身材
stir / stɜː / v. 搅拌
stomachache / 'stʌməkeɪk / n. 肚子痛；胃痛
storm / stɔːm / n. 暴风雨
stove / stəʊv / n. 烤炉/箱
straight and flat 平直的
stray dogs 流浪狗
stretch / stretʃ / v. 伸展
stretching exercises 伸展运动
striped / straɪpt / adj. 有条纹的
striped sweatshirt 条纹运动衫
stroll by 漫步于……
strong accent 很重的口音
strong coffee 浓咖啡

stubbornly / 'stʌbənlɪ / adv. 顽固地；倔强地
stuck / stʌk / v. 被堵住
stuffed animal 填充动物玩具
subject pronouns 人称代词主格
substitute words 代词
suck out of 从……中吸出
suffer from 忍受；遭受
suit / suːt / n. 西服
surviving / sə'vaɪvɪŋ / adj. 健在的
swan / swɒn / n. 天鹅
sweatpants / 'swetpænts / n. (美)宽松长运动裤
sweatshirt / 'swetʃɜːt / n. 运动衫
sweep up 扫除；打扫
symptom / 'sɪm(p)təm / n. 症状
synonym / 'sɪnənɪm / n. 同义词

T

tablespoon / 'teɪb(ə)lspuːn / n. 调羹；汤匙
take a cruise 乘坐邮轮
take a photo 拍照
take advantage of 利用
take care of 照顾；抚养
take no notice 不理会；没注意
take off 卸下；拿掉
take the place of 代替；取代
Tanzania / ˌtænzə'niːə / n. 坦桑尼亚
teenager / 'tiːneɪdʒə / n. 青少年
tent / tent / n. 帐篷
text messaging 手机短信息发送
the African interior 非洲内部
the average person 一般人
the distant past 远古
the holy city of Mecca 麦加圣城
the imperative 祈使句
the Inca Trail 印加古道
the laws of the jungle 丛林法则
the Mabotsa Valley 玛波塔撒山谷
the Nile River 尼罗河
the pill of immortality 长生不老药
the Potala Palace 布达拉宫(拉萨)
the rescue center 救护中心
the science fair 科学博览会
the shakes 混合饮料
The Simpsons 《辛普森一家》(美国动画片)
the Statue of Liberty 自由女神像

Vocabulary

the theory of relativity 相对论
three times a week 一周三次
thumb / θʌm / n. 拇指
Tibet / tɪ'bet / n. 西藏
tie / taɪ / n. 领带
tight / taɪt / adj. 紧的
time flies 时光飞逝
toddler / 'tɒdlə / n. 学步的小孩
toe / təʊ / n. 脚指
toilet / 'tɔɪlɪt / n. 厕所
top floor 顶楼
tortoise / 'tɔːtəs / n. 乌龟
tough / tʌf / adj. 牢固的; 结实的
tourist / 'tʊərɪst / n. 旅行者
toy giraffe 长颈鹿玩具
traffic jam 交通阻塞
trail / treɪl / n. 小径
train / treɪn / v. 训练
trans-Siberian 穿越西伯利亚的
travel overland 走陆路
trek / trek / n. 艰苦跋涉
trend / trend / n. 趋势
trendy / 'trendɪ / adj. 时髦的; 流行的
trendy clothes 流行服饰
trip over 被……绊倒
tropical diseases 热带病
tube / tjuːb / n. 管
tuna / 'tjuːnə / n. 金枪鱼
turn 18 18岁了
twice as much time as 两倍的时间
typical dishes 特别的菜肴

U

unexploded land mines 未爆破的地雷
ungrateful /ʌn'greɪtfʊl / adj. 忘恩负义的
up to 忙于……; 在做……
urban legend 都市传奇
used to 过去常常

V

Valentine's Day 情人节(圣瓦伦丁节)
valley / 'vælɪ / n. 山谷
Venetian gondolas 威尼斯贡多拉游船
view / vjuː / n. 景色
violent / 'vaɪəl(ə)nt / adj. 暴力的

volunteer / ˌvɒlən'tɪə / n. 志愿者

W

wait in line 排队等候
wait up for (为……而)熬夜等候
walk / wɔːk / n. 步行
warm-blooded 温血的
warm-blooded animal 温血动物
war-torn areas 遭受战争破坏的地区
watch / wɒtʃ / n. 手表
water filter 滤水器
waterproof / 'wɔːtəpruːf / adj. 防水的
waterproof jacket 防水夹克
weak / wiːk / adj. 虚弱的
wear a kilt 穿苏格兰裙
wedding cake 结婚蛋糕; 喜饼
well-paid job 高薪工作
What a bummer! 真糟糕! 真扫兴!
What's new? 有什么好事?
whistle / 'wɪs(ə)l / n. 口哨
white cheese with nuts 带坚果的白奶酪
win first prize 获得一等奖
winning lottery ticket 中奖彩票
wonder / 'wʌndə / n. 奇迹; 惊奇
work out 锻炼
wrist / rɪst / n. 手腕
write a survey report 撰写调查报告

X

X-files 《X档案》(美剧)

Z

Zambia / 'zæmbɪə / n. 赞比亚

Audioscript

Unit 1 Good luck, bad luck

Page 3, Exercise 2 01_02

Reporter: I'm here talking to Bill Morgan, an engineer from Chicago. His amazing story started earlier this year when he had a heart attack. Bill, how are you feeling?
Bill: I'm feeling great!
Reporter: But things were pretty bad just a few months ago.
Bill: That's right! I had a heart attack when I was only 30 years old. In fact, I nearly died. I was in a coma for several days. The doctors didn't think I was going to live. But to everyone's surprise, I suddenly woke up 12 days later.
Reporter: And how did you feel?
Bill: Amazingly, I felt great. I just wanted to get back to work. Fortunately, I got my old job back, so that was good.
Reporter: And then you got engaged.
Bill: That's right. A few days after I got out of the hospital, I decided to ask my girlfriend to marry me... and she said yes!
Reporter: And things just got better and better.
Bill: That's right. About two weeks later, I bought a lottery ticket from the local convenience store. It was the last ticket in the store. You can imagine my surprise when I saw that I was the winner of a $35,000 car!
Reporter: Wow! That's great! Did you need a new car?
Bill: Actually, I did!
Reporter: But your luck didn't stop there.
Bill: No. Some reporters came to interview me. They wanted me to buy another ticket, so they could take my picture next to the new car. So I bought another one. I scratched it off, and it was the winning ticket!
Reporter: Wow! That's amazing!
Bill: I know! It was so amazing that the reporters didn't believe me!
Reporter: What did you do?
Bill: I shouted, "I won $100,000!" And then I started crying.
Reporter: Well, Bill, that really is an amazing story. Are you sure it's true?
Bill: It's true, all right. Every word.

Page 10, Exercises 2 and 3 01_09

Maya: Hey, Kate! I haven't seen you in a long time. How are you?
Kate: Hi, Maya! Oh, things aren't too bad.
Maya: What's new?
Kate: Well, I'm getting married next month.
Maya: You are? Congratulations! Who's the lucky guy?
Kate: His name is Nick. His grandfather's a millionaire.
Maya: That's amazing!
Kate: Yes, but unfortunately he died last week.
Maya: Wow. That's really a shame.
Kate: Yes, it is. He lived a long life, but we're still very sad. So, what's new with you?
Maya: Not much. I just found out that I didn't get the promotion I wanted at work.
Kate: Oh... That's too bad.
Maya: Thank you. And I've been sick all week.
Kate: Really? I'm sorry to hear that. I hope you get well soon.
Maya: Thanks. But the good news is that I just bought a lottery ticket and I won $500!
Kate: Really? That's great news!
Maya: Thanks! Now I'm going to get a new TV with the money!

Unit 2 My favorite things

Page 15, Exercises 2 and 3 02_02

Nancy: Do you collect anything as a hobby, Greg?
Greg: Yes, I do. I have a large collection of t-shirts. Um... they're all rock band t-shirts. I'm really into music, so all of the t-shirts are of different bands that I like.
Nancy: So, how many rock band t-shirts do you have?
Greg: I'm not sure. I think I have about 215.
Nancy: That's so cool!
Greg: Yeah, thanks. I had more, but I lost some when I was on vacation.
Nancy: Oh, no! What a bummer! Well, at least you still have the rest of them. And where do you keep them all?
Greg: In the closet in my bedroom. I have a big closet! They're organized by color, and I wear a different one every day.
Nancy: No way! How long have you collected them?
Greg: Let's see... I've collected them since I was in high school.
Nancy: Have you seen all of the bands play in concert?
Greg: No, I haven't. But I've seen a lot of them. How about you? Do you have a collection?
Nancy: Well, yes, I do!
Greg: Wait! Let me guess...Hello Kitty.
Nancy: No! My sister collects Hello Kitty. I have a cool collection of sunglasses. I think I have about 80 pairs.

Audioscript

Greg: Wow! That's awesome! And how long have you collected them?

Nancy: Oh, I've collected them for years. My cousin gave me a pair of pink sunglasses for my 6th birthday and I've loved them ever since! But I don't wear them every day—only on special occasions. I don't want them to get broken or scratched. Last year I wore my favorite pair to school one day, and they got scratched.

Greg: Oh! That's too bad!

Page 22, Exercise 1 and 2 [02_09]

Tara: Hey, Pete. What kinds of things are you interested in?

Pete: Well, I'm really into music.

Tara: What kind of music do you like?

Pete: Well, my favorite singer is Elvis. In fact, I'm an avid collector of Elvis memorabilia.

Tara: Really? What kinds of thing?

Pete: Oh, you know, t-shirts, clocks, pens, mirrors... you name it!

Tara: Wow! That's so cool!

Pete: What about you? What kinds of things do you like?

Tara: I'm a really big fan of music too.

Pete: Really? What kind of music?

Tara: Actually, I like all kinds of music. I'm very interested in musical instruments, especially guitars. In fact, I collect guitars as a hobby.

Pete: That's awesome! How did you get interested in guitars?

Tara: Let's see... I fell in love with guitars after seeing my first rock concert... And I have been hooked ever since!

Unit 3   Memorable experiences

Page 27, Exercises 3 and 4 [03_02]

Ava: So, Tim, tell me about one of your childhood memories—something that happened to you that you will always remember.

Tim: Let's see... well, I remember something that happened to me when I was about four years old.

Ava: Oh yeah? What happened?

Tim: Well, it was in the summer. I was walking with my sister over an old bridge that crosses a river near our house. The rail on the bridge was broken, and I wasn't watching where I was going.

Ava: Uh-oh. I think I know what happened next.

Tim: Yes, you can probably guess. I fell off the bridge into the river.

Ava: Oh, no! Then what happened?

Tim: Not too much more. But I remember I was wearing red plastic sandals. And I remember that I saw these red plastic sandals and the blue sky, you know, as I was falling.

Ava: Were you scared?

Tim: No, just surprised, I think. And my sister didn't see me fall! She continued walking over the bridge and talking to me! Luckily, there were some people swimming in the river. They saw me fall in and rescued me.

Ava: That was lucky!

Page 34, Exercise 2 and 3 [03_08]

Ron: Hey, Jen. What did you do last weekend?

Jen: Well, most of the weekend was boring, but there was a terrible accident on Sunday!

Ron: Really? What happened?

Jen: Well, Tim and I were walking over the old bridge, and he fell off it!

Ron: Really? That's terrible! How did it happen?

Jen: Well, he wasn't paying attention. He was leaning on a rail, and it broke!

Ron: Oh, no! Is he OK?

Jen: Yes, he's fine. There were some people swimming in the river and they helped him.

Ron: Wow! He really got lucky!

Jen: Yes, he did! But he wasn't so lucky when we got home.

Ron: Really? What happened?

Jen: Well, my mom wasn't very happy when she found out why he was wet. So he got in trouble. He's not allowed to watch TV for a week!

Ron: Oh, no! Poor Tim!

Unit 4   I love chocolate!

Page 39, Exercises 3 and 4 [04_02]

Monica: Hey, Brandon. Can I ask you a favor?

Brandon: Sure. No problem.

Monica: Thanks! I'm having some friends over for dinner and ...

Brandon: ...you don't know what to cook?

Monica: Yeah! Well, actually, I know what I'm making for the appetizer and main course. It's the dessert I need ideas for. I want to make something delicious, but easy. You always have such good ideas!

Brandon: Well, how about making chocolate sauce? It's easy and cheap. And you can serve it with ice cream or fruit.

Monica: That sounds perfect. Can you tell me how to make it?

Brandon: OK. You need 4 ounces of chocolate.

Monica:	What kind of chocolate?
Brandon:	Baker's chocolate. You can find it at the supermarket. It's made with less sugar than regular chocolate.
Monica:	OK. What else? Water?
Brandon:	No! Chocolate sauce isn't made with water! You need half a cup of cream, half a cup of milk, and a teaspoon of honey. Cut the chocolate into small pieces, and put it in a pan. Pour in the other ingredients and heat gently. Make sure it doesn't boil or it will be ruined.
Monica:	OK. That sounds easy.
Brandon:	Yes. It's really easy. Remember to stir the mixture until it's smooth. Then when it's ready, it can be served on ice cream or fruit—or both. It's really good.
Monica:	Yeah, it sounds delicious! Thanks!

Page 46, Exercise 2 and 3 [04_08]

Conversation 1

Rob:	It's my birthday. Would you like a chocolate?
Sara:	Yes, please. I'll have that one—the square one.
Rob:	But that's my favorite!

Conversation 2

Don:	Oh…I don't have any water.
Tim:	Here, have some of mine.
Don:	Thanks very much.

Conversation 3

Josh:	I'm going to the store. Do you want anything?
Liza:	No, thanks. I have everything I need.
Josh:	Are you sure?
Liza:	Yes. Thanks, anyway.

Unit 5 How can we help?

Page 51, Exercises 3 and 4 [05_02]

Brad:	Hey, Sara!
Sara:	Hi, Brad! How was your spring break?
Brad:	It was great! I went down to Mexico with my roommate!
Sara:	Awesome. That sounds like fun!
Brad:	Yes, we spent lots of time on the beach, and we went to lots of fun parties! How about you? What did you do for spring break?
Sara:	I went down to Florida, actually.
Brad:	That's great! Did you have fun?
Sara:	I did have a great time, but I didn't go to any parties.
Brad:	You didn't? What did you do?
Sara:	I went on a service trip with nine other students.
Brad:	A service trip? What's that?
Sara:	It's a vacation where you work to help others.
Brad:	Really? That's awesome. What did you do? Did you volunteer somewhere?
Sara:	We worked for Habitat for Humanity.
Brad:	Habitat for Humanity? Isn't that the organization that builds houses for poor people?
Sara:	Yes, that's it. We built a house for a family that lost their house in last year's hurricane. They are poor and have five children, so Habitat for Humanity helped them. The family just moved in yesterday.
Brad:	Wow! That's amazing!
Sara:	Yeah! And the best part is that we were helping people in need, and we still got out of this cold and snowy weather!
Brad:	That's wonderful, Sara. I'd like to go on a service trip for my next vacation.
Sara:	You should! Dr. Collins in the French department is organizing the next one to Haiti. The volunteers will work in the schools. I'll give him your name if you're interested.
Brad:	That would be great, Sara! Thanks!

Page 58, Exercise 2 and 3 [05_08]

Conversation 1

Eve:	Excuse me. Would you mind helping me, please? How does this thing work?
Ned:	I'm sorry, I can't help you. I don't know how it works.
Eve:	Oh, well. Thank you anyway.

Conversation 2

Dad:	Hey, Tina. Can you give me a hand? I'm cleaning up.
Tina:	Sorry. I'm doing my homework.
Dad:	Come on! It won't take long.
Tina:	I'm really busy. I'll help later.

Conversation 3

Jodie:	Excuse me. I was wondering if I could ask you a few questions.
Marc:	I'm sorry, I'm in a rush.
Jodie:	OK. Thank you anyway.

Audioscript

REVIEW 1

Page 64, Listening, Exercises 2 and 3 `05_R1_01`

Once, someone gave me a model boat. It was made in Spain. My friend bought it when she was on vacation there. It was a souvenir from a museum. It's a small boat with a sail. I have it in my bedroom, on the table next to my bed. I really like it a lot. I haven't been to Spain, but I would like to go one day.

Page 65, Conversation, Exercises 2 and 3 `05_R1_02`

Nora: Hey, Tina! What are you doing this summer?
Tina: Well, you know I'm graduating next week, right?
Nora: You are? Congratulations!
Tina: Thanks! I'm really excited because after graduation I'm going on a hiking trip in Costa Rica to celebrate.
Nora: Wow! That's amazing!
Tina: Yeah—I'm looking forward to it. I'm an avid hiker, and I'm also a big fan of unusual animals so I think it will be the perfect trip for me.
Nora: It sounds like it! Who are you going with?
Tina: Well, Janet was planning to go with me, but she just broke her leg.
Nora: Really? That's terrible! Poor Janet!
Tina: I know... So I'm looking for someone to go with me. Hey! Would you like to go?
Nora: Wow! Thanks very much! That would be great!

Unit 6   World languages

Page 67, Exercises 3 and 4 `06_03`

Nancy: So, Amal, just how many languages do you speak?
Amal: Um... let me see... three... no... four.
Nancy: Four?
Amal: Yeah. My native language is Arabic because that's what my parents speak at home. And I speak fluent French because that's what I spoke at school.
Nancy: You speak French? I didn't know that. I speak French too!
Amal: You do?
Nancy: Well, I speak broken French. I went to Paris a few years ago on vacation, and I picked up a few expressions and a little slang. Anyway... what are the other two languages?
Amal: Well, English obviously.
Nancy: Yes. And number 4?
Amal: Italian. I'm taking a class on the Internet. It's really good.
Nancy: Italian? That's cool. Wow! You're really good at languages.
Amal: Well, so are you! Japanese, English, and what else?
Nancy: That's all.
Amal: No, that's not all. I heard you talking to the waiter at the Chinese restaurant last night.
Nancy: Oh... no... I'm bad at Chinese. I mean, I can get by, but I'm certainly not fluent.

Page 67, Exercise 5 `06_04`

Nancy: So, do you like studying Italian on the Internet? How does that work?
Amal: Well, I do grammar exercises and I read news articles. But the best thing is that I listen to songs and watch movies. It's good because it's fun and I don't get bored.
Nancy: Yeah, but I'm not sure I'd like studying on the Internet. How do you practice speaking? I mean, I like talking to people in person. For example, I'm trying to improve my Chinese at the moment. so I meet up with a Chinese friend two times a week to practice. And I practice whenever I get a chance, like last night in the restaurant.
Amal: That's good. It's important to really talk to people, isn't it?
Nancy: I think so. And I have a Chinese e-pal.
Amal: What's an e-pal?
Nancy: You know, a friend that I can practice Chinese with on the Internet. We chat on the Internet and write emails to each other.
Amal: Oh, so you do use the Internet to study!
Nancy: Yeah, I guess you're right! It's really good too, because my Chinese e-pal tells me about interesting websites and blogs in Chinese.
Amal: Hey, that's cool.
Nancy: Yup. And she recommends books and magazines too.
Amal: Hmm, I think I'll get an Italian e-pal.

Unit 7   Are you fashionable?

Page 79, Exercise 2 `07_02`

Pat

Hi, I'm Pat. Because I'm a lawyer, I have to wear clothes that give a serious, formal image. So I usually wear a plain blue or black suit. Sometimes I wear pants, but I prefer skirts. I also wear plain shirts, usually white or blue.

Kim

My name is Kim. I think I'm pretty lucky because I can wear what I want to work. So I usually wear the same clothes I wear at home—sneakers, plain shirts, and old, faded jeans.

Audioscript

Sam
My friends call me Sam. In my job I have to train people five or six hours a day. Of course, I wear comfortable clothes for that—never tight clothes. You know, something like a comfortable t-shirt and bright pants.

Unit 8 That's life!

Page 90, Exercise 2

A: What do you know about Queen Elizabeth's family?
B: Well, I know that her husband is Prince Philip and they have four children—Charles, Anne, Andrew, and Edward.
A: And grandchildren?
B: I think she has eight, but the most famous ones are her grandsons, William and Harry.
A: Their mother was Princess Diana, right?
B: Yes, Diana was married to Charles. They had two kids.
A: So Princess Diana was the Queen's daughter-in-law?
B: Exactly.

Page 91, Exercises 2 and 3

Ken: Dylan!
Dylan: Hi, Ken! Long time no see.
Ken: Yeah, I haven't been here since last summer.
Dylan: So how's it going? How have you been?
Ken: Great! We have a new baby son, and we moved last year.
Dylan: Wow! Congratulations.
Ken: Thanks. But what about you? What have you been up to?
Dylan: Not much, really. We still live in the same place and no kids yet—just a cat. I was in the U.S. for a couple of weeks last month...
Ken: For work?
Dylan: Yes. I had always wanted to go there, and then this opportunity came up. And you? Are you still working at the bank?
Ken: Yes, I've been there for five years now.
Dylan: Really? Time flies, doesn't it?
Ken: Yes, you're right. Anyhow...

Unit 9 Do you know a good story?

Page 103, Exercises 3 and 4

The Eagle and the Tortoise, an African folktale
The tortoise and the eagle did not know each other. The eagle lived high on a mountain, and the tortoise lived under some rocks on the ground. The eagle heard that the tortoise was very generous and kind, so he decided to visit him. The tortoise and his family made the eagle very welcome. They gave him food and drink and were very hospitable. The eagle returned again and again to the tortoise's house, but each time he laughed, "Ha! Ha! I can visit the tortoise on the ground, but he can never reach my nest on the mountain!" Soon all the animals were talking about the selfish and ungrateful eagle. They decided to help the tortoise. "Next time the eagle visits, offer him a basket of food to take to his family. Then climb into the basket and you will hear how he laughs at you," they explained.
The tortoise did what the animals suggested. As the eagle was flying home, he repeated his usual cry, "Ha! Ha! I can visit the tortoise on the ground, but he can never reach my nest on the mountain!"
When they arrived at the eagle's nest, the tortoise came out of the basket. "Take me home. You have insulted me and my family's hospitality. You are not my friend!"
"Take you home? Ha! Ha! I will pick you up and throw you to the ground," the eagle replied. So the tortoise bit the eagle hard on the leg. "Let go, let go!" the eagle begged. "Only after you take me home," replied the tortoise. And he bit the eagle harder.
The eagle flew high into the sky and tried to shake the tortoise from his leg. But it was no use; the tortoise wouldn't let go. Finally, the eagle took the tortoise back to his house. As he flew away, the tortoise said, "I welcomed you, but you did nothing for me and my family. You laughed at our hospitality. You have lost a friend and I have lost a problem."

Unit 10 Home, sweet home

Page 115, Exercises 2 and 3

Tim: Hello. Mary?
Mary: Yes? This is Mary.
Tim: Hi. This is Tim. I'm calling about the apartment you advertised to rent.
Mary: Oh, yes, good. What would you like to know?
Tim: Well, um... everything. Could you tell me about it, please?
Mary: Yes, of course. It's on the top floor of a building in SoHo. It's on a quiet street. There are a few stores close to the building—you know, pharmacy, bookstore... it's about five minutes from the subway.
Tim: And what about the apartment itself? What's it like?
Mary: The apartment itself is really nice. It's fully furnished. It has a lot of natural light and a large balcony. It's fabulous in the summer! It's an old apartment, but I painted it recently. So it's ready to move in.
Tim: And there's just one bedroom. Is that right?
Mary: No, actually there are two bedrooms. One is a

225

Audioscript

good size and the other one is a bit smaller. Then there's the living-dining-kitchen area. It's quite spacious.

Tim: OK, fine. Sounds good. When can I come and see it?
Mary: Um, let's see… tomorrow afternoon would be good for me. How about at 5 o'clock?
Tim: Five o'clock is fine for me. Can I meet you there?
Mary: Yes, perfect. We can meet there.
Tim: And what's the best way to get there? On the subway?
Mary: Yes. Take the subway to the Prince Street station. Here, I'll give you the address. Do you have a pen?
Tim: Just a second… right…

Page 124, Example 10_09
My grandmother is amazing. She's almost 90 years old and she's still going strong. She loves to spend time with her fourteen grandchildren and four great grandchildren. I hope I have half her energy when I'm her age.

Page 124, Practice 10_10
My neighbors are driving me crazy. They're so noisy. They play loud music. Their TV is on all the time. The children jump on the floor. I'm not sure what I should do. I could talk to them again, or I could talk to the apartment manager. That's it! I will talk to the manager.

REVIEW 2

Page 127, Listening 10_R2_01
1. Which table should we put in the dining room?
   A. Maybe this one. It's bigger than the other one.
   B. It's on the small table by the TV.
   C. Put it on the table by the window.
2. Well, I'd better get going. How about getting together next week?
   A. Yes, me too. I'll be in touch.
   B. I'm going to the cinema.
   C. OK. I'm not doing anything next week.
3. Did I ever tell you about the time I was attacked by a tiger in Nepal?
   A. I went to Nepal on vacation two years ago.
   B. No, what happened?
   C. The last time I saw a tiger was at the zoo.
4. What languages do you speak?
   A. I've been studying English for five years.
   B. I find speaking more difficult than reading and writing.
   C. English is my native language. And I can get by in French.
5. What do you usually wear during the week?
   A. Monday to Friday I have to wear formal clothes to work.
   B. I prefer casual clothes to formal clothes.
   C. Last week I wore a new pair of jeans.

Unit 11   Doing it for charity

Page 131, Exercises 2 and 3 11_02
Interviewer: So, Andy, how do you feel about your sponsored trek across the Kalahari Desert?
Andy: Well, I feel pretty nervous. I mean, it's a long trip, and it'll be really hot. But personally, I'm looking forward to doing something this difficult.
Interviewer: Are you doing any special training to prepare for the walk?
Andy: I was a little out of shape, so I'm working out at the gym, going swimming, and taking an exercise class.
Interviewer: When exactly do you start your trek?
Andy: I leave on June 1st, and I expect to finish in a month.
Interviewer: Are you going to take any special equipment with you?
Andy: Well I'm not going to take many clothes, but I'm going to take lots of water and a compass!
Interviewer: And exactly why are you going to do this sponsored trek?
Andy: With the money I make from this trek, the charity, Work for All, plans to start special cooperative work projects to help poor people.
Interviewer: Well, good luck!

Page 137, Pronunciation, Exercise 1
1. It'll be very hot.
2. I'm going to donate a lot of money.
3. We'll start training next week.
4. We're going to swim for charity.
5. He's going to organize the event.

Unit 12 How do you stay healthy?

Page 143, Exercises 3 and 4
Instructor: Good morning class. How is everyone today?
Woman 1: Good.
Man: All right. Tired!
Woman 2: Tired!
Instructor: OK. Let's get started. Everyone stand up straight with your feet about shoulder width apart.
Woman 1: Like this?

Audioscript

Instructor:	Yeah, that's right. Good. Today we're going to do a few stretching exercises that can help you if work a lot on the computer during the day.
Man:	That's just what I need. My neck is killing me.
Instructor:	Well then, this should really help you. All right. First, raise your left arm over your head.
Woman 2:	Like this?
Instructor:	No, raise your arm up over your head. That's it. Good. Now, slowly bend your arm so that your hand touches the back of your neck. Good. Now hold your left elbow with your right hand and gently... slowly... push your elbow so that your hand moves down between your shoulders. Good. Hold for five seconds... four... three... two... one. Great. Good job everyone! This exercise is excellent for stretching your arms, shoulders, and upper back.
Woman 1:	That felt good.
Woman 2:	Yeah.
Instructor:	OK. Listen everyone. Let's do another exercise. This one stretches your arms and wrists. Ready? Put your arms out in front of you at about shoulder height.
Woman 1:	Like this?
Instructor:	No, lift your arms up a bit higher. There... that's it. At shoulder height. OK. Relax and gently bend your wrists so your fingers point up. Remember to keep your fingers straight and relaxed. That's it. Now, rest... and repeat... arms up, bend your wrists. Good. How was that?
Man:	Good. I could really feel the stretch.

Unit 13 Space travel

Page 155, Exercises 2 and 3 [13_02]

Marta

Interviewer:	What do you think, Marta? Would you like to travel to the Moon on vacation?
Marta:	Um... I don't think that's really a possibility, in my case.
Interviewer:	Why not?
Marta:	Well, I don't have enough money.
Interviewer:	OK, but in theory, would you like to travel to the Moon?
Marta:	Uh... not really. I don't think the Moon would be a very nice place. I mean, I guess it would be very cold there. I prefer the beach. Also, a big problem for me would be you can't leave when you want to. So I think going to the Moon for me is definitely not an ideal vacation.

Earl

Interviewer:	So Earl, would you like to travel to the Moon on vacation?
Earl:	Um... I always find flying a little traumatic. So flying in a rocket I think would be even more traumatic. It's a very long way to go.
Interviewer:	So you wouldn't like to go?
Earl:	Uh... I guess once you're there on the Moon it could be interesting, you know, interesting views, but really I prefer Earth. I prefer to walk in nature. I like to hear waves breaking on the beach, birds singing, and see the sun setting and all that. I don't think that's what I would get if I went to the Moon.

Vanessa

Interviewer:	Vanessa, would you like to travel to the Moon on vacation?
Vanessa:	Sure I'd go to the Moon on vacation. Why not? You have to try everything in this life. The views of Earth would be amazing. I'd like to leave Earth and get away from the effects of gravity, to be able to jump really high. I think I'd find the trip there quite frightening, but all in all it would be a great experience. And I imagine that a hotel on the Moon would be... like... a fivestar hotel, you know, with lots of facilities. Imagine playing golf on the Moon!
Interviewer:	OK, thanks Vanessa.

Page 161, Pronunciation, Exercise 1

1. They said that they'd go by train.
2. They say they go by plane.
3. It's very cold.
4. It'd be very cold.
5. We'd drive to the beach.
6. We drive to the beach.
7. I told you I'd do it.
8. I told him I do it.

Page 161, Pronunciation, Exercise 2

1. They said that they'd go by train.
4. It'd be very cold.
5. We'd drive to the beach.
7. I told you I'd do it.

Audioscript

Unit 14 What have you been doing?

Page 167, Exercises 3 and 4

Woman

Well, it takes me about forty, forty-five minutes to get ready in the morning. After the alarm goes off, I like to listen to the news. Then I take a shower and get dressed. Um... it only takes me about ten minutes to go to work because I live very close to where I work, which is good. But I always stop to get coffee on the way. And um... watching TV? I don't spend a lot of time watching TV, maybe an hour. Every evening I watch the news. Uh... how much time do I spend shopping? Hmm... probably about half an hour a day; maybe a bit more on Saturday, maybe an hour. That's shopping for food. And um... what do I do while I'm waiting? Well, if I'm standing in line, for example, waiting to buy a ticket, well, I think about work.

Man

Well, my kids wake me up every morning. I don't need to set an alarm! It only takes me about 15 minutes to get ready for my day. I wash my face, brush my teeth, and put on some clothes. Uh... it doesn't take me any time to get to work either because I work at home. I'm a house husband, and my wife goes out to work. Uh... TV? I watch a lot of TV, maybe three or four hours a day. Um... especially with my kids. They like to watch a lot of TV. Shopping? I normally do one big shopping on Saturday, in the afternoon, maybe two or three hours. And while I'm waiting in line, I talk to my kids. I'm always with my kids so I talk to them and, um... tell them stories and jokes.

Page 173, Pronunciation, Exercise 1

A. 2 ½
B. 715
C. 5:13
D. 9:50

Unit 15 Great adventures

Page 179, Exercise 2

Gary: And radio listeners, if you've just joined us, we're discussing some great stories from a new book, called *Female Explorers of the 19th and 20th Centuries*. Can you tell us about any women who traveled to Asia, Marcia?

Marcia: Yes, Gary—one amazing woman was Alexandra David-Néel, a French explorer born in Paris in 1868. Have you heard of her?

Gary: Well, no, I have to admit that I haven't, Marcia.

Marcia: Alexandra David-Néel was born in Paris on October 24th, 1868. As a young woman, she was very interested in Asia and Asian languages. So when she was given some money as part of an inheritance, she decided to use it to fulfill one of her great ambitions—to travel to Tibet. Now at that time, Tibet was forbidden to foreigners—closed to people from other countries. David-Néel tried to make the journey into Tibet four times, but each time she was discovered and sent back. In 1924, she decided to try again. This time, she traveled with her adopted Tibetan son, Yongden. They carried food, a knife to cut firewood, a tent, and leather to repair their boots. They traveled at night. During the day, they hid so that no one would see them. On their trip, they had many adventures. Four months later, they reached Lhasa, the capital city of Tibet. Now they had one last problem—how could they enter the city without being seen?

Gary: And? What did they do?

Marcia: Well, Gary, suddenly, while they were thinking of a plan, a sandstorm began. It covered Lhasa, and everyone rushed into their houses for protection. This was their opportunity, and they entered the city. They had arrived! David-Néel and Yongden spent two months in Lhasa. They visited the famous Potala Palace and enjoyed the festivals celebrating the Tibetan New Year. They were very worried that they might be discovered and ordered to leave so they told no one who they really were. When, finally, it was time to go, they left the city as quietly and secretly as they had arrived. Now they had another long journey to India and home.

Gary: And I bet that, after that trip, all she wanted to do was get home, have a long hot bath, and set off again!

Marcia: You're absolutely right, Gary! David-Néel continued traveling in Asia for years and wrote many books about her adventures. She died in 1969 at the age of 101.

Photo Credits

SS = Shutterstock® Images
2 ©Andrei Marincas/SS, ©celarviewstock/SS, ©Jane Rix/SS, ©VIPDesignUSA/SS, ©Odelia Cohen/SS, ©Vphoto/SS, ©Jozsef Szasz-Fabian/SS, ©karam Miri/SS, **3** ©bikerriderlondon/SS, ©jerrysa/SS, ©Mike Avlas/SS, ©Fabio Bernardi/SS; **4** ©Monkey Business Images/SS; **7** ©Igor Zakowski/SS; **8** ©Arpi/SS, ©Steve Snowden/SS; **10** ©tonobalaguerf/SS; **11** ©dott.Razcan/SS; **14** ©Antonin Vodak/SS, ©jaimaa/SS, ©vilax/SS, ©Raymond Kasprzack/SS, ©Tatiana Popova/SS, ©Leenvdb/SS, ©nomeko/SS, ©Jennifer N. Kidd/SS,©Thomas M Perkins/SS, ©Triff/SS; **15** ©Page2, ©Pixel 4 Images/SS, ©Page2, ©Alexander Kalina/SS, ©Valery Lebedev/SS, **16** ©Zuura/SS, **17** ©Nastya22/SS; **18** ©Eric Isselée/SS, ©humbak/SS, ©GETTY/ABC Photo Archives/GETTY, ©istock/MentalArt/istockphoto; **19** ©HomeStudio/SS, ©Tan, Kim Pin/SS, ©Margo Harrison/SS; **20** ©Dongliu/SS, ©Pan Xunbin/SS, ©gualtiero boffi/SS; **21** ©DNFStyle Photography/SS; **22** ©GETTY/Michael Ochs Archives/GETTY; **23** ©Stuart Elflett/SS; **24** ©Andrejs Pidjass/SS; **25** ©Gaydukov Sergey/SS,©Patricia Hofmeester/SS, ©Tina Rencelj/SS; **26** ©Maridav/SS, ©krivenko/SS, ©dundanim/SS, ©Andresr/SS, ©Forester Forest/SS, ©OntaYdur/SS, ©Yuri Arcurs/SS, ©Sandra Gligorijevic/SS, ©Henrik Larsson/SS; **28** ©Johanna Goodyear/SS, ©Sapsiwai/SS, ©Jaimie Duplass/SS, ©Edw/SS,©Jaimie Duplass/SS, ©Damian Herde/SS, ©xyno6/istockphoto, ©NinaMalyna/SS; **30** ©Mike Brake/SS, ©Bryant Jayme/SS, ©Jerome Scholler/SS; **31** ©JelenaA/SS; **32** ©Joyce Marrero/SS, ©aldorado/SS, ©Lukas Hlavac/SS, ©Alon Brik/SS; **33** ©John Kobal Foundation/GETTY, **35** ©Iafoto/SS; **38** ©soulgems/SS,©GWImages/SS, ©aniad/SS, ©Stuart Monk/SS, ©Olga Lyubkina/SS, ©ZEF/SS, ©Pete Saloutos/SS, ©Esteban De Armas/SS: ©Petros Tsonis/SS; **39** ©Anthony DiChello/SS, ©karam Miri/SS; **40** ©Siarhei Fedarenka/SS, ©Elena Elisseeva/SS, ©PeterG/SS,©Joe Belanger/SS, ©Elena Elisseeva/SS, ©Lisa F. Young/SS, ©iofoto/SS, ©Olga Utlyakova/SS, **42** ©Alena Brozova/SS;**43** ©Jules_Kitano/SS, **44** ©Shebeko/SS, ©Warren Goldswain/SS; **45** ©joingate/SS;**46** ©visi.stock/SS; **50** ©kaetana/SS, ©Andrew Gewntry/SS, ©Suzanne Tucker/SS, ©Robert J. Daveant/SS, ©Robert A. Mansker/SS, ©jon le-bon/SS, ©Jerry Sharp/SS, ©paul prescott/SS, **51** ©James Peragine/SS, ©Kurhan/SS, ©James Peragine/SS, ©gualtiero boffi/SS, ©Hannamariah/SS;**52** ©jcjgphotography/SS, ©Dean Mitchell/SS; **53** ©vgstudio/SS; **54** ©Lucian Cuman/SS; **55** ©Katar/SS; **56** ©JeremyRIchards/SS; **58** ©AVAVA/SS, ©Monkey Business Images/SS, ©keellla/SS; **64** ©Igor Sirbu/SS, ©MARGRIT HIRSCH/SS, ©BW Folsom; **65** ©Blaj Gabriel/SS **67** ©Robert Kneschke/SS; **70** ©Jakrich/Dreamstime.com; **71** ©StockLit/SS; **73** ©CREATISTA/SS; **75** T ©Rlippiett/Dreamstime.com, TM ©Sam DCruz/SS, MB ©Christopher Howey/Dreamstime.com, B ©Charles Outcalt/Dreamstime.com; **78** (1) ©Karkas/SS, (2) ©Kayros Studio "Be Happy!"/SS, (3) ©BortN66/SS, (4) ©Elnur/SS, (5) ©Karkas/SS, (6) ©Worakit Sirijinda/SS, (7) ©artproem/SS, (8)©terekhov igor/SS, (9) ©Picsfive/SS, (10) ©Andresr/SS, (man at computer) ©junjie/SS, (girl with orange sweatshirt) ©photomak/SS; **79** (1)©jackhollingsworthcom, LLC/SS, (2) ©konstantynov/SS, (3) ©Lisovskaya Natalia/SS, (A) ©Vasiliy Koval/SS, (B) ©GG Pro Photo/SS, (C) ©Edyta Pawlowska/SS; **80** (A) ©SergiyN/SS, (B) ©Eduard Titov/SS, (C) ©ecxcn/SS, (D) ©Vinicius Tupinamba/SS; **82** (gold miner) ©viridian1/iSTOCK,(jeans) ©viviamo/SS, (girl jumping) ©Svemir/SS, **84** T ©Junial Enterprises/SS, B ©James Steidl/SS; **86** L ©elenabo/SS, R©Ronald van der Beek/SS; **87** ©Tyler Olson/SS; **90** ©POOL/Reuters/CORBIS; **91** T ©Aleksey Fursov/Dreamstime.com, B ©visi.stock/SS; **92** T ©Stephen Coburn/SS; **93** ©Galina Barskaya/SS; **94** ©PT Images/SS; **95** ©Yuri Arcurs/SS; **96** (A)©StockLife/SS, (B) ©Monkey Business Images/SS, (C) ©ampyang/SS; **97** ©juan carlos tinjaca/SS; **98** ©Yeko Photo Studio/SS; **99** B ©sculpies/SS; **102** (A) ©Zhukov Oleg/SS, (B) ©igorkosh/SS, (C) ©4736202690/SS, (D) ©Kruglov_Orda/SS, (E) ©EricIsselée/SS, (F) ©Lindsey Eltinge/SS, (G) ©FloridaStock/SS, (H) ©Ultrashock/SS, (I) ©alexxi/SS, (J) ©Michiel de Wit/SS, (K) ©Erik Lam/SS, (L)©Eric Isselée/SS, **105** ©David Evison/SS; **108** (A) ©Stevies/Dreamstime.com, (B)©Masi Gianluca/Dreamstime.com, (C) ©Nico Smit2/Dreamstime.com, (D) ©Tudorica Alexandru/Dreamstime.com, (E) Stevies/Dreamstime.com, (F) ©Stevies/Dreamstime.com; **110** ©Dontsov Evgeny Victorovich/SS; **115** B ©Atlaspix/SS; **118** (stones and water) ©Marilyn Barbone/Dreamstime.com; **119** T ©David Hilcher/Dreamstime.com; **120** T ©Chris Hill/SS, M ©chungking/SS, B ©kkymek/SS; **122** ©CandyBoxPhoto/SS; **123** ©Albert H. Teich/SS; **124** ©Brian Eichhorn/SS; **129** ©Halina Yakushevich/SS; **130** (A) ©Mirco Vacca/SS, (B) ©Galyna Andrushko/SS, (C) ©upthebanner/SS;**67** L©Francesco Ridolfi/SS, M ©joingate/SS, R ©Francesco Ridolfi/SS; **132** (A) ©Kushch Dmitry/SS, (B) ©Galyna Andrushko/SS, (C) ©ImageFocus/SS, (D) ©Catalin Petolea/SS, (E) ©Tatiana Popova/SS, (F) ©ANATOL/SS, (G) ©Diana Taliun/SS, (H) ©Wolfe Larry/SS; **133** ©zurabi/SS;**134** T ©Katseyephoto/Dreamstime.com, B ©Kenishirotie/SS; **135** L ©Sergey Peterman/SS, R ©Vladimir Kozieiev/SS; **136** (1) ©yasar/Dreamstime.com, (2) ©Franck Boston/SS, (3) ©Kushnirov Avraham/Dreamstime.com, (4) ©Bruce Hempell/Dreamstime.com, (5) Joe Gough/Dreamstime.com, (6) ©Drazen Vukelic/Dreamstime.com, (7) ©Trutta/Dreamstime.com, (8) ©Oleg Kozlov/Dreamstime.com;**138** T©S1001/SS, B ©Tad Denson/SS;**139** ©Christopher Jones/SS; **142** T ©Andresr/SS, BR©Diedie/SS, BL ©Vibrant Image Studio/SS; **144** (1) ©Warren Goldswain/SS, (2) ©Blaj Gabriel/SS, (3) ©dendong/SS, (4) ©Piotr Marcinski/SS, (5) ©swissmacky/SS, (6) ©cristovao/SS, (7) ©Juriah Mosin/SS, (8) ©Alexander Raths/SS; **145** L©hightowernrw/SS, R ©Radu Razvan/SS; **146** T ©Andresr/SS, B ©Artur Bogacki/SS; **147** T ©EDHAR/SS, **149** ©East/SS; **151** ©Dmitriy Shironosov/SS; **152** (LA skyline) ©sheff/SS, (NY skyline)©upthebanner/SS; **154** T ©Peter Hansen/SS; **156** B©Andrea Danti/SS, **157** ©1971yes/SS; **158** ©Triling Studio LTd./SS; **160** T ©HO/Reuters/CORBIS, (1) ©LianeM/SS, (2)©Roman Gorielov/SS, (3) ©Igor Dutina/SS, (4) ©Rob Stark/SS, (5) ©Nayashkova Olga/SS, (6) ©Nikola Bilic/SS, (7) ©Arkady/SS; **163** ©Steve Heap/SS; **166** T ©Petrenko Andriy/SS, M ©Poleze/SS, B ©Rena Schild/SS; **167** (1) ©Monkey Business Images/SS, (2) ©Maridav/SS, (3) ©Tomasz Trojanowski/SS, (4) ©Yuri Arcurs/SS, (5) ©Losevsky Pavel/SS; **168** (1) Ian D Walker/SS, (2) ©More SimilarImages/SS, (3) ©Bigelow Illustrations/SS, **169** ©Andresr/SS; **170** (time) ©andrey_l/SS, (hour glass) ©James Steidl/SS; **171** (woman looking at watch) ©Edw/SS; **172** ©Milan Jurkovic/Dreamstime.com; **173** ©iofoto/SS; **175** ©Ivanova Natalia/SS; **179** T ©Aron Brand/SS, B ©wong sze yuen/SS; **180** (A) ©S.M./SS, (B) ©SergeyIT/SS, (C) ©Shannon M Rush/SS, (D)©picturepartners/SS, (E) ©Maxim Godkin/SS, (F) ©Jovan Nikolic/SS, (G) ©Rosli Othman/SS, (H) ©Pontus Edenberg/SS, (I) ©Chris Turner/SS, (J)©mikeledray/SS, (K) ©Mark Herreid/SS, (L) ©Volegzhanina Elena/SS, (M) ©karam Miri/SS, (N) ©S.M./SS; **182** (lion) ©Helen E. Grose/SS; **183** ©Jiri Haureljuk/SS, **184** (A) ©Christopher Meder - Photography/SS, (B) ©Natalia Bratslavsky/SS, (C) ©4745052183/SS, (D) ©Charles T. Bennett/SS, (E) ©Sergey Khachatryan/SS, (F) ©efiplus/SS, (G) ©TracingTea/SS, (H) ©andras_csontos/SS; **185** T ©Galyna Andrushko/SS, B ©place-to-be/SS; **187** TL ©cynoclub/SS, TM©Dmitri Kamenetsky/SS, TR ©Kharidehal Abhirama Ashwin/SS; **190** ©zhu difeng/SS; **191** ©LockStockBob/SS; **192** L ©Alexander Gatsenko/SS,R ©Dmitrijs Dmitrijevs/SS; **193** ©Michael Ransburg/SS

Audio Track List

TakeAway English, Student Book 1

Track	Unit	Section	Exercise
01_01	Unit 1	Start	2
01_02	Unit 1	Listening	2
01_03	Unit 1	Vocabulary	2
01_04	Unit 1	Grammar	2
01_05	Unit 1	Reading	2, 3
01_06	Unit 1	Culture	2
01_07	Unit 1	Pronunciation	1
01_08	Unit 1	Pronunciation	2
01_09	Unit 1	Conversation	2, 3
02_01	Unit 2	Start	2
02_02	Unit 2	Listening	2, 3
02_03	Unit 2	Vocabulary	2
02_04	Unit 2	Grammar	2
02_05	Unit 2	Reading	2, 3
02_06	Unit 2	Song	3
02_07	Unit 2	Pronunciation	1
02_08	Unit 2	Pronunciation	2
02_09	Unit 2	Conversation	1, 2
03_01	Unit 3	Start	2
03_02	Unit 3	Listening	3, 4
03_03	Unit 3	Vocabulary	2
03_04	Unit 3	Reading	3, 4
03_05	Unit 3	Culture	3
03_06	Unit 3	Culture	5
03_07	Unit 3	Pronunciation	1
03_08	Unit 3	Conversation	2, 3
03_09	Unit 3	Test Takeaway Practice	
04_01	Unit 4	Start	2
04_02	Unit 4	Listening	3, 4
04_03	Unit 4	Vocabulary	2
04_04	Unit 4	Reading	2, 3
04_05	Unit 4	Song	2
04_06	Unit 4	Pronunciation	1
04_07	Unit 4	Pronunciation	2
04_08	Unit 4	Conversation	2, 3
05_01	Unit 5	Start	2
05_02	Unit 5	Listening	3, 4
05_03	Unit 5	Vocabulary	2
05_04	Unit 5	Reading	3, 4
05_05	Unit 5	Culture	2
05_06	Unit 5	Pronunciation	1
05_07	Unit 5	Pronunciation	2
05_08	Unit 5	Conversation	2, 3
05_R1_01	Review 1	Listening	2, 3
05_R1_02	Review 1	Conversation	2, 3
06_01	Unit 6	Start	2
06_02	Unit 6	Start	3
06_03	Unit 6	Listening	3, 4
06_04	Unit 6	Listening	5
06_05	Unit 6	Vocabulary	2
06_06	Unit 6	Grammar	3
06_07	Unit 6	Reading	2
06_08	Unit 6	Song	3, 4
06_09	Unit 6	Pronunciation	
06_10	Unit 6	Conversation	1
07_01	Unit 7	Start	1
07_02	Unit 7	Listening	2
07_03	Unit 7	Vocabulary	2
07_04	Unit 7	Reading	2, 3
07_05	Unit 7	Culture	2, 3
07_06	Unit 7	Pronunciation	1
07_07	Unit 7	Conversation	2
08_01	Unit 8	Start	2
08_02	Unit 8	Listening	2, 3
08_03	Unit 8	Vocabulary	2
08_04	Unit 8	Reading	2, 3
08_05	Unit 8	Song	2, 3
08_06	Unit 8	Pronunciation	1
08_07	Unit 8	Pronunciation	2
08_08	Unit 8	Conversation	2, 3
09_01	Unit 9	Start	2
09_02	Unit 9	Listening	3, 4
09_03	Unit 9	Vocabulary	2
09_04	Unit 9	Vocabulary	4
09_05	Unit 9	Vocabulary	5
09_06	Unit 9	Grammar	4
09_07	Unit 9	Reading	2
09_08	Unit 9	Reading	3
09_09	Unit 9	Reading	5
09_10	Unit 9	Culture	2
09_11	Unit 9	Pronunciation	
09_12	Unit 9	Conversation	1, 2
10_01	Unit 10	Start	2
10_02	Unit 10	Listening	2, 3
10_03	Unit 10	Vocabulary	1
10_04	Unit 10	Reading	2, 3
10_05	Unit 10	Song	3, 4
10_06	Unit 10	Pronunciation	1
10_07	Unit 10	Pronunciation	2
10_08	Unit 10	Conversation	2
10_09	Unit 10	Test Takeaway Example	
10_10	Unit 10	Test Takeaway Practice	
10_R2_01	Review 1	Listening	1
11_01	Unit 11	Start	2
11_02	Unit 11	Listening	2, 3
11_03	Unit 11	Vocabulary	2
11_04	Unit 11	Vocabulary	3
11_05	Unit 11	Reading	3
11_06	Unit 11	Culture	2, 3
11_07	Unit 11	Pronunciation	1
11_08	Unit 11	Pronunciation	2
11_09	Unit 11	Conversation	1, 2
12_01	Unit 12	Start	1
12_02	Unit 12	Start	2
12_03	Unit 12	Listening	2
12_04	Unit 12	Listening	3, 4
12_05	Unit 12	Vocabulary	2
12_06	Unit 12	Reading	2, 3
12_07	Unit 12	Song	3, 5
12_08	Unit 12	Pronunciation	
12_09	Unit 12	Conversation	1
12_10	Unit 12	Conversation	2
13_01	Unit 13	Start	1
13_02	Unit 13	Listening	2, 3
13_03	Unit 13	Vocabulary	1
13_04	Unit 13	Reading	3, 4
13_05	Unit 13	Culture	2, 3
13_06	Unit 13	Pronunciation	1
13_07	Unit 13	Pronunciation	2
13_08	Unit 13	Conversation	1, 2
14_01	Unit 14	Start	2
14_02	Unit 14	Listening	3, 4
14_03	Unit 14	Vocabulary	3
14_04	Unit 14	Reading	2, 3
14_05	Unit 14	Song	2, 3
14_06	Unit 14	Pronunciation	1
14_07	Unit 14	Pronunciation	2
14_08	Unit 14	Conversation	2, 3
15_01	Unit 15	Start	2
15_02	Unit 15	Listening	2
15_03	Unit 15	Vocabulary	2
15_04	Unit 15	Reading	3, 4
15_05	Unit 15	Culture	3
15_06	Unit 15	Pronunciation	1
15_07	Unit 15	Pronunciation	2
15_08	Unit 15	Conversation	2, 3
15_R3_01	Review 2	Reading	1, 2